CW00600888

A Bilingual Guide to the
Japanese Economy

A Bilingual Guide to the Japanese Economy

Published by Kodansha International Ltd., 17-14 Otowa 1-chome,
Bunkyo-ku, Tokyo 112-8652.
No part of this publication may be reproduced in any form or by any
means without permission in writing from the publisher.
Copyright ©1995 by NHK Overseas Broadcasting Department
Economic Project and Daiwa Institute of Research Co., Ltd., Economic
Research Department
All rights reserved. Printed in Japan.
First Edition 1995

ISBN 4-7700-1942-4
99 00 20 19 18 17 16 15 14

対訳：英語で話す日本経済 Q&A

A Bilingual Guide to the Japanese Economy

NHK国際局経済プロジェクト・大和総研経済調査部

講談社インターナショナル

Tokyo • New York • London

序文

　「焼け跡から経済大国へ」。第2次世界大戦で焼け野原になった日本は，その後のわずかな期間のうちに目覚ましい経済成長を遂げ，戦後の奇跡といわれました。かつて，「アメリカがくしゃみをすれば風邪をひく」といわれるほどひ弱だった日本経済も，今やアメリカやEUと並び，世界経済の動向に大きな影響を与えるほど巨大になりました。

　日本の製品は世界各地に輸出され，近年では，大企業ばかりでなく多くの中小企業も海外への進出を図っています。日本への関心，特に経済への関心は高まるばかりです。

　そこでNHKの国際放送「ラジオ日本」では，民間のシンクタンク大和総研の協力を得て，日本経済についてやさしく解説する番組を制作し，1993年の4月から1年間にわたって放送しました。戦後の経済の急成長の秘密は何なのか。経済が拡大する過程でどういう問題につき当たったのか。そして，そこに働く人々の暮らしぶりはどうなのかなどについてわかりやすく伝え，日本経済の姿を理解してもらいたいと思ったからです。

　本書はこの番組をもとに，データを一部新しいものに変えるなど，加筆修正してまとめたものです。

　経済活動の分野で，国際化と相互依存の関係はますます強まっています。外国の人に日本経済を理解してもらう際に本書を役立てていただければ幸甚に思います。

NHK国際局制作センター部長
桑江　勝巳

Preface

"From burned ruins to economic superpower." Japan was a scorched plain at the end of World War II, and the startling economic growth that it achieved in such a short time is nothing less than a miracle. Whereas Japan's economy was once so weak that it was often said that "when America sneezes, Japan catches cold," the Japanese economy today ranks alongside that of America and the European Union in terms of its impact on the world economy.

Japanese products are exported to every region of the world, and in recent years not only large enterprises but even small and medium-size enterprises have been making inroads overseas. Interest in Japan has grown, particularly as regards to its economy.

In response to this interest, NHK's internationally broadcast "Radio Japan," in cooperation with the private think-tank Daiwa Institute of Research created a series of programs aimed at explaining the Japanese economy in simple terms. This year-long series was broadcast starting in April 1993. What were the secrets of Japan's rapid economic growth following the war? What issues did Japan encounter as a result of its economic growth? What effect did this have on the lives of Japan's workers? It was hoped that these explanations would help people to better understand the situation of Japan's economy as a whole.

This volume is based on these broadcasts, which have been partially revised and supplemented with new data.

In the field of economic activity, the themes of internationalization and mutual coexistence are growing ever stronger. We hope that this volume will be of help to non-Japanese readers who seek a better understanding of the Japanese economy.

Katsumi Kuwae

NHK, Overseas Broadcasting Department,
News & Program Production Division
Director

まえがき

　バブル経済の崩壊を受けて始まった景気後退は，1991年5月から1993年10月までの30カ月間続き，戦後で2番目に長い不況となりました。しかも経済企画庁が景気回復の宣言をしたのは，実際に景気が上昇し始めたときより11カ月も後の1994年9月になってからでした。

　本書のもとになった番組「日本経済ミニ事典」が放送されたのは，1993年4月からの1年間でしたから，「平成不況」といわれる不況の真っ只中だったわけです。この間，不況を乗り切るために企業のリストラの必要性が叫ばれ，一方では海外から，日本の貿易黒字がいつまでも減らないのは経済システムに問題があるからだとの批判も浴びました。終身雇用制度や年功序列型賃金など日本式経営の根幹をなすものが揺らぎ始め，サラリーマンの意識にも大きな変化が起き始めました。

　本書は，こうした最新の動きも織り込みながら，戦後の日本経済の発展を支えたものは何だったのか，今どんな課題を抱えているのかをわかりやすく紹介しようと試みたものです。

　第1部では日本式経営を取り上げました。戦後しばらくは，日本製品と言えば「安かろう，悪かろう」が相場でした。それが今では，「Made in Japan」といえば品質の良さを代表するものになっています。なぜそうなったのでしょうか。主に欧米諸国の会社経営との比較で見ていきます。

　第2部では働く人々の姿を取り上げています。日本では全体の70%から75%がサラリーマン家庭といわれます。世界で最も豊かな国のひとつになったといわれる日本のサラリーマンですが，その実態はどうなのでしょうか。

　第3部は戦後の経済政策についてです。「日本株式会社」というこ

Introduction

The economic recession which began with the collapse of the so-called "Bubble Economy" lasted 30 months from May 1991 through October 1993, the second longest economic slump since the end of World War II. Moreover, the Economic Planning Agency's declaration that the economy was recovering did not occur until September 1994, fully 11 months after business activity first began to increase.

The program "A Mini-Guide to the Japanese Economy," upon which this book is based, was broadcast starting in April 1993, precisely during the so-called "Heisei Recession." During this period the necessity of restructuring in order to overcome the economic downturn was being advocated at the same time that Japan was inundated with criticism from abroad concerning its economic system, which prevented any reduction whatever in its trade surplus. The system of lifetime employment and the payment of wages according to seniority, which form the basis of Japanese-style management, began to crumble, and the consciousness of employees toward their jobs began to change radically.

This volume takes these recent developments into account while attempting to explain in easily understandable terms what sustained the development of Japan's economy after the war, as well as what issues the economy now faces.

The first section deals with Japanese-style management. Shortly after the war, Japanese goods were known for being "cheap" and "poor in quality." Today, the label "Made in Japan" indicates a product of high quality. How did this change come about? Comparison are made primarily with Western nations.

The second section deals with those who work. It is said that between 70% and 75% of all Japanese households are headed by a

とがよくいわれましたが，日本の経済発展の中で政府はどういう役割を果たしたのでしょうか。

　最後の第4部では国際社会の中での日本経済を取り上げました。貿易摩擦や外国人労働者などについて解説しています。

　なお，難しいといわれる経済のことを楽しく理解していただくために，毎回クイズを出題しました。クイズに出てくるデータは日本経済の実態を示す重要な数字です。是非，読者の皆さんも挑戦してみてください。また，和文と英文の中のキーワードを対照させましたので，利用してください。

ＮＨＫ国際局経済プロジェクト
チーフ・ディレクター　中村　治

salaried worker. What is the actual situation of these workers in Japan, one of the wealthiest nations in the world?

The third section is concerned with postwar economic policy. We have often heard the term "Japan Inc." and this section deals with the role that the government has played in Japan's economic development.

The fourth and final section examines the Japanese economy within international society, discussing such issues as trade friction and non-Japanese laborers in Japan.

Economics is often thought to be difficult, and to make it enjoyable and easy to understand, each chapter includes a quiz. The data in each quiz consists of important statistics indicating the true state of the Japanese economy, so I hope that everyone will try to answer the questions in each quiz. I also hope that you will make use of the keywords contrasted in the Japanese and English texts.

Osamu Nakamura
NHK, Overseas Broadcasting Department,
Economic Project Senior Program Director

執筆者 Writers

NHK 国際局 経済プロジェクト
NHK Overseas Broadcasting Department, Economic Project

中村　治
NAKAMURA Osamu (Senior Program Director)

松永　日出男
MATSUNAGA Hideo (Program Director)

北泉　マリ
KITAIZUMI Mari (Program Director)

(株) 大和総研経済調査部
Daiwa Institute of Research Co., Ltd., Economic Research Department

翻訳者 Translators

(株) NHK情報ネットワーク, バイリンガルセンター
NHK Joho Network, Inc., Bilingual Center

(株) 翻訳情報センター
Translation Services, Inc.

目次 ——————————— Contents

装　幀　菅谷貞雄
本文イラストレーション　高橋　満

日本式経営の特徴
JAPANESE-STYLE MANAGEMENT

1 | サラリーマン社長

日本企業の社長の月収は，新入社員の何倍くらいで
しょうか。

① 10倍　② 50倍　③ 100倍

● 社長の月収

● 社長の登用にも
　違い

A：第1部では，戦後日本経済が急速に発展，拡大す
る原動力となった日本企業の特徴についてお話し
します。第1章では，その日本企業の**社長**とはど
んな人かについてご紹介しましょう。まずクイズ
の答えですが，正解は**①**の10倍です。1991年に民
間の調査機関である政経研究所が行った調査によ
りますと，日本の企業の社長の**月収**は，平均で
190万円。**新入社員**は18万1000円で，約その10分
の1です。

Q：アメリカではどのくらいなのですか。

A：アメリカの場合は，平均すると約50倍です。日本
に比べるとかなり高いですね。ちなみに日本の平
均的な労働者の月収は，同じく'91年に行われた
総務庁の家計調査によりますと，34万3000円で
す。社長の月収は，それに比べれば約5.5倍高い
だけで，トップの地位はますます平均的な労働者
の中に埋没していきます。

Q：社長といえば雲の上のような存在に思えますが，
意外と差が小さいですね。

A：そうですね。これは，特に日本の企業の特徴とい
えるかもしれません。というのは，日本の大企業

18

President as an Employee

> **How much more does the president of a Japanese company make than an entry-level employee?**
>
> ① 10 times　② 50 times　③ 100 times

A : In the first part of this book, we'll begin by discussing the characteristics of Japanese companies which powered Japan's economic recovery and development after World War II. In this chapter, we'll take a look at the **presidents** of Japanese companies. The correct answer to the question is number one, 10 times. A 1991 survey by a private research organization, Seikei Research Institute found that the average **monthly salary** of presidents of Japanese companies is ¥1,900,000. A **new employee's** salary is ¥181,000, about 1/10th that amount.

Q : What are the comparable averages in the United States?

A : The presidents of American firms make about 50 times more than new employees, much more than the Japanese ratio. Incidentally, according to a report by **the Management and Coordination Agency** on family budgets in 1991, the average worker in Japan earns a monthly salary of ¥343,000 and the presidents of firms earn 5.5 times more than that. This means that the top echelon salary in a Japanese company is fairly close to that of the average worker.

Q : One would imagine that there would be a big gap between the president and a rank-and-file employee, but actually the gap is small.

A : That's right. This is especially a characteristic of most Japanese companies. Most top executives in major firms join the company

のトップは，学校を卒業してすぐに入社した後，20年から30年かけて，階段を一歩一歩上がるようにしてその地位に到達した人が，ほとんどだからです。

Q：外国の企業の**経営者**はどうなんでしょうか。

A：欧米では，いろいろな会社を渡り歩いて実績を上げた人が，トップの地位を獲得するというシステムになっています。しかも，こうした競争に参加できるのはMBA（経営学修士）という，企業の**経営，財務，人事管理**などに関する教育を専門的に受けたごく一部の人々に限られています。

Q：こうしたシステムのもとでは，地位をめぐる競争が極めて厳しいという話を聞きますが。

- アメリカの社長は

A：トップの地位も安泰ではなく，業績が悪ければ解任されるといった事態も多いですね。また，**ヘッドハンティング**と言われる**人材**の引き抜きが多いのも，日本とは違うところです。1993年3月，世界最大のコンピューターメーカー，IBMのトップが，**業績不振**のために交代しました。新しく**会長**になったガーストナー氏は，IBMに引き抜かれる前は，大手食品会社のRJRナビスコの会長をしていました。ガーストナー氏は，ナビスコの会長になる前には，大手金融サービス会社，アメリカンエキスプレスの社長も務めた実力経営者です。

Q：なるほど。そうした厳しい競争に勝ち抜いた人には，それにふさわしい報酬が与えられるというわけですね。

A：そのとおり。その結果，経営者と一般の社員との格差が大きくなります。格差が大きすぎるという批判も一部にはありますけどね。

- 収入格差が小さいメリット

Q：日本のように，トップと社員の収入の格差が小さいということは，どんなメリットがあるのでしょうか。

A：「**仲間意識**」や「**企業一家**」という意識が強くな

20

immediately after graduation, then work for 20 to 30 years, rising gradually through the ranks.

Q : How about the **management** in foreign companies?

A : In Europe and the United States, people who change jobs and get good results get the top positions. But only a limited number of people are competitive in this area. Most have graduate degrees such as MBAs. In graduate school they make a special study of company **management, finance** and **personnel management**.

Q : I've heard that competition for those positions is really fierce under this system.

A : Yes, top executive positions are definitely not secure and people get fired if they can't produce good results. U.S. corporations often go "**headhunting**," poaching **talented people** from other companies. This is not a common practice in Japanese corporations. In March 1993, a top executive at IBM, the world's largest computer manufacturer, was replaced because of **poor business results**, and Louis V. Gerstner became the new **chairman**. He had been chairman at RJR Nabisco, a large food products company before being drafted by IBM. Mr. Gerstner is a skillful manager, and served as the president of American Express, a financial service company, before moving to Nabisco

Q : I see. The people who are selected in these large fierce competitions are generously rewarded, aren't they?

A : Yes, that's right. But as a result, it widens the gap between the executives and regular employees. Some people find this gap to be a problem.

Q : What are the merits of having a small gap in salary between executives and regular employees such as Japanese companies have?

A : The consciousness of "**fellowship**" or "**the company being**

ポイント

るることです。これが，日本式経営の大きな特徴の
ひとつですね。日本の会社では，**管理職**と一般の
社員が同じ事務所で机を並べて仕事をしたり，同
じ食堂で一緒に食事をするというパターンが大半
です。そのため，「会社は社員全体によって支え
られている」，あるいは「会社は社員の生活を維
持する器」という意識が強くつちかわれます。

・デメリット

Q：それでは，デメリットは？

A：このシステムですと，入社した時点では誰でもト
ップになる可能性があるわけですが，昇進の際に
は，**減点主義**による選別が行われがちなんですね。
その結果，競争に勝ち残って経営者になる人は，
できるだけ失敗をしないようにしようという傾向
が強くなり，何か決断をするにあたっては，守り
の姿勢をとることが多くなるというマイナス面が
あります。

like your own family" becomes stronger. This is one of the features of Japanese management. In most Japanese companies, **administrators** and regular employees sit side by side in the same office and eat in the same company cafeteria. This fosters the feeling that the company is supported by all employees and that the company is a means to support the livelihood of all employees.

Q : What then are the demerits?

A : According to this system, at the point of entering the company, everyone has an equal chance of climbing the corporate ladder. But at promotion time, the company tends to select people by the **demerit system**. As a result, people get promoted to management positions by making the fewest mistakes, and this promotes a conservative and defensive stance in their decision making.

2 | 優れた品質管理

> アメリカのある調査会社は，毎年，新車のトラブル
> がどの程度起きているかを調べて，「品質のよい車の
> ベストテン」を発表しています。さて1994年の調査
> で，日本車はベストテンの中に何車入っていたでし
> ょうか。

A：戦後しばらくは，「安かろう，悪かろう」といわ
　　れていた日本製品，その品質がよくなったのはな
　　ぜでしょうか。この章では品質管理についてお話
　　します。クイズの正解は，8車です。この調査は，
　　ＪＤパワーという調査会社が実施しているもの
　　で，正確にいいますと10位には2つの車が同点で
　　並んでいるので，11車中8車が日本車でした。残
　　る3車はアメリカ車です。

Q：やはり日本車の品質はいいのですね。車に限らず，
　　日本の製品の品質がよいのはどうしてなんですか。

● アメリカから
　QCを導入、
　TQCに改良

A：戦後間もなく，アメリカからＱＣ（**品質管理**）を
　　取り入れたことが，大きく作用しています。ただ
　　しＱＣを実施するにあたって，日本の企業のやり
　　方はアメリカとかなり違うので，同じ品質管理で
　　もＴＱＣ（**全社的品質管理**）といっています。

Q：両者はどう違うのですか。

A：アメリカの初期のＱＣは，製品を作った後の出荷
　　の段階の検査で，**不良品を取り除く**ことに限定さ
　　れていました。しかし日本の場合は，生産の段階
　　で不良品を出さないためにはどうしたらよいかと

Superior Quality Control

> U.S. research company surveys the problems of new cars every year and then ranks the top ten cars in term of quality. Can you guess how many Japanese cars were ranked in the top ten in the 1994 survey?

A : For quite a while after World War II, people regarded Japanese products as cheap and of poor quality. How has quality improved? Our subject in this chapter is quality control. The answer is eight Japanese cars. J D Power and Associates carried out this survey. Actually two cars were tied for tenth in the survey, so eight Japanese cars and three American cars were nominated.

Q : Japanese cars really are of high quality, aren't they? Why are not only Japanese cars but also products in general of such high quality?

A : In the years immediately after World War II, the introduction of a U.S. system called **"quality control"** or "QC" greatly affected quality. As it is quite different from the U.S. system in actual practice, however, the Japanese call it **"total quality control"** or "TQC."

Q : How are the two systems different?

A : In the early days in the United States, quality control was limited to inspecting products at the shipment stage and removing the inferior ones. On the other hand, Japanese concentrated their efforts on reducing **inferior products** as much as possible at

いう点に力点を置いたんです。したがって**製品設計から資材の仕入れ，生産，在庫管理，そして出荷**に至るまで，いろいろと工夫したわけです。また品質管理には，企業のトップから従業員に至るまで，全社的な取り組み体制がとられました。それで**ＴＱＣ**，全社的品質管理というわけです。

Q：品質管理に力を入れることで，**生産性**の低下を招く心配はありませんか。

A：欧米ではそういう考え方もあったようですが，品質管理を徹底すれば，不良品は大幅に減少します。その結果，従来なら不良品が出るたびに**生産ライン**を停止しなければならないところを，その必要がなくなるので，かえって生産性の向上につながったということです。

・ TQC成功の理由

Q：日本のＴＱＣが，成功したのはなぜなのでしょうか。

A：これはやはり日本式経営の大きな特徴である**終身雇用制**と切り離して考えることはできないでしょう。ＴＱＣの土台となっているのは，職場ごとにつくられた**ＱＣサークル**の活動です。この活動は，従業員自身が改善すべき点を見つけ，会社に提案をしていくものです。そのためには一人一人の従業員が自分の仕事に習熟するとともに，自分の仕事が全体の中でどんな位置を占めているのかをよく知っていなければ，機能しません。その点，日本の企業は終身雇用制のもとで，定年までの間に社員にいろいろな職場を経験させ，幅広い技能を習得させる社員教育を行っていますからね。

Q：従業員の定着率があまりよくない欧米では，難しいということですか。

A：それもあるでしょうし，欧米の場合，たとえ同じ企業に長くいる人の場合でも，ひとつの専門分野にずっといることが多いですね。そうなると，他の工程のことはあまりわからないということにな

the production stage, from **product design, stocking materials,** actual **production,** and **inventory control,** all the way to the **shipment** stage. The entire company, from the top executives to the regular employees, grappled with quality control. And that's what is meant by total quality control.

Q : Was there no possibility of decreasing their **productivity** because of such concentration on quality control?

A : That's what European and U.S. companies thought. But thorough quality control cuts down the number of inferior products substantially. As a result, they don't have to stop the **production line** which they used to do whenever an inferior product came through, so overall productivity rises.

Q : What brought about the success of Japanese TQC?

A : I don't think you can separate its success from the **lifetime employment system,** one notable factor of Japanese management. TQC is based on **QC circle** activity, which is organized in each section of the company. When employees find areas that need to be improved, they submit proposals to the company. For this to succeed, each worker has to be well trained in his job and know what function his job has in relation to the entire company. In Japanese companies, employees under the lifetime employment system gain experience in a variety of areas and learn a wide range of skills by the time of their retirement.

Q : That means TQC might be difficult in Europe and the United States, where workers don't stay in one company for a long time.

A : Well, that may be true. Even if a worker does stay in one company for a long time, in most cases he specializes in one field for that period. So he tends not to know much about other sections in the company. Providing complete **repair service** to gain

りがちです。このほかにも，日本製の品質が良い
のは，**アフターサービス**が徹底していて，ユーザ
ーから不満や要望があった場合には，それを生産
現場にフィードバックすること，それに生産工程
のロボット化が進んだことも大きな理由でしょう。

● 外国もTQC導入

Q：外国でも，このTQCという品質管理のやり方を
取り入れていると聞いていますが。

A：そのとおりです。QCの発祥の地アメリカでも日
本式経営に対する関心は高く，すでに多くの企業
が日本のTQCの考え方を逆輸入しています。初
めに述べた自動車の**品質調査**でも，アメリカ車の
評価はここ数年着実に上昇しています。これも品
質管理によるところが大きいと思われます。

feedback from customers' complaints and demands on the factory also improves quality. Another major element here is the increased use of robots in production.

Q : I hear that companies in other countries are also implementing TQC.

A : That's right. Companies in the U.S., the birthplace of quality control, are really interested in Japanese-style management. Many companies have already reimported the concept of TQC back to the United States. In the past several years, American cars have been improving steadily in the **quality survey** I mentioned at the beginning of the chapter. This probably has a lot to do with quality control.

3 | 日本の研究開発

WIPO（世界知的所有権機関）がまとめた統計によると，1991年1年間に全世界で約125万件の特許の出願がありました。さてこのうち日本は，約何％を占めているでしょうか。

① 10%　② 20%　③ 30%

ポイント

A：日本製品の国際競争力が強まった背景には，**研究開発**に力を入れたことが指摘されていますが，その実態はどうでしょうか。クイズの答えは③の30％で，件数は38万件です。厳密にいえば，この出願件数は日本で受け付けたもので，その中には外国人の分も入っています。しかし逆にアメリカの件数には日本人の出願したものが入っていますから，傾向として日本が多いことには，変わりありません。

Q：どうして日本はこんなに多いのですか。

A：研究開発費そのものは，欧米に比べて突出しているわけではありませんが，企業が**応用研究**や**商品化**に力を入れているからだといわれています。

● 研究開発費の
　現状

Q：その研究開発費の現状はどうなんですか。

A：官民合わせた日本の研究開発費は，1991年で12兆7000億円。GNP（国民総生産）に占める割合は2.77％で，アメリカ，旧西ドイツの2.65％を上回っています。しかし以前はアメリカや旧西ドイツの方が高く，日本が両国を抜いたのは1989年

Japanese Research and Development

> According to statistics from the World Intellectual Property Organization (WIPO), there were approximately 1.25 million patent applications worldwide in 1991. What percentage of these were from Japan?
>
> ① 10%   ② 20%   ③ 30%

A : Focusing on **research and development** (R and D) has been a factor in the strong international competitiveness of Japanese products. What is the actual situation? The answer to the quiz is number three, 30%. A total of 380,000 patents applications were submitted in Japan. Strictly speaking, this is the number of patent applications Japan received, which includes applications submitted by foreigners. The United States statistics also include patent applications by Japanese. But overall, the number is larger in Japan.

Q : Why are there so many patent applications in Japan?

A : It's not that research and development expenditures are much larger than in the United States and Europe, but companies in Japan put most of their efforts into **applied research** and **developing products.**

Q : How much is government and private enterprise spending on R and D?

A : Combining government and private enterprise, Japan spent ¥12.7 trillion on R and D in 1991, or 2.77% of its **gross national product** (GNP). This is more than in the United States and former West Germany at 2.65% of their GNPs. But until 1989, the percentage spent in the United States and former West Germany

になってからです。近年になって日本の研究開発が活発になったことを裏付けています。日本の場合，**研究開発費**のうち**民間企業**のものが全体の4分の3を占めています。

Q：その日本企業の研究開発の特徴といえば何でしょうか。

● 日本の重点は
　生産技術開発

A：**生産技術**の開発に重点を置いていることです。新製品はもちろん既存の製品についても，生産の方法を改善し，合理化，省力化を行ってコストを削減していく努力です。その結果，生産性は上がり競争力が上がります。日本企業が世界で圧倒的なシェアを持つ製品も現れました。大和総研の推定によると，日本製のＶＴＲは70％に達していますし，**感熱紙型のファクシミリ**のシェアは，全世界の市場の90％を超えています。

Q：90％とはすごいですね。

A：このほか，日本の研究開発をアメリカと比べますと，政府機関と企業の共同研究が比較的盛んなことがいえると思います。たとえば，**半導体**や**光ファイバー**，それに次世代コンピューターなどの分野では，政府と企業とが共同で技術開発を行っています。

Q：この点アメリカはどうなんですか。

● アメリカは基礎
　研究と軍事研究

A：アメリカは，**基礎研究**や**軍事研究**，それに宇宙開発などの**国家的なプロジェクト**には，非常に力を入れていて，その成果はご承知のとおりです。しかし民生品を作るための産業技術については，これまで政府は基本的に介入しないという方針でした。そんなこともあってアメリカの産業技術の競争力は日本などに後れを取る結果となってしまいました。クリントン政権は，1993年2月に新しい

was higher than in Japan, and this was the first time that Japan surpassed them. This shows just how active Japanese R and D has become in recent years. Furthermore, in Japan's case, three-fourths of all **R and D expenditures** are provided by **private enterprise.**

Q : What are the special features of Japanese R and D?

A : Japan emphasizes development of **product technology.** This means that Japan puts its greatest efforts into improving production methods and making production more efficient in order to cut costs for new and existing products. As a result, productivity and competitiveness increase. Japanese companies now put out some products which hold a dominant share of the world market. Daiwa Institute of Research estimates that Japanese video tape recorders account for 70% of the world market share and **thermal facsimile machines** account for over 90%.

Q : Ninety percent is pretty impressive.

A : Also joint research between the government and the private sector is more prominent in Japan than in the United States. For example, the Japanese government is working with the private sector to jointly develop technology for **semiconductors, optical fibers** and high-tech computers.

Q : Does the government participate in this way in the United States?

A : The United States puts a lot of effort into **basic research, military research** and **national projects** such as space development. I'm sure you're aware of their achievements. But the U.S. government's policy is not to interfere with development in industrial technology for producing consumer goods. This is one of the reasons why the United States lags behind Japan in industrial technology competitiveness. In February 1993 the Clinton administration put forth a new policy to promote scientific tech-

● 日本の研究開発
　の問題点

科学技術振興策を打ち出しましたが，この中で，今後は民間の技術開発を政府が支援する方針を打ち出しています。

Q：日本の研究開発の問題点といえば，「基礎研究にはあまり力を入れず，研究成果だけを横取りする」という外国からの批判がありますね。

A：技術面で日本の高度成長を支えたのは，欧米からの基礎技術の輸入とその応用にあったことは，間違いない事実ですね。例えば冒頭に紹介した特許についていえば，確かに出願件数は多いものの，特許の使用料をどれだけ外国に支払っているか，あるいは逆に受け取っているかを表す**技術貿易の収支**を見ると，日本はずっと**赤字**，つまり支払うほうが多いという状態が続いています。基礎研究の弱さを示しています。

Q：アメリカは逆に**黒字**というわけですね。

A：ええ。アメリカでは，外国から得る特許料収入が外国に支払う**特許料**の5倍近くにのぼっており，大幅黒字です。また日米2国間を見ても，この特許料の収支はアメリカ側の大幅な黒字です。ただし，日本もアジア向けに**国産技術**の輸出が増えているほか，基礎研究にもしだいに力を入れ始めていますから，技術貿易の赤字幅はしだいに減り始めています。いずれにしても，基礎研究については今後いっそうの努力が必要でしょう。

nology, part of which is to aid the private sector's technological development in the future.

Q : Other countries criticize Japanese R and D, saying that Japan's basic research is weak and it uses other countries' basic research to put out final products.

A : Yes. It's undeniable that applied research on basic technology imported from the West has supported Japan's high economic growth on the technological front. For example, the number of patents mentioned at the beginning of the chapter is large, but if we consider the **balance of technological trade**, which shows how much a country pays and receives for patent royalties, Japan has always had a **deficit**. This means Japan pays out more than it receives and it shows what a weak research base Japan has.

Q : On the other hand, the United States has a **surplus**, doesn't it?

A : That's right. The United States has a huge surplus, receiving almost five times more money than it pays on **patent royalties**. On a bilateral basis between the United States and Japan, the United States has a huge surplus in the balance of patent fees. But Japan is increasing its exports of **indigenous technology** to Asian countries and is beginning to put more effort into basic research, which should reduce technological trade deficit proportionately. In any case, Japan will have to put a lot more effort into its basic research from now on.

4 | ハイテク化，ロボット化

> **1993年のデータで，アメリカのロボット台数は約5万台ですが，日本はおよそ何台でしょうか。**
>
> ① 8万台　② 16万台　③ 37万台

● 日本のロボット化のきっかけ

A：日本は産業のハイテク化が進み，**産業用ロボット**の導入も多いといわれています。クイズの答えは，③の37万台です。

Q：アメリカの7倍以上ですね。

A：そうです。日本ロボット工業会の調べによると，いま世界中で使われているロボットはおよそ61万台といわれていますが，そのうちの60％近くが日本にあります。ロボットは今や自動車や電気機械，食品などあらゆる産業で使われています。**溶接**や**組み立て**，**検査**など，人の手の代わりとなって働いているのです。

Q：日本ではロボット化がどうしてこんなに進んだのでしょうか。

A：そのいちばんの原因は2度の石油ショックでしょう。それまでの日本経済は，**重化学工業**を中心に驚異的な成長を遂げてきました。石油などエネルギーを大量に使う産業に支えられてきたのです。その石油の価格が，第1次石油ショックの後には5倍以上にはね上がりました。日本は石油をほとんど輸入に頼っていますから，企業の経営が急速に悪化してしまったわけです。

High Tech and Automation

> According to data for 1993, the United States had about 50,000 industrial robots. Approximately how many robots did Japan have?
>
> ① 80,000 ② 160,000 ③ 370,000

A : It is said that technology is advancing within Japanese industry and the number of **industrial robot** is increasing. The answer to the quiz is number three, 370,000 robots.

Q : That's over seven times the number of robots in the United States.

A : That's right. According to a survey of the Japan Robot Association, there are approximately 610,000 robots in use worldwide, and more than 60% of those robots are found in Japan. Robots are used in every industry from automobiles to electric appliances to the food industry. They do jobs that people used to do, such as **welding, assembly** and **products inspection**.

Q : Why is Japanese automation so advanced?

A : The biggest factor was the two oil crises. Until that time, the Japanese economy had achieved spectacular growth led by the **heavy chemical industries**. The economy was supported by industries which use great quantities of energy, such as oil. After the first oil shock, oil prices rose by more than 500%. Since Japan depended on imports for almost all of its oil, company management suffered a sudden, heavy blow.

ポイント

● 省エネ、省力化
　も後押し

● 工場のオートメ
　ーション化

● ロボット化の
　影響

Q：そこで省エネルギー，省力化の問題が出てきたわ
　　けですね。

A：はい。企業は生産コストをできるだけ削減するた
　　めに，生産設備の徹底した見直しを行いました。
　　この過程でロボットの導入が進んだのです。それ
　　から省エネルギーという課題を抱え，エネルギー
　　をあまり使わない**産業構造**へとシフトしていきま
　　した。その代表が**エレクトロニクス産業**で，時代
　　をリードする成長産業として注目を集めました。
　　かつて学生の間で就職先の人気ナンバーワンだった
　　鉄鋼産業は影をひそめ，代わってエレクトロニク
　　スや**サービス産業**に学生が集まりだしたのです。

Q：そしてこのエレクトロニクス技術の発達で，工場
　　のオートメーション化がさらに進んだのですね。

A：エレクトロニクス化には高度な**精密加工技術**が必
　　要になります。人間から機械へのシフトにさらに
　　はずみがついたというわけです。

Q：工場の様子もずいぶん変わったようですね。

A：ええ，高性能の産業用ロボットの導入，**コンピュ
　　ーターによる設計**や**製造技術**の導入などで工場の
　　様子は一変しました。産業用ロボットの心臓部で
　　あるロボットコントローラーを月産6500台生産し
　　ている工場が山梨県にありますが，ここでは生産
　　ラインの無人化が実現しています。生産ラインの
　　主力は200台のロボットと220台のパソコンです。
　　こうしたロボット化で資材の効率的利用が可能に
　　なり，生産に携わる人間の数も減り，いっそうの
　　省エネルギー化，省力化が進みました。ある国の
　　経済の規模を見るのにGDP（**国内総生産**）とい
　　う概念を使います。つまり，その国の人たちが1
　　年間にどれだけのモノやサービスを生産したかを
　　見るわけです。このGDP1単位を生産するのに
　　必要なエネルギー量は，日本では'73年を100とす

Q : That's when industries started trying to simultaneously conserve energy and streamline operations.

A : That's right. Industries thoroughly reexamined equipment in order to cut production costs. During this process, industry began introducing robots. Since they had to conserve energy, they shifted to an **industrial structure** that didn't use as much energy as the **electronics industry**, a growth industry for the future. This put a damper on the **steel industry**, which until that time had been the most popular industry among college graduates looking for employment, and new graduates began to look for jobs in the electronics and **service industries**.

Q : So with the progress in electronics technology, factories became even more automated, right?

A : Yes. **High-precision processing technology** accompanied advances in the electronics industry. This added further impetus to the shift from humans to machines.

Q : Factories have really changed, haven't they?

A : Yes. The introduction of high-performance industrial robots and **computer-aided design** and **manufacturing, CAD** and **CAM**, changed the design and structure of factories. One factory in Yamanashi Prefecture produces 6,500 robot controllers, the "brains" for robots, every month. The factory has a completely automated production line made up of 200 robots and 220 personal computers. Such automation makes it possible to use materials more efficiently, and the number of people involved in production has been reduced. The result is savings of energy and streamlining of the production process. **Gross domestic product** (GDP) is an index of the scale of a nation's economy. It measures the total annual output of goods and services. The amount of energy required to produce one unit of GDP has fallen from 100 in 1973 to 67 in 1989.

ると，'89年には67にまで下がりました。

Q：しかし，ロボットの導入は，今までその仕事に従
事していた人の職を奪うことになりませんか。

A：確かにそういう面も否定できませんが，日本の企
業の場合，そうした余った労働力を企業内の他の
分野に移すことで吸収してきました。工場の余っ
た労働者を**ソフト開発**に回したり，営業に回した
りですね。日本式の経営のひとつといわれる「終
身雇用制度」や「企業内研修制度」によって，大
量の失業者を出すことなく危機を乗り切ってきた
のです。

Q : But doesn't automation take jobs away from people?

A : Well yes, that's true, but in Japanese industry, the surplus labor
force has been absorbed in other sections of the companies, by
transferring laborers from the factory to **software development** or sales. Japan averted mass unemployment through the
Japanese system of lifetime employment and in-house training.

5 | 終身雇用制度

労働者の雇用について，「働けるかぎり働いてもらってきた」「定年まで働いてもらってきた」など，終身雇用制度を採っている日本企業の割合はおよそ何％でしょうか。

① 50%　② 70%　③ 90%

- 終身雇用制度とは

- 昇進、昇給とリンク

A：この章では日本企業の従業員の雇用制度「終身雇用制度」についてご紹介します。終身雇用制度というのは，学業を終え，ある企業に就職した勤労者が定年になるまでずっとその一つの企業に勤め続けるという就労形態のことです。まずクイズの答えですが，正解は③の90％です。特に大企業の場合，この数字はさらに大きくなりますから，ほとんどの企業が終身雇用制度を採用しているといってもよいでしょう。

Q：欧米のように，勤労者が条件の良い企業に次々と転職してしまうということはないのですか。

A：理解しなければならないのは，終身雇用制度は，昇進・昇給と密接に結びついていることです。日本の企業では，若いときは比較的給料が低く抑えられていますが，30代半ばくらいから急速に給料水準が上昇するのが普通のパターンです。そして転職した人，つまり途中から入社した人は，それ以前の経歴があまり評価されません。したがって転職する人は少ないのです。若いときは安い給料に我慢しても，長い期間同じ会社にいた方が有利なシステムになっているわけです。

The Lifetime Employment System

> What percentage of Japanese companies observe life-time employment, keeping employees as long as the employees are able to work or until they reach retire-ment age?
>
> ① 50%   ② 70%   ③ 90%

A : In this chapter we will look at the Japanese employment system. In this form of employment workers take jobs with an employer following their schooling and continue with that employer until **retirement age**. The correct answer is number three, 90%. This is especially true for large companies, so it's safe to say that almost all companies use the **lifetime employment system**.

Q : Aren't there some cases where people change jobs in order to get better conditions as in Western countries?

A : What we have to understand is that the lifetime employment system is closely tied to **promotions** and **pay raises**. Salaries in Japanese enterprises are relatively low for younger workers, but normally the salary level rises dramatically when a worker reaches his mid-thirties. Companies don't recognize previous **work experience** when workers switch jobs. That's why few people change jobs. So under this system it's beneficial to employees to continue to work for the same company for a long time, even if they have to put up with low salaries when they are young.

- 戦後に定着

- メリット

- デメリット

- 欧米企業の雇用形態

Q：終身雇用制度はいつごろからある制度なのですか。

A：それほど昔からではなく，第2次大戦後，それも1950年以降，日本経済が著しく成長する中で，こうした形が定着しました。ただ，この制度は法律で決められているものではなく，あくまでも慣行なのです。

Q：終身雇用制度にはどんなメリットがあるのですか。また，日本の経済成長にどんな役割を果たしたのですか。

A：従業員にとっては，突然の解雇の心配なしに勤務でき，長期の生活設計ができることがいちばんのメリットでしょう。企業にとっては，優秀な労働力を長期間にわたって確保でき，従業員の企業に対する忠誠心を維持できることが最大のメリットです。特に研究開発，技術開発のように長期にわたる努力が必要な分野では，従業員が自分の雇用と地位に関して安心して，長期間研究に専心できることが必要です。このように安定した**職場環境**が穏やかな**労使関係**を生み，企業内に技術やノウハウが蓄積され，日本は高度経済成長をスムーズに達成することができたのです。

Q：デメリットについてはどうですか。

A：不況になっても従業員の解雇が難しいので，企業の業績回復が遅れます。また，賃金の高い中高年者を多く抱え込むと，その人件費が経営を圧迫します。近年，日本の労働力の年齢構成はそういう状態になりつつあります。このほか，新しい事業に進出したい企業にとっては人材を集めにくいということもあります。

Q：いずれにせよ欧米の企業の**雇用形態**とは，かなり違うようですね。

A：欧米の企業では，業績が悪化した場合は，不要な

Q : How long has lifetime employment been the rule?

A : It began not that long ago. It is a postwar phenomenon that actually became common only after 1950, and it basically accompanied high economic growth. It's important to note that it is merely a custom and is not prescribed by law.

Q : What are the merits of the lifetime employment system? And what role did it play in the growth of the Japanese economy?

A : The biggest merit is that workers can work without fear of sudden dismissal and make long-term plans for their lives. The biggest merit for the company is that it can secure a superior labor force for a long period of time and maintain employees' loyalty to the company. Particularly in the areas of research and development, and technology development which require work over the long term, workers must be able to devote themselves to their research without worrying about their job security or position. This stable **working environment** has led to good **labor-management relations**. Also the company accumulates technology and know-how. One of the reasons Japan was able to achieve smooth high economic growth was because of this system.

Q : What are the demerits of this system?

A : Since it's difficult to let employees go in times of recession, business recovery in the company is retarded. Also, the budget for salaries is stretched if the company has a lot of middle-aged and older employees with high salaries. The age structure of the Japanese labor force continues to head in this direction. This system also makes it difficult for new businesses to gather talented people.

Q : This system must be really different from the **employment systems** in Western countries.

A : Companies in the West reduce personnel when business is poor

従業員は解雇します。反対に，事業を拡大したり新規の分野に進出するときは，それに必要な従業員を随時採用します。高い給料で募集すれば，適切な質と量の従業員を集めることができるのです。しかし，従業員の定着率は日本のようには高くないため，企業にとっては**経営設計**がやりにくい面もあるでしょう。

Q：終身雇用制度が揺らぎ始めた，という人もいますが。

A：ある音響機器メーカーが業績不振のために，勤続年数が長く給料の高い従業員を事実上解雇し，サラリーマン社会に衝撃を与えました。また中高年齢層を減らすために，優遇条件を付けて**希望退職**を募集する企業も増えています。

● 終身雇用制度
　の今後

Q：そうしますと長期的に見て，この制度は変わっていくのでしょうか。

A：いろいろと手直しはするでしょうが，企業としてはメリットの大きい制度ですから，できるだけ維持していくだろうと思います。しかし，従業員の考え方に変化が出てきています。日本生産性本部が1993年春に就職した新入社員を対象に行ったアンケート調査では，最近の**不景気**にもかかわらず，「状況しだいで会社を移る」と答えた人が30％もいました。現実に転職するかどうかはまた別の問題ですが，終身雇用制度に対する意識が変わるきざしではありそうです。

and employ personnel as needed when they expand operations or enter a new field. They can attract the right number of people with the appropriate skills by advertising high salaries. In contrast with Japan, not as many workers stay with one company for a long time, so this makes **management planning** difficult.

Q : Some say lifetime employment in Japan has been weakening.

A : Because of the economic slowdown, a certain company specializing in audio equipment was forced to dismiss longtime employees who had high salaries. This came as a shock to salaried workers. In addition, an increasing number of companies are offering attractive benefits to lure some employees in older age groups into **voluntary retirement**.

Q : This system will probably change in the long term, won't it?

A : There will probably be some adjustments, but the system is beneficial to companies, so they want to maintain it as long as they can. However, employees' attitudes are changing, too. The Japan Productivity Center carried out a survey of new employees in spring 1993. Despite the current **recession**, 30% of the pollees replied that they would switch companies if the situation called for it. Whether they would actually change jobs or not is another question, but it's one sign that attitudes towards the lifetime employment system are changing.

6 | 年功序列型賃金

日本の大企業で，同期入社の社員について「入社後
10年程度はできるだけ同時に昇進させる」というや
り方をとっているのは，何割ぐらいあるでしょうか。

①　20%　②　40%　③　60%

● 年功序列型賃金
　とは

A：この章では，勤続年数が長くなるにつれて地位も
　給料も上がっていく「**年功序列型賃金**」について
　ご紹介します。クイズの正解は，②の40%です。
　これは，従業員が1000人以上の大企業を対象にし
　た調査の結果です。

Q：入社後10年といえば，大学卒であれば32～33歳で
　すよね。その年齢まで昇進に差をつけない企業が，
　40%もあるとは驚きですね。

A：この調査は**労働省**が1987年に実施したものです
　が，それによると，さらに「入社後15年後までは
　同時昇進」と答えた企業が10社に1社の割合であ
　るんですよ。

Q：この制度の背景にある考え方は，勤続年数が同じ
　人は企業への貢献度は同じだというのでしょうか。

A：基本的な考え方は，そのとおりです。各人に能力
　の差があることは認めるが，35歳ぐらいまでは企
　業の中で与えられる仕事の量と質にあまり違いは
　ない，したがって企業に対する貢献度も余り変わ
　らないという考え方なんです。それに賃金や昇進
　に差をつけると，社員の間に反感や対立が生じる

Seniority Wage System

What percentage of large Japanese corporations simultaneously promote colleagues who entered the company about ten years after they entered?

① 20% ② 40% ③ 60%

A : In this chapter we'll discuss the **seniority wage system**, under which salaries and position rise with the length of service within the company. The answer is number two, 40%. This figure applies to companies that have over one thousand employees.

Q : Let's see, ten years after entering the company means that they would be 32 or 33 years old if they graduated from college. I'm surprised that 40% of companies don't make any distinction in promotions between employees for such a long period of time.

A : According to a survey by **the Ministry of Labor** in 1987, one out of ten companies answered that they promote collegues simultaneously for the first 15 years after entering the company.

Q : Is the principle behind this system that employees who have worked for the same amount of time make the same degree of contribution to the company?

A : Yes, that's the basic idea. Companies do acknowledge the differences in abilities among employees, but all employees receive about the same amount and difficulty of work until they are about 35. So companies think that their degree of contribution to the company is about the same. Also if they single out employees for wage raises or promotions, it will cause animosity among

● メリットは職場
との一体感

● 制度見直しの
動き

ので，職場の一体感を損なう恐れがあるというわけです。

Q：この制度のメリット，ほかにはどういう点がありますか。

A：年功序列型の賃金制度というのは，終身雇用制度とワンセットのものなので，そのメリットも重複するところがありますが，従業員にとっては**降格**や**減給**がなく，かつ将来の**昇進**や**昇給**がおおむね計算できるので，安心して生活設計を立てることができるのが最大のメリットでしょう。一方，企業にとっては，従業員に安心感を持たせることによって企業への忠誠心を高めることができること，それと従業員が落ち着いて勤務するので，将来の幹部を従業員の中からじっくりと選べることも大きなメリットでしょう。

Q：そのようなメリットがありながら，なぜ近年この制度を見直そうとする動きがあるのでしょうか。

A：終身雇用と年功序列の制度は，企業が安定的に成長し，しかも**業務内容**が大きく変わらないというときにはメリットが大きいのです。1950年代以降，日本の企業は毎年生産量が増え，売上高も増え，従業員数も増えました。業務が拡大するにつれて職場も増えたので，終身雇用制度の維持が可能となりました。つまり毎年多くの従業員が入社するので，多くの課長や係長といった管理職が必要となり，このため年功序列型の昇進，昇格制度によって処遇できたのです。ところが低成長時代に入った近年は，生産量や売上高が安定的に伸びず，従業員も簡単に増やすことができません。そうなりますと，ポストも仕事も増えないのに，勤務年数とともに給料だけが高くなる年功序列型賃金制度を維持することは，企業にとって大変負担が大きいものになってきたわけです。

employees which in turn, could destroy the feeling of unity in the workplace.

Q : Are there other merits to this system?

A : The seniority wage system goes hand in hand with the lifetime employment system. So that merits complement each other, but the biggest merit is the employees don't have to worry about **demotions** or **salary reductions**. In addition, employees can generally calculate their **promotions** and **pay raises**, so they can feel secure about their household finances. On the other hand, the company increases the employees' loyalty to the company by providing this sense of security. Another merit for the companies is that they can take time in selecting future executives.

Q : With all these merits, why has there been a recent movement to reevaluate this system?

A : The lifetime employment system and the seniority wage system are beneficial when the company enjoys steady growth and there is not much variety in **work contents**. Since 1950, production, sales and numbers of employees have steadily increased in Japanese enterprises. So it has been possible to maintain the lifetime employment system because the number of positions for new employees has steadily increased. Since new employees entered the company every year, companies needed many leaders and managers. So they were able to promote employees in line with the seniority system. But now that growth has slowed, and production and sales aren't rising steadily, companies can't increase their number of employees so easily. They are really hard pressed to maintain the seniority wage system as their employees get older and salaries grow larger, because there are no positions for them and there is less work to do.

ポイント

● 年俸制導入の
　動きも

● 「年功序列型」
　の将来は

Q：年功序列制度を見直す動きとして，具体的にはど
　んなものがあるんでしょうか。

A：欧米の企業で採用されている「**年俸制**」を導入す
　る企業が増えています。日本生産性本部が1992年
　10月に行った調査によりますと，日本の大企業の
　うち10％がすでに年俸制を導入。また30％の企業
　が導入を計画，残る企業のうちの半数も関心を持
　っていると答えています。今のところ，対象を管
　理職に限っている企業が大半です。

Q：見直しの動きとしてほかには？

A：年功序列型賃金のデメリットのひとつは，能力の
　ある若い人に対して仕事に見合った報酬が支払わ
　れないため，やる気をそいでしまうという点です。
　このため能力のあるものを従来より早めに昇進さ
　せたり，「**歩合制**」を導入する企業も増えています。

Q：この制度は，将来どうなるんでしょうか。

A：**通産省**の**外郭団体**である日本能率協会が1993年に
　実施した調査によりますと，年功序列的な**人事評
　価**，昇進について，「積極的な転換が必要」と答
　えた大企業の経営者は30％，「できれば転換すべ
　きである」と答えた経営者は62％にものぼりまし
　た。こうした結果から見ますと，いずれは年功序
　列型から能力や業績を重視した制度に変わってい
　くものと思われます。しかし，年功序列型という
　のは，新卒の大学生を一括して採用するといった
　従業員の採用制度や**退職金制度**などとも密接に結
　びついたものですから，その変わり方は，徐々に，
　しかもなし崩し的なものになるのではないでしょ
　うか。

Q : What exactly are companies doing to reevaluate the system?

A : A number of companies are introducing the **annual salary system** used in the United States and Europe. According to a survey conducted by the Japan Productivity Center in October 1992, 10% of Japanese companies have already introduced the annual salary system. Thirty percent planned to introduce it, and just about half of the remaining companies expressed interest in the system. Management positions are the main targets right now.

Q : What else is being reevaluated?

A : One of the demerits of the seniority wage system is that talented young people lose their motivation because they are not given salaries that truly reflect their contributions. So an increasing number of companies are introducing a **commission system**, while others have started to promote talented people faster.

Q : What do you think will happen to this system in the future?

A : The Japan Management Association, an **auxiliary organ** of **the Ministry of International Trade and Industry**, in 1993 conducted a survey on **personnel evaluation** and promotion according to the seniority system. Thirty percent of managers from large companies replied they have to change the system. Sixty-two percent of managers answered that they should change the system if possible. Based on these results, it seems that companies will move away from the seniority system to one that emphasizes accomplishments and ability. But since other practices such as employing new graduates all at once and the **retirement benefit system** are closely connected, the system will probably change little by little.

7 | 人材育成

日本の企業が重点的に能力開発訓練を行う対象は，
次の3つのうちのどれでしょうか。

① 課長層　② 新入社員　③女子社員

ポイント

A：終身雇用制度や年功序列制度を支えているものの
ひとつに，日本の企業が熱心に取り組む「**人材育
成**」があります。クイズの答えは，①の課長層で
す。日経連（**日本経営者団体連盟**）が1990年に
行った調査（複数回答も可）では，「課長層の能
力開発が重要」と答えた企業が，67％で第1位で
した。一方，「女子社員の能力開発」と答えた企
業は42％，「新入社員の教育」と答えた企業は
40％でした。

● 社員の能力開発
に熱心

Q：課長には能力の備わった人を採用するというのが
欧米企業の戦略ですが，なぜ日本の企業は課長層
の能力開発にそれほど力を入れるのでしょうか。

A：まず，**課長は企業活動の現場の指揮官**であること。
そして課長は企業戦略の企画や改革の発案の中心
的存在であること。さらに課長は将来の**部長**や経
営者の候補者であり，経営幹部への最初の登竜門
であることなどから，日本の企業では課長の地位
は重いのです。したがって，能力開発も重点的に
行うわけです。

Personnel Training

In which section of personnel do Japanese companies especially emphasis training? Select your answer from the choices below.

① managerial level employees   ② new employees
③ female employees

A : Japanese companies put great effort into the **training of personnel** because it is a major element that supports the lifetime employment system and the seniority system. The answer to the quiz is number one, managerial level employees. In a 1990 survey by Nikkeiren, **the Japan Federation of Employers' Associations,** companies were asked to mark as many choices as were applicable. Sixty-seven percent, the highest percentage of companies, answered that they emphasized developing the abilities of section chiefs. Forty-two percent replied that they emphasized women employees and 40% answered that they stressed new employees.

Q : Western firms employ managers with the appropriate capabilities. Why then do Japanese companies put so much effort into training their own managers?

A : First of all, **managers** are the on-the-spot directors of company activities. They also are key players in planning corporate strategy and reform. Furthermore, managers are future candidates for **general managers** and executive positions. Since it's the first step up the ladder of managerial positions, the position of section chiefs are very important in Japanese companies. Therefore, companies put considerable emphasis on developing their abilities.

ポイント

Q：ところで日本の企業では，一般に課長職に限らず，従業員に対する教育訓練に熱心だと聞いていますが，それはなぜなのでしょうか。

A：これまで日本企業の終身雇用制や年功序列型賃金制度についてお話ししましたが，この制度を最大限に生かすためには，従業員の能力開発が大変重要になってきます。欧米の企業のように，必要なときに必要な人材を採用するのとは違い，日本では高校や大学を卒業したばかりの人たちを定期採用するのが普通です。そしてこの人たちが将来，**係長**や課長になっていくのですから，その職にふさわしい能力をあらかじめ身につけさせておく必要があるのです。

Q：そのような教育は誰が行うのですか。

A：彼らの上司，または勤続年数の長い従業員です。大企業の課長の**評価基準**のひとつに，部下の教育をちゃんと行っているか，というのがあります。後輩を自分の後任が務まるように育て上げることが，課長に義務づけられているといってもよいでしょう。部長には課長を育て上げる義務があり，社長も自分の後任を社内で育て上げることが求められるのです。

● 外国企業は

Q：外国の企業の人材育成はどうなっているのですか。

A：外国では普通，従業員は自分の持っている知識や技術を他の従業員に教えたがらないといわれます。もし教えると，自分の競争者をひとり増やすことになり，次には自分が解雇される心配が出てくるからです。しかし日本では，終身雇用制度が普及していることや，同じ**部署**に長期間とどまることが少ないため，解雇の不安はなく，むしろ後継者の育成の方が重要になります。

Q：企業としてもこのような教育システムにはメリットが多いのですか。

Q : I have heard that Japanese companies are serious about educating and training all employees, not just the section chiefs. Why is that?

A : Well, we've already looked at the lifetime employment system and the seniority wage system. It's vital to develop employees' abilities in order to use these systems to the full. In contrast with firms in the West, which employ the right personnel for the job when necessary, Japanese companies regularly hire new employees who have just graduated from high school or college. Because these people are the **sub-section chiefs** and section chiefs of the company, companies have to make sure in advance that employees have the necessary abilities for the job.

Q : Who does the educating?

A : Their superiors or employees who have worked for the company for many years. One **standard for judging** section chiefs in large companies is whether they are educating the younger employees properly. It's fair to say that it's the responsibility of the section chief to train the younger employees so that they can take over his position. Then it's the department head's duty to teach the section chiefs, and the company president's duty to bring up his own successor within the company.

Q : What about the education system in non-Japanese companies?

A : In other countries, employees don't want to teach other employees their own knowledge and skills because that adds one more person to the competition, and then they have to worry about keeping their job or position. On the contrary, Japanese employees don't have to worry about dismissal because of the lifetime employment system and because they rarely serve in the same **section** for a long time. Educating younger employees is more important than worrying about dismissal.

Q : Are there many benefits for the companies?

A：後輩に教える知識や技術が企業の中に蓄積されていきますので，これが日本企業の強さの秘密でもあるのですね。特に，製造業にはこの傾向が強いので，日本製品の輸出競争力の強さにつながっているのです。

● 社員教育は
　現場主義

Q：ところで，日本の企業ではどんな**社内教育**を行っているのですか。

A：研修や講習会での教育ももちろんありますが，**オン・ザ・ジョブ・トレーニング（OJT）**が主体です。職場で先輩社員が教育しながら，それぞれの改善点も一緒になって考えていくのです。生産技術が社内に蓄積されながら高められていくというわけです。

Q：なるほど。しかし現場での教育に力を入れていきますと，その人の能力がひとつの分野に限られてしまうことになりませんか。

A：日本の企業の社内教育にはもうひとつ特徴があります。それは，従業員の**配置転換（ジョブ・ローテーション）**をたびたび行うことです。こうして，どの職場でも役立つ**ゼネラリスト**が育つのです。特に将来の幹部要員は，企業内の多くの職場を経験して優秀なゼネラリストになることを求められるのです。

● 人材育成、
　今後の課題

Q：それぞれの職場のリーダーから幹部まで，すべて企業内で育成するのですね。企業の人材育成の方法は今後も大きく変わることはないのでしょうか。

A：**産業構造**が変化するにつれ，企業がそれまでやってきた事業ではもはや大きな成長が望めなくなってきています。しかしこれまでの企業内教育制度では，新しい事業に進出しようとしても社員教育ができません。社内に先生がいないのですから。日本の大企業もこの点を十分認識しており，日経

A : The secret of Japanese companies' strength is that knowledge and skills taught to younger employees accumulates inside the company. Because this trend is especially prominent in manufacturing, Japanese products can compete in the export market.

Q : What kind of **in-house education** do Japanese companies have?

A : Of course it includes training and lectures, but the main activity is **on-the-job training** (OJT). Experienced employees teach the younger ones while actually working, and they work together to improve the company's business performance. This is how they accumulate production skills and improve those skills at the same time.

Q : I see. But if they emphasize this on-the-job training so heavily, aren't their skills limited to one area?

A : There is another unique aspect of Japanese in-house training, namely, frequent **job rotation**. The process cultivates generalists who are useful in any area within the company. Especially for future executives, Japanese companies require highly skilled **generalists** who have working experience in many areas of the company.

Q : So employees are trained in different departments of the company by everyone from departmental managers to executives. What are the chances that this method of personnel training will change in the future?

A : With the change in the **industrial structure**, Japanese companies can't expect to expand their business in their current fields. Even if they try to move into new fields, companies can't train employees under the current in-house educational system. They don't have anyone inside the company to teach employees. Large Japanese companies are well aware of this limitation, and as

ポイント

連の調査でもおよそ50％の企業が，5年後の最大
の課題は「新しい事業転換に即応した人材育成」
としています。しかし難しい課題です。

Q：新規事業を始めるには新しい教育訓練の方法が必
　要だというわけですね。
A：もうひとつ問題があります。ＯＪＴとかゼネラリ
　ストの養成が中心になっているので，新しい発明
　や発見に結びつきにくいのです。日本の企業は，
　応用技術には強いが**基礎技術**には弱いとよくいわ
　れますが，こんなところにも原因があるのでしょう。

shown in a survey by the Japan Federation of Employers' Associations about 50% of companies say their biggest challenge in the next five years will be to educate personnel who can be immediately effective when the company moves into new areas. It looks like a very difficult problem.

Q : They'll have to use new educational and training methods when they move into new fields.

A : Yes, and there's one more problem. Since this system focuses on OJT and bringing up generalists, it's difficult to come up with new inventions and discoveries. It's often said that Japanese companies are strong in **applied technology** but weak in **basic technology**, and this system may be one of the reasons why.

8 | 企業別労働組合

政府機関や民間企業の雇用者のうち，労働組合に加入している人の割合(組織率)は，日本，アメリカおよびイギリスで，それぞれ何%でしょうか。

① 16%　② 25%　③ 44%

● 各国の組合
　組織率

A：この章では，日本の**労働組合**についてご説明しましょう。まずクイズの答えですが，正解は日本が25%（'90労働省調べ），アメリカ16%（'90アメリカ労働省調べ），イギリス44%（'89イギリス労働省調べ）です。アメリカの組織率は，地域によって違いが大きく，製造業の歴史の古い北東部では25%を超えているのに対して，海外からの労働者の増加の著しい中西部では14%以下にとどまっています。

Q：日本の労働組合の組織率も地域によって違いがあるのですか。

A：いいえ。日本の場合は，地域よりもむしろ業種によります。平均では25%ですが，**公務員**は73%，電気，ガス，水道業のような公共事業を行なう大企業では61%です。一方，従業員が30人未満の小さな企業では，ほとんど組合がありません。

● 企業別組合と
　職種別組合

Q：日本の労働組合は，それぞれ企業ごとに組織されているのが大きな特徴ですね。

A：この点は，企業の枠を超えて，職種別に横のつながりを持った組合をつくっている欧米諸国と大きく違います。ひとつの大企業の中には，工場で働

In-house Unions

> **What percentage of workers in government and private corporations belong to labor unions? Pick the correct percentages for Japan, the United States, and Great Britain.**
>
> ① 16%　② 25%　③ 44%

A : In this chapter we'll introduce Japanese **labor unions**. First of all, the correct percentages are: Japan 25% (1990, Ministry of Labor), the United States 16% (1990, Labor Department),Great Britain 44% (1989, Department of Employment).　The percentage of labor union membership in the United States varies according to region. In the Northeast, which has a long history of manufacturing, membership is over 25%. On the contrary, in the Midwest, where the number of laborers from abroad is rising rapidly, membership is less than 14%.

Q : Does membership vary according to region in Japan as well?

A : No, it doesn't. Rather than region, in Japan, it varies according to the type of industry. The average is 25%, but it's 73% among **public employees**, and 61% in large utility companies such as electric, gas and water companies. However, there are almost no labor unions in companies which have less than 30 employees.

Q : One major characteristic of Japanese labor unions is that they are in-house unions.

A : Yes, this is totally different from labor unions in Western nations which have horizontal relationships between workers with the same type of job in different companies. In Japan, a union inside

く人，販売をする人，事務をする人などさまざまな職種がありますが，日本ではこのような人々が一緒になって，ひとつの企業でひとつの組合をつくっています。

Q：「**企業別組合**」と，「**職種別組合**」では，現実にはどんな違いが出てくるのですか。

A：職種別組合のイギリスでは，労働組合数はおよそ300なのに対し，企業別組合の日本では，7万2000もあります。日本では，企業別の小さな組合が多いことになります。しかしあまりにも小さな企業では，組合を維持していくだけのコストを負担できないため，組合をつくれないところも多いのです。その点，職種別組合ですと，小企業の従業員でも組合に入れます。

Q：企業ごとに組合が組織されていて，それぞれの組合の規模が小さいとなると，経営者との交渉力が弱くなりませんか。

A：必ずしもそうはなりません。経営者が交渉を拒否し，労働組合が**ストライキを行う**と，その企業だけがダメージを受け，競争している他の企業に市場のシェアを奪われてしまいます。これでは経営者は困ります。組合員もまた，企業の一員という意識が強いので，自分たちの企業がひどいダメージを受けては困るわけです。

Q：経営者も労働組合も，適当なところで妥協しようということになるのですね。

- 労働争議の
  発生頻度

A：1990年のＩＬＯ（**国際労働機関**）のデータで「**労働争議**によって操業できなくなった日数」を比べてみると，日本はアメリカのおよそ40分の1にとどまっています。日本では4月に**会計年度**が始まるので，ほとんどの企業でこの時期に賃金引き上げを決める交渉が行われますが，そうした場でも，他企業並みに条件が満たされると妥協することが

a company covers all occupations in that organization, that is, factory workers, salespeople, and office workers. All the workers in that company form one union within the company.

Q : What is the difference between **in-house unions** and **trade-specific unions**?

A : There are 300 trade unions in Great Britain, but under the in-house union system in Japan, there are 72,000 unions. Japan has a large number of small unions which are limited to one company, but in companies that are really small, employees can't afford to maintain a union, so they don't form one. Employees of small companies can join a union under the trade union system.

Q : But if unions are formed within a specific company and the respective unions are rather small, aren't they in a weaker bargaining position with management?

A : That's not necessarily true. Labor unions can **go on strike** if management refuses to negotiate, and because only that company would be damaged the company would lose market share to its competitors. That would be threatening to management. Also, union members feel that they themselves would suffer if they damaged their own company.

Q : So both management and labor have to make the appropriate compromises.

A : According to data from **the International Labor Organization (ILO)**, if we compare the number of days in 1990 when work was hindered due to **labor-management problems,** the ratio Japan to the United States is less than 1 to 40. In Japan the **fiscal year** begins in April, and most companies negotiate wage-raises at this time. The unions and companies negotiate and usually agree when the conditions reach the same level as other

多いのです。組合の元委員長をしていた社長もいますから、お互いに話し合いもスムーズにいく可能性が大きいというものです。

Q：こうした点が時に「馴れ合い」と批判されるゆえんですね。組合の元幹部がその会社の社長になるというのは、外国の人にとっては驚くべきことではないでしょうか。

A：これも日本独自の**人事制度**から生じることなのです。企業別労働組合の委員長や幹部も、組合員の中から選挙で選ばれた、その企業の従業員です。委員長も年功序列制度により、やがて昇進して管理職となり、組合を脱退します。そして取締役となって、経営側の代表として、組合と交渉を行います。組合の元幹部が社長となる例はそう珍しくありません。

Q：日本の労働組合は、変わっていくのでしょうか。

● 日本の組合の
　問題点

A：問題点はいくつか指摘されています。まず、組織率の低下です。日本の労働組合の組織率は平均25％ですが、これは25年前に比べると10％低下しています。その原因のひとつには、若い従業員の組合離れがあります。労使の交渉による賃上げの決定にも「年功序列」の原則が適用されるのが普通なので、若い人にとっては、せっかく組合活動をしても、あまりその恩恵にあずかれないというわけです。そのほかに、サービス業のように各従業員の労働環境のばらつきが多くて、組合の組織化が難しい業種で働く人が増えてきています。また、企業別組合では、**パートタイマー**や**臨時工**は組合員になれません。さらに、いま日本では中高年層の割合が高くなってきていますが、こうした人たちは管理職に昇進した後、組合から離れます。つまり労働組合の支持基盤が小さくなってきているわけです。一般的にはこのような傾向にあるの

companies. In companies where the company president used to be the chairman of the labor unions, negotiations tend to go even more smoothly.

Q : That's why many people criticize the negotiations as collusion. Westerners would certainly be surprised to hear that former executives in labor unions can become presidents of companies.

A : Well, this is also specific to the Japanese **personnel system.** The chairman and executives of in-house unions are elected to their posts by other union members and at the same time they are employees of that company. The chairman is also promoted by the seniority system, and when he reaches the management level, he retires from the union. He negotiates with the union as a director, a representative of the management. It's not that rare for a former chairman of a labor union to become company president.

Q : Do you think Japanese labor unions will change in the future?

A : Several problems have been pointed out in the system. One is the decline in the rate of union membership. The average rate of union membership in Japan is 25%. This is 10% below what it was 25 years ago. One reason is that young employees tend to drift away from the unions. Even in wage-raise negotiations, the decision is usually based on the seniority system. So even if young employees are active in the union, they don't really receive many benefits. Also, in service industries the working environment is so diverse that it is difficult for employees to form a union. Furthermore, **part-time workers** and **temporary workers** can't join an in-house union. At present, a large percentage of union members are older, so when they become administrators, they will retire from the union. This means that the support base for labors unions is growing smaller. This is typical of unions now, but during the recent recession a new movement in labor unionism has appeared.

● 新しい組合の
　出現

ですが，ここ数年の不況で労働組合をめぐっては，新しい動きも出てきているのです。

Q：と，いいますと？

A：例えば管理職が集まって**管理職組合**をつくる例があります。というのも，業績の悪化で余剰人員を削減するために，中高年齢層を狙った指名解雇が多くなっているからです。これらの年代の人の多くは管理職に昇進して，組合からは離れているので，雇用の確保に関して組合からの支援を受けられません。また，これまでの企業別組合という枠を超えて，さまざまな企業で働くパートタイマーの人たちで結成された組合や，外国人労働者が集まってつくっている組合も出現しています。

Q : What kind of movement?

A : For instance, administrators have created **unions of adminis-trators** because companies, in an effort to reduce surplus work-ers, have specifically designated middle-aged and older workers for dismissal. Such workers have already retired from the unions after becoming administrators so they cannot gain support from the unions in their efforts to keep their jobs. Another type of union that has appeared is for foreign workers and part-time workers in various companies and goes beyond the bounds of ordinary in-house labor unions.

9 企業系列

世界で最も生産台数の多い自動車メーカーは，日本のトヨタ自動車で，1991年の生産台数は約400万台，第2位はアメリカの自動車会社ＧＭで約370万台です。ところで従業員数はＧＭの方が多いのですが，トヨタの何倍ぐらいでしょうか。

　① 1.5倍　　② 3倍　　③ 10倍

A : 「Keiretsu」という英語ができるほど有名になった，日本の「企業系列」についてご紹介します。クイズの正解は，③の10倍です。ちなみにトヨタの従業員数はおよそ7万3000人，ＧＭは75万人と10倍以上です。

Q : 車の生産台数があまり違わないのに，どうしてこんなに差があるのですか。

A : トヨタの生産効率は，世界の自動車メーカーの中でも最高の水準といわれていますが，しかし，いくらなんでもＧＭの10倍はありません。この差は，両者の**生産体制**の違いによるものです。

Q : どう違うのですか。

● 欧米との生産
体制の違い

A : 車は大変多くの部品を組み立てて作ります。ＧＭなど欧米のメーカーは，この部品の約50％を自社で作っていますが，トヨタなど日本のメーカーの場合，自社で作るのは約20％で，残りは部品メーカーから購入しているのです。

Q : なるほど。それで日本の**自動車メーカー**は，少ない従業員でも大きな生産量を上げられるというわけですか。

Keiretsu

> In 1991, Japan's Toyota Motors produced almost 4 million cars. The U.S. auto manufacturer General Motors came in second with 3.7 million cars. How many times more employees does GM have than Toyota Motors?
>
> ① 1.5 times ② 3 times ③ 10 times

A : The Japanese word "keiretsu," meaning affiliated companies, is now well-enough known to be used in English and this is the subject of this chapter. The answer is number three, 10 times. Toyota has 73,000 employees, while GM employs 750,000 people, 10 times more than Toyota.

Q : Why is there such a great difference in the number of employees when the number of cars produced is almost the same?

A : Toyota is said to be the most efficient automobile manufacturer in the world in terms of production. But it is not 10 times more efficient than GM. The difference is due to the two types of **production systems**.

Q : How are they different?

A : Many parts are needed to assemble a car. European and U.S. manufacturers, like GM, make 50% of their parts in-house. Japanese manufacturers, like Toyota, make only 20% of their parts in-house and procure the remainder from parts manufacturers.

Q : I see, that's why Japanese **auto manufacturers** have such a high volume of production with so few employees.

● 企業系列とは

● 企業グループ
　との違い

A：そうです。そしてこの点が日本的な特色なんですが，組み立てを行う大手メーカーと部品メーカーが，「企業系列」という大変密接な関係で結ばれているのです。

Q：「企業系列」といえば，アメリカの企業や政府から，これがあるから日本市場への参入が難しいと問題にされていますね。具体的にはどういう関係なんですか。

A：単なる**取引関係**とは違い，大手組み立てメーカーが傘下の部品メーカーに資本参加したり，経営陣を派遣したりします。また技術指導のほかに，製品の開発までも協力して行います。こうした系列関係は，自動車だけではなく電子機器や家庭電器などの組み立て産業から，製鉄業や化学産業などの素材産業に至るまであります。

Q：株式の保有による**親会社**，**子会社**の関係とは違うのですか。

A：普通，親会社というのは，子会社に対する出資の割合が50％を超えて，経営面での支配権を握っていますが，系列の場合は部品メーカーの株の3分の1程度を所有しているに過ぎません。系列の特色は，何よりも**生産工程**での協力関係にあります。トヨタの場合は，コストを切り詰めるために在庫を自分のところでできるだけ持たずに，分刻みで部品メーカーに部品を納入させます。ですから機能的にはむしろ「**本社工場と分工場**」の関係に近いですね。

Q：日本には三菱，三井，住友のような大きな企業グループがありますね。これも今まで話してきた系列なのでしょうか。

A：若干違います。これらの**企業グループ**は，傘下に多数の系列子会社を持った大企業の集まりです。

A : Yes, this is a characteristic Japanese feature. Large assembly manufacturers and parts manufacturers have a very close systematic relationship known as "keiretsu."

Q : U.S. corporations and government criticize the keiretsu system as one of the things that makes it difficult to enter the Japanese market. What exactly is the keiretsu system?

A : Well, it's not just a **business relationship**. The large assembly manufacturer funds the parts manufacturer and sends management to their company. In addition, they also direct their technology and help develop products. The keiretsu relationship isn't just specific to the auto industry, it's also seen in other assembly industries, such as the electronic machinery and electrical appliance industries, and in material industries such as the steel and chemical industries.

Q : How is this different from the relationship of a **parent company** that holds stock in a **subsidiary**?

A : Usually a parent company funds over 50% of a subsidiary's expenses. They also direct the management. In the keiretsu system, the manufacturer holds only about one-third of the parts manufacturer's stock. But one characteristic of the keiretsu system is the cooperation in the **production process**. For example, Toyota tries not to stock parts in order to curtail costs and has the parts manufacturer deliver the parts at the exact time needed. So the relationship is almost like that between a **main factory** and a **branch factory**.

Q : There are large company networks in Japan like Mitsubishi, Mitsui and Sumitomo. Are these the keiretsu we were just talking about?

A : No, they're a little different. These **company groups** are umbrella networks that have large companies with several

グループ内の会社同士で少しずつ株式を持ち合っていますし，役員を派遣することもありますが，互いに支配，被支配の関係にあるわけではありません。取引の面でも，クールな関係といえるでしょう。

Q：欧米の企業には，日本のような系列関係はあるんですか。

A：もちろん欧米の企業の間にも，原材料や部品の納入で企業間の連携はありますし，販売面でも関係の深い会社はあります。しかし日本の系列企業間にあるような緊密な関係はないようです。

● メリット

Q：企業系列のメリットはどこにあるのですか。

A：メリットを説明する前にひとこと。これまでは自動車産業の例を紹介してきましたので，**組み立てメーカー**と**部品メーカー**という言い方をしましたが，系列関係は素材産業にもありますので，これからは**系列親会社**と**系列子会社**という言い方にします。さて企業系列のメリットですが，まずは，製品の開発や生産技術の向上について系列子会社まで巻き込んだ形で行うので，欠陥品の出る割合が低くて国際競争力の強い製品を作れます。また通常，系列子会社の方が従業員の給料が低いので，系列親会社にとっては自社で作るより，コストが下がります。一方，系列子会社にとっては，製品の納入先が決まっていることは，経営の安定化につながります。

● デメリット

Q：デメリットはどんな点ですか。

A：系列親会社にとってデメリットはほとんどありません。しかし系列子会社にとっては，販路を拡げようと考えても系列親会社に反対されることもあります。また自分の会社の生産技術や製造コストなどが，系列親会社にほとんどわかってしまうの

keiretsu subsidiaries under them. The companies within the group hold each others' stock and they exchange personnel. But no single company controls another one. And they don't have such close business relations.

Q : Do U.S. and European companies have this kind of keiretsu system?

A : Of course, they have relationships between their raw material and parts suppliers. And some companies have close relationships in sales transactions. But these contacts are nowhere near as tight as the relationships between Japanese keiretsu companies.

Q : What are the merits of the keiretsu system?

A : I want to make one point before I explain the merits. I've been using the auto industry as an example, so I used the phrases **"assembly manufacturer"** and **"parts manufacturer,"** but since there are also keiretsu in the materials industry, I'm going to use the phrases **"keiretsu parent company"** and **"keiretsu subsidiary"** from now on. Now for the merits. First of all, since the keiretsu parent company closely cooperates in product development and improving production technology with the keiretsu subsidiary, the defect rate is low, which allows companies to make products that are good enough to compete internationally. Usually employee wages are lower in the keiretsu subsidiary, so it is cheaper for the keiretsu parent company to have the parts made in the keiretsu subsidiary than in-house. On the other hand, the keiretsu subsidiary has steady business because the client for their products is pre-determined.

Q : What are the demerits?

A : There are almost no demerits for the keiretsu parent company, but there are some for the keiretsu subsidiary. For example, the subsidiary may want to expand its sales, but the parent company opposes. Also the parent company knows all the details about the subsidiary's production technology and costs. So the man-

ポイント

● 今後の企業系列

で，経営の独立性は少なからず制約されるでしょう。こうした点が，欧米の企業には受け入れにくいところでしょう。

Q：これまでの話によると，コストの低い自動車や家電製品を作るには，企業系列が有効に働いてきたといえるようですが，今後もうまく機能していくのでしょうか。

A：**バブル経済**が崩壊して厳しい経営環境となった現在，企業系列にも新しい変化が起きています。系列親会社側は，品質の良さはもちろん，できるだけ安い部品を作る系列子会社をと考え，一方，系列子会社側は，収益を上げるために販売量を少しでも増やそうと考えて，系列外の企業との取引を始めるケースも出てきました。またこのほか，日本のメーカーの中で外国へ工場立地をする企業が増えていますし，先ほども触れたように系列に対する外国からの批判が強まっています。そうした点を考えると，系列関係も徐々に希薄になっていくことは避けられないだろうと思います。

agement doesn't have much independence. This type of thing is very difficult for U.S. and European companies to accept.

Q : I've heard the keiretsu system is very beneficial for producing low-cost cars and electrical appliances. Do you think it will function as well in the future?

A : The **bubble economy** has collapsed and the business environment is very harsh right now, so some changes are beginning to appear in the keiretsu system. The keiretsu parent wants to have a keiretsu subsidiary that makes products as inexpensively as possible, without neglecting quality, of course. On the other hand, some keiretsu subsidiaries are trying to expand sales by making transactions with companies outside their keiretsu network. Also an increasing number of Japanese manufacturers are building factories overseas. And as I mentioned before, foreign countries have increasingly criticized the keiretsu system. Taking these points into consideration, I think it possible that the keiretsu system may gradually weaken.

10 | 企業の株式持ち合い

日本の証券市場に上場している企業の株式のうち,
個人投資家が所有する株式は何%くらいでしょうか。

① 24%　② 48%　③ 96%

A：企業の本来の所有者といえば**株主**ですが,この株
　主の実態も日本と欧米諸国とではずいぶん違いま
　す。この章では株主の実態に焦点を当てます。**東
　京証券取引所**によると,1993年度の**個人投資家**
　が所有している株式は,全体の23.7%で,**①**が正
　解です。一方,銀行や他の企業が所有する**株式**は,
　全体の65%にも達していました。

Q：アメリカでは,個人投資家が全体の50%以上の株
　式を所有しているというのに,だいぶ違いますね。

● 日米株主の違い

A：そうなんです。連邦準備制度理事会によれば,こ
　れに**年金基金**や**投資信託**など,もともと個人の資
　金を集めた**機関投資家**による所有株式を含める
　と,アメリカの場合,実質的な個人所有の株式は
　全体の90%近くになります。日本では,こうした
　株式を合わせても全体の27%程度にしかなりませ
　ん。株式の過半数を所有して**上場企業**の実質的な
　所有者になっているのは,アメリカでは個人投資
　家,日本では銀行や企業となります。

Q：日本では昔からこうだったのですか。

● 日本も昔は
　個人投資家が主

A：日本でも30年ほど前には,投資信託も含めると,
　個人投資家がおよそ55%の株式を所有していまし
　た。しかし,この30年間に個人投資家の持ち株の

Cross-Shareholding

> Among Japanese companies whose stock prices are listed in the stock exchanges, about what percentage of stock is owned by individual investors?
>
> ① 24%   ② 48%   ③ 96%

A : The actual owners of corporations are their **stockholders**. The realities are different in Japan and Western nations and in this chapter we are going to focus on stockholding in Japan. According to **the Tokyo Stock Exchange** for fiscal 1993, **individual investors** owned 23.7% of all stocks. The correct answer is number one. Approximately 65% of all **stocks** were owned by banks and other companies.

Q : This is quite different from the United States, where individual investors own over 50% of all company stock.

A : That's right. According to the Board of Governors of the Federal Reserve System, including stocks owned by **institutional investors** who collect money from individuals, such as **pension funds** and **investment trusts**, individual investors own nearly 90% of all corporate stock. Even if you include these stocks in the Japanese figure, it still totals only 27%. So the majority of corporate stockholders of **listed enterprises** in the United States are individual investors, but in Japan the majority are banks and other corporations.

Q : Was it always like this in Japan?

A : Thirty years ago, individual investors, including investment trusts, owned 55% of Japanese stocks. But during the past thirty years, the percentage of individual stockholders has drastically

比率がどんどん減って，代わって銀行や企業が大株主になってきたわけです。

Q：なぜなのでしょう。

A：原因はいろいろ指摘されています。まず，個人投資家にとっては，**配当が少ない日本企業の株式**に魅力がなくなったのでしょう。なにしろここ何年かは，**配当利回りは1％**にも満たないのですから。それと，個人の**金融資産**の蓄積が貧弱だったため，資産の安全性が最重視され，預貯金に対する志向が強く，**株式投資**に消極的でした。

Q：では，銀行や企業は配当利回りをあまり重視しないのですか。

● 株式の持ち合い
　とは

A：重視しないわけではありません。日本では，企業は取引先の銀行や企業と，株式をお互いに1％から5％くらいずつ持ち合っているのが普通です。それもかなり長期間にわたって保有しているため，配当利回りは，現時点では低いとはいえ，株式購入時の**株価**でみれば高くなっています。

Q：なぜ株式の持ち合いをするのですか。

● メリット

A：株の買い占めによる企業の**乗っ取り**を防ぐために考え出されたようです。例えば，30社の企業が，お互いの株を2～3％ずつ持ち合っていれば，全体で企業の持ち株比率は60～70％になります。こうなると乗っ取りは不可能になります。企業買収のために高値で株を売却するよう持ちかけられても，それに応じる企業はまずありません。そうすればその企業の信用を失うことにもなります。

Q：株式の持ち合いのもとではお互いに大株主ですから，**経営実績**や**利益配分**に対してお互いに批判を差し控える傾向もあるでしょうね。

A：そのとおりですね。日本の企業は，株主に対する配当よりも，**内部留保の積み増し**と，それによる投

decreased, and instead, banks and other corporations have taken over as the majority stockholders.

Q : Why did this happen?

A : People point to several reasons. First of all, individual investors have lost interest in Japanese corporate stocks because **dividends** have dropped to such low levels. The **dividend yield** has been below 1% in the past several years. Because individual **financial assets** were poor, investors preferred secure savings to **stock investment**.

Q : Does that mean banks and other corporations are not as concerned about dividend yields?

A : That is not actually true. What happens is that Japanese corporations usually hold from 1% to 5% of the stocks of the banks and other corporations they do business with. Since they hold these stocks for the long term, even if the dividend they receive is currently low, it is high when considered in the light of the **price of the stock** at time of purchase.

Q : Why do companies hold each other's stock?

A : This is one strategy for preventing corporate **takeovers** through cornering shares. For example, if 30 companies hold between 2% and 3% of each other's stock, this adds up to 60% or 70% of the total stock issued. This makes a takeover impossible. Even if a certain investor approaches a company asking it to sell at a high price the stock it holds in a partner company, no company would accept, because if it did, that company would lose its credibility.

Q : With cross-holdings, companies become one another's major shareholders and this is why they are inclined to refrain from mutual criticism concerning **business performance** and **profit-sharings**.

A : That's right. By attaching greater importance to **accumulating internal reserves** and investment than to stock dividends,

ポイント

資を重視することで，高い成長を維持してきました。中長期的な視点による経営で株価の上昇を支えられてきたのも，こうしたことが背景にあるからです。企業にとっては，このほかにも株式の持ち合いによるメリットがあります。例えば，企業は株主である銀行から融資を受けやすくなりますし，企業同士でいえば，原料や製品の販売や購入を通じて関係を強化することができます。こういった業務上のプラスを求めて，株式の持ち合いがいっそう進んだようですが，外国から見ると，株式の持ち合いというのは，なかなかわかりにくい現象です。また，株式の持ち合いが，企業買収によって日本進出を目指す外国企業には障害と映るようです。

● 今後の株式の
　持ち合い

Q：株式の持ち合い構造は今後も続くのでしょうか。

A：この構造のもとでは，持ち合っている株式の価格が上昇すればお互いに利益がありますが，株価が大きく下落すると多額の損失を出すことになります。幸運にも，1990年までは，日本の**株式市場**はおおむね上昇基調にありました。企業にとっては**含み資産**が増え続け，いつもお互いによい状態だったわけです。株式の買い占めによる乗っ取りを防ぎ，株主からの批判も避けられ，また，業務上のプラスもあり，経営者にとってはとてもメリットがあったわけです。

Q：しかし，1990年の初めから株価は下落しましたね。

A：そうなんです。持ち合っている株式を相手方の了解なしに売ることはできないのが実態なわけですから，下落した株式を抱えた銀行や企業は大きな損失を被りました。最近，こうした株式の持ち合いに対する反省気分が出てきています。ただ，安定株主を維持する方法として，これに代わるものが今のところないので，株式の持ち合いが今すぐにも簡単に崩れることはないでしょう。

Japanese corporations have been able to sustain high growth. They are also able to increase the price of their stock over the long run through management which takes a medium or even long-range point of view. There are other benefits in cross-shareholding. For example, it's easier for companies to obtain financing from a bank which is a shareholder. Because companies buy and sell raw materials and products from one another, they can strengthen mutual relations.These business merits provide incentive to continue cross-shareholdings. On the other hand, this practice is very difficult for foreign companies to understand. They view it as a barrier to gaining access to the Japanese market by purchasing corporations.

Q : Will this structure of cross-shareholdings continue in the future?
A : Mutual shareholding companies profit within this structure if stock prices increase, but they suffer heavy losses when stock prices plummet. Fortunately, the Japanese **stock market** rose fairly steadily until 1990. Companies were able to increase their **latent assets** constantly, so all the parties involved profited. They were also able to prevent takeovers and avoid criticism from stockholders. So this was good for business and beneficial to management.

Q : But stock prices plunged at the beginning of 1990, didn't they?
A : That's right. Since the group stockholders could not sell their holdings without their partner company's consent, banks and companies left with stocks suffered major losses. The practice of holding each other's stock is being reevaluated. However, at present there is no other way to secure steady stockholders, so I do not think that this practice will be dismantled so easily.

11 | シェア拡大主義

通産省が行った，日本の証券市場に上場している大企業466社に対するアンケート調査があります。どの企業も自社の製品の販売にしのぎを削っていますが，「販売の面でいちばん大きな問題は何か」という質問に対して最も多かった答えは何だったでしょうか。

① 他業界からの参入（新規参入）
② 輸入品との競合
③ 日本国内の同業他社との競争

A：日本企業には，採算よりもシェア，**市場占有率**を重要視する傾向があります。クイズの正解は③の「日本国内の同業他社との競争」で，およそ3分の2の企業がこのように回答しています。

●「同業他社比較」を最重視

Q：国内企業同士のシェア争いは大変激しいといわれますが，なぜでしょう。

A：日本企業は自社製品の販売実績を計るために，「同業他社比較」「前年比較」「予算比較」という3つのモノサシを使うことが多く，なかでも「同業他社比較」で売れ行きやシェアが落ちることは，販売担当役員の最も大きなマイナス点となるのです。ですから同業他社比較の実績だけは落とさないように全力を挙げるのです。業界全体が不況のときは，他の会社もふるわないので，販売が落ち込んでもしかたがない。しかし，景気が良いとき

Expanding Market Share

All companies fiercely compete to sell their products. In Japan 466 major companies listed on the securities market were surveyed by the Ministry of International Trade and Industry about their biggest concern regarding sales. What do you think the most common answer from these companies was?

① The new entry of other firms
② Competition from imported goods
③ Competition with domestic companies in the same trade

A : Japanese companies tend to regard **market share** as more important than **profit**. The answer to the quiz is number three. Almost two-thirds of those surveyed said that their greatest worry is competition from other Japanese companies selling similar products.

Q : Why is the competition among Japanese companies to expand market share so fierce?

A : Japanese companies have three means of measuring sales of their products: comparison with other companies in the same sector, comparison with figures from the previous year, and budget comparison. When market share falls in comparison with other companies in the same sector, it's especially bad for the person in charge of sales. So the head of the sales department makes great effort to insure that the sales performance doesn't fall in comparison with competitors. When the entire industry is in a recession, and other companies are suffering as well, noth-

に，自社の販売額が前年比較でいくら伸びたとしても，他社と比べたときのシェアが落ちることは我慢できない，といわれます。

Q：なぜ，それほどシェア競争にこだわるのですか。

A：実はシェア競争は，メーカーだけの問題ではなく，日本独特の**流通システム**にも関係があるのです。特に大企業は，その企業の製品をおもに取り扱う**卸問屋や小売店を特約店**として組織化していて，なかにはメーカーが役員派遣や資本参加を行っているところもあります。シェアが落ちれば，末端の特約店も他社の特約店に対して劣勢になります。消費者の間にも，シェアの大小でそのメーカーを評価するような風潮がありますから，シェアの低下を放置しておけば，最悪の場合，その会社の流通ルートが崩壊するかもしれないのです。

Q：しかし，いくらシェアを守るためでも，極端な値引きなどすれば採算が悪化するでしょう。そのときは撤退ということも考えるのでしょうか。

A：先ほどと同じ調査で，「製品によっては採算が悪化しても撤退しない」と答えた企業が100社のうち62社を占めているので，撤退はよほどの採算割れがなければやらないでしょう。撤退するとなると従業員の雇用の問題も生じてきます。ともかくシェアと特約店さえ確保しておけば，あとは，他社の動向を見ながら値上げをしたり，新製品を出したりして採算の向上が図れますからね。

Q：日本の企業というのは，採算よりも，シェアを重要視するということなんですね。

● 採算よりシェア

A：このことは，日本の企業がまだシェアの固まっていない新規分野についてどんな**販売戦略**をとるかを見ればよくわかります。通産省の調査によると，「当初から一定水準以上の利益が見込めなければ進出しない」とする企業は16％にすぎません。3

ing can be done about falling sales. But when the economy is in an upswing, Japanese companies can't tolerate having their market share fall, even if total sales are higher than the previous year.

Q : Why do Japanese companies adhere so tightly to market share?

A : Actually, the struggle for market share is not just a problem for manufacturers, but is also related to Japan's **distribution system**. Large companies in particular organize **special agents** as **wholesalers** and **retailers** which mainly carry one company's products. Some companies dispatch executives and finance their special agents, so if their market share decreases, the special agents' stores will lose ground to the special agents of other large companies. Consumers also tend to evaluate manufacturers on their market share. So in a worst case scenario, if that share declines and remains low, the distribution system for that company could collapse.

Q : A company could offer discounts to protect its market share, but that would lower profits. Would it withdraw from the market in such a situation?

A : In the same survey, 62 out of 100 companies said that depending on the product, they would not withdraw, even if profits were low. They would only pull out if they had to sell below cost. Withdrawing from a market would also lead to unemployment problems. In any case, if they can secure their share and maintain their special agent stores, they can plan to increase profits later by raising prices and putting out new products while watching trends in other companies.

Q : Japanese companies really place more emphasis on their market share than on profits, don't they?

A : If you look closely at **marketing strategy** for completely new fields, where no company has entered the market, you'll be able to see this pattern clearly. A Ministry of International Trade and Industry survey indicated that only 16% of companies would not enter a field where there's no expectation of a certain level of

～4年は利益をあてにしていない企業が多いのです。同じ新規分野に複数の企業が進出するとなると，各社とも自社の利益をあげることよりも，まずはシェアの獲得を目指して，猛烈な販売競争を行うのです。こうした激しい販売競争があるために，企業は常に製品に改良を加えて顧客にアピールしようとし，その結果，製品の品質が向上するというメリットもあるわけです。

Q：しかしそうなると，いったんシェアが固まってしまった製品については，新規参入は難しいでしょうね。

A：かりに参入しても，既存の各社がシェアの防衛を行いますので，大きなシェアのとれる見込みはほとんどありません。特に外国の企業にとっては，日本の市場は新規参入しにくく感じられるでしょう。**特約店制度**があるために，流通ルートを確保するのが難しいうえに，前年実績により担当者の給料が決まる外国企業の人事制度のもとでは，採算を考えないシェア拡大競争や，3～4年も利益の望めない新規事業への進出などは，普通はとりえない政策でしょうから。

Q：日本の企業は外国にも多く進出していますが，そこでもシェア争いをしているのでしょうか。

● 外国でも日本
企業の争い

A：カメラや半導体メーカーなど，日本企業が世界シェアの多くをとっている商品では，国内の競争の延長戦が外国でも行われています。外国の市場でも日本企業同士で競争しているのです。その結果，安くて良い製品が供給されるのは消費者にとっては喜ばしいことでしょうが，つまりは，日本企業全体のシェアが拡大するということにつながるわけで，外国の企業はこうした日本の企業行動には批判的です。

profit from the outset. Most companies don't count on profits for three to four years. When companies try to penetrate a new field, they launch fierce marketing wars to secure a share of the market rather than profit. As a result of this fierce marketing competition, companies are always trying to improve their products and appeal to customers. This leads to the merit of higher product quality.

Q : But on the other hand, once a product has a firm share of the market, it makes it difficult for new companies to enter the market.

A : Even if a company tries to enter a new market, its competitors will defend their share, so it's almost impossible to expect a large piece of the market. Foreign companies especially feel the difficulties of entering a new field in the Japanese market. First of all, it's difficult to secure a distribution route because of the **special agent system.** In addition, since foreign companies usually base the salary of their sales personnel on the previous year's business performance, it's not reasonable to pursue market share and not think about profit, or to enter a new field where a profit cannot be expected for three or four years.

Q : Many Japanese companies have entered markets overseas, do they compete for a market share in the same way?

A : In cameras and semiconductors, for example, where Japanese companies hold a large share of the world market, their strategy overseas is an extension of their domestic struggle. Japanese companies compete among themselves in foreign markets as well. Consumers are happy to have inexpensive, high quality products as a result of the competition. This practice increases the total market share held by Japanese firms, but foreign companies don't look kindly upon such Japanese business practices.

12 | 日本企業のリストラ

> 日本の大手石油化学会社13社は1992年，不況のため2年前に比べて利益が47%も減りました。さて，それではこの2年間に従業員の数はどう変わったでしょうか。
>
> ① 30%以上減った
> ② ほとんど変わらなかった
> ③ 5%ほど増えた

 ポイント

A：企業を取り巻く環境が厳しくなったとき，日本の企業はどんな行動をとるのでしょうか。「企業の**リストラ**」についてお話しします。クイズの正解は，③の「5%ほど増えた」でした。

Q：日本的な経営では，利益が半減した程度では従業員の解雇は行わないということなんですか。

A：そうです。バブル経済崩壊後の不況で「リストラ」という言葉は頻繁に聞かれますが，実際にはこの例に見られるように，組織のスリム化はなかなか実行されていないようです。

• リストラとは

Q：これまでも不況のときに行われてきた**人員削減**とか，**不採算部門**からの撤退といった不況時の対策とどう違うのですか。

A：とる対策はよく似ていますが，問題を構造的に捉えるのかどうかという点が違います。リストラとは，「好不況にかかわらず，収益の見込める戦略的な部門を拡大する一方で，不採算部門から撤退することにより，事業を再構築する」という意味です。

Japanese Corporate Restructuring

> Because of the depressed business environment, 1992 profits in thirteen Japanese petrochemical companies were down 47% compared with two years earlier. In what way did the number of employees fluctuate?
>
> ① Over 30% reduction   ② No change   ③ 5% increase

A : The situation that confronts Japanese companies now is quite severe. How will Japanese companies cope? In this chapter let's look at **restructuring**. The correct answer is number three, a 5% increase.

Q : That means that in Japanese-style management, companies don't lay off employees even though profits have been cut in half.

A : That's right. We've been hearing about "restructuring" frequently during this recession following the burst of the bubble. But as we can see from the figure, companies have a very difficult time in streamlining their organization.

Q : How is this different from anti-recession measures, such as **personnel reduction** and pulling out of **unprofitable sectors**?

A : The actual policies are very similar, but the difference lies in whether they deal with it as a structural problem. Restructuring refers to the building of a new business structure, regardless of economic conditions, by expanding in strategic areas which are profitable, and withdrawing from unprofitable fields.

Q：いつごろからいわれるようになったのですか。

A：日本では1986年の円高以降，構造的な経営改革をしないと事態を乗り切れないという危機感から，よくこの言葉が使われるようになりました。しかしバブル経済の好況期になると，新規の戦略部門の拡大は行われたものの，肝心な不採算部門からの撤退はほとんど行われませんでした。バブル崩壊とともに再び，不採算部門からの撤退が注目されるようになったのです。

Q：具体的な動きは出ているのですか。

A：トラックを主に生産しているいすゞ自動車が，1992年末，乗用車の生産を中止することを決めました。リストラの中で，不採算部門からの撤退という動きが，日本でも出始めていますが，日本企業の場合，従業員の雇用を確保しなければならないという前提があることから，欧米の企業に比べるとリストラが徹底しないきらいがあります。

● 欧米企業の
リストラ

Q：欧米の企業の徹底したリストラとは？

A：不採算部門の従業員を解雇して閉鎖してしまうか，あるいは従業員も含めた形で不採算部門を売却したりします。アメリカのモンサント社は1985年以降，それまでの主力部門であった化学製品部門を次々に売却する一方，食品・医薬品・農薬分野の企業を買収し，短い年月でリストラを成功させました。日本の場合，企業の売買は，日本特有の**人事制度**や**株式の持ち合い**，それに取引先への影響を懸念して，容易には進みません。

Q：リストラの中で，不採算部門からの撤退のほかにも難しいことは何ですか。

● 日本企業の場合

A：全社的に**人件費**をいかに削減するかでしょう。日本企業の場合，終身雇用制の前提のもとで従業

Q : When did this word start being used?

A : Companies have been using the word since 1986 when the yen began appreciating. At that time they began to fear that they would not be able to surmount these difficulties, if they didn't reform the structure of their management system. When business was booming during the speculative economy, companies were venturing into strategic new fields, but few began the vital process of pulling out of unprofitable areas. But with the collapse of the bubble economy, they are once again focusing on withdrawal from unprofitable fields.

Q : What are they actually doing?

A : Isuzu Motors, Ltd., which mainly manufactures trucks, decided to stop producing passenger vehicles at the end of 1992. So there are some attempts to restructure in Japan. But Japanese companies operate on the principle that they must keep their employees' jobs secure, so they tend not to restructure drastically, like European and U.S. companies do.

Q : How do European and U.S. companies restructure?

A : Well, they lay off employees and shut down unprofitable areas of the company. Or they sell off those unprofitable areas, which includes the employees in that section. Monsanto in the U.S. succeeded in restructuring within a very short period. In 1985 they began selling off sections of their major field which is chemical products, then they began buying companies in the food, medical and agricultural chemical fields. In Japan, however, companies can't buy and sell companies so easily because of their unique **personnel** and **cross-shareholding systems**, not to the mention the fear of the effects on their partner companies.

Q : What other problems do Japanese firms have in restructuring, besides withdrawing from unprofitable sectors?

A : One is how to cut back on the **personnel costs** throughout the entire company. Japanese companies under the lifetime employ-

ポイント

● 日本式経営との
　調和が課題

員の解雇はできるだけ避けなければなりません。したがって不況のときでも，まず最初に取り組むのは，取締役の報酬を減らしたり，部長や課長といった管理職の給料をカットすることですね。

Q：しかしそれだけでは，人件費の削減には限界があるでしょう。

A：大企業であれば，従業員を**子会社**や**関連会社**に出向させます。また業績の好調な全く別の企業に，従業員を集団で貸し出すことさえあります。それでもダメなときには人員の削減に乗り出しますが，退職金の上積みをするなどの措置をとり，あくまでも希望退職者を募るという形をとります。

　　最近企業が積極的に取り組み始めているものに，給料の高い管理職ポストの削減や，**総務**とか**企画**といった管理間接部門のスリム化があります。しかしこうした対策も，日本式経営のひとつである年功序列型賃金などと深くかかわってくるため，なかなか抜本的な改革にはなりません。

Q：どうやらリストラを大胆に進めることは，日本企業には難しいようですね。企業を取り巻く環境が，今後ますます厳しくなる中，日本企業はどう対応しようとしているのでしょうか。

A：日本式企業経営もバブル経済崩壊後の不況を機に，いろいろな点で限界が見え始めているようです。このため企業は，これまでの経営手法を少しずつ変えつつあります。しかし日本式経営の特徴のひとつは，「他の企業に準ずる」ことでもありますので，1社だけで急進的な改革を行うことはビジネス社会から浮き上がることになり，思うようには進みそうにありません。いずれは，欧米の企業経営とは異なった新しい経営手法をつくり出していくのでしょうが，それにはまだ時間がかかりそうです。

ment system try to avoid laying off personnel if at all possible. So even during recessions, their first response is to reduce executives pay or cut the salaries of their management, such as those of department and section chiefs.

Q : Are these measures alone sufficient for cutting down personnel expenses?

A : If it's a large company, they send employees on temporary transfer to **subsidiaries** and **affiliated companies**. In some cases, a company may actually loan a team of employees to another stable company. If these measures are insufficient, employees are asked to retire voluntarily and given incentives such as extra severance pay.

Recently, companies have begun to aggressively tackle the problem, reducing the number of high-salaried management posts and streamlining the management-related sections such as **general affairs** and **planning**. But even these measures are closely related to the Japanese seniority wage system, and it is extremely difficult to carry out radical reforms.

Q : Japanese companies don't seem to be very good at bold restructuring. How should they deal with the increasingly severe business climate in the coming period?

A : After the bubble burst and the recession became serious, Japanese companies began to see the limitations of their management methods. As a result, they are gradually changing their traditional methods. But one characteristic of Japanese management is that they follow the crowd. If one company on its own carried out radical reforms, it would lose the support of the business community, and its business performance would suffer. In the future, companies will develop a new management method, different from that of U.S. and European companies, but this will probably take some time.

サラリーマン社会の実態
THE WORKING WORLD

13 | 長時間労働

労働省によれば，先進国の中で労働時間がいちばん短いといわれるドイツでは，1992年の年間総労働時間はおよそ1570時間でした。そのドイツ人と比べて，日本人は年間でどのくらい余計に働いているでしょうか。

① 250時間　② 450時間　③ 750時間

ポイント

● 欧米諸国の
　労働時間

A：第2部では，サラリーマンの仕事ぶりや生活，そして意識の変化などにスポットを当てます。この章では，「働き過ぎ」と欧米諸国からよく批判される「**長時間労働**」についてご紹介します。正解は，②の450時間です。年間の総労働時間を1992年の数字で比べると，日本の2017時間に対してアメリカは1957時間，イギリスは1911時間，そしてフランスは1682時間です。

Q：1日8時間働くとして，日本人はドイツ人より年間でおよそ60日も余計に働いているということになりますね。

A：しかも実際はこれだけではないんです。日本には「サービス残業」や，休日に朝早くから得意先の相手をする「接待ゴルフ」などの習慣もあって，実際の労働時間は数字に表れたものよりもっと長いと考えられているのです。

Q：その**サービス残業**というのは何ですか。

● サービス残業
　とは

A：サービス残業というのは，残業時間を実際よりも少なめに申告することで，賃金には計算されない時間外労働のことです。最近では，不況による業

Long Working Hours

According to the Ministry of Labor, of all the industrialized nations, Germany is said to have the shortest working hours. The average working hours per year in 1992 was 1,570 hours. How many more hours did the Japanese work than the Germans?

① 250 hours ② 450 hours ③ 750 hours

A : In the second section, we will focus on working conditions, lifestyles of workers, and changes in worker attitudes. We'll give special attention to the **long working hours** of Japanese workers—a fact which draws criticism from the West. The correct answer to the quiz is number two, 450 hours. According to 1992 statistics on total annual working hours, the Japanese worked an average of 2,017 hours, Americans worked 1,957 hours, the British, 1,911 hours and the French, 1,682 hours.

Q : Assuming an eight-hour workday, that means that the Japanese worked about 60 more days a year than the Germans.

A : Actually, these figures do not cover overtime work without pay and working on days off. Nor does it include hours spent entertaining clients by taking them to play golf and such. So Japanese working hours are higher than the figures actually show.

Q : What is **"overtime without pay"**?

A : Employees often report a lower number of overtime hours than those actually worked, and they are not paid for these hours. Because of depressed business performance during the recent

績の悪化から残業代を抑えようという企業も多く，全般に，このサービス残業は増えているものと見られます。このほかに，長い通勤時間を加えると，実際に仕事に要する時間はもっと長くなります。

Q：長時間労働に関連して，最近では「**過労死**」という言葉が新聞によく登場しますが。

A：これは働き過ぎからくる過労が原因といわれています。それでなくても，長時間労働は家族の生活を犠牲にすることになりますし，働き過ぎて健康を害することにもなります。

● 長時間労働の
　背景

Q：この長い労働時間の背景には何があるのですか。

A：いくつかの要因が考えられます。日本の多くの企業では，景気がよくなって仕事量が増えたからといって，正社員を急に増やすことはしません。仕事が減ったときにクビにするということができないからです。必然的に，アルバイトや派遣社員を活用しますが，それでも十分でなく，結局，正社員の仕事量が増え，労働時間も長くなることになります。また，終身雇用制度のもとで転職が一般的でなかったことから，個人の力が企業に比べて非常に弱く，個人は企業のいうことを聞かざるをえない立場にあります。さらに，多くの企業では終身雇用制度をとっており，個人としても企業に依存していれば安心ということがあります。

Q：ところで，この働き過ぎといわれる日本ですが，最近では「**時短**」，つまり労働時間の短縮ということがよくいわれるようになりましたね。

A：ひとつには，日本人は働き過ぎだという海外からの批判があります。人が休んでいる間にも働いて安い製品を作るのは，フェアではないというものです。もうひとつは，個人の生活重視という最近の風潮があります。日本は経済的な豊かさという

recession, many companies are trying to hold down their over-time expenses. So in general, the amount of overtime without pay seems to be on the rise. If you add in the long commuting times, this makes a long working day.

Q : The word "karoshi" or **"death from overworking,"** has been in the newspapers a lot recently.

A : "Karoshi" is said to be caused by working too much. The long working hours come at the expense of family life and also damage health.

Q : Why do the Japanese work such long hours?

A : There are several reasons. Many companies do not hire new regular employees when business is good, because they cannot dismiss workers when business declines. Inevitably, companies turn to part-time or temporary workers, but even then, regular employees are required to work harder and longer. Because job-changing is not common under the lifetime employment practice, the individual is in a much weaker position than the company, so the employee has to abide by the company's instructions. Yet, because of this lifetime employment system, the individual can feel secure about his job.

Q : Though it is often said that the Japanese work too much, **reducing working hours** has been a hot topic recently.

A : One reason is criticism from abroad. The international community claims it's not fair to work longer hours to produce cheap goods while other workers are resting. Another reason that the reduction of working hours has been in the news is the recent trend toward placing greater emphasis on one's personal life.

ことではすでに世界の最高水準に達しています。例えば，1992年の1人当たりのＧＤＰ（国内総生産）で見ますと，日本は2万8220ドルで，アメリカの2万3120ドルやフランスの2万2300ドルなどを上回っています（世界銀行の調査）。しかし，こうした経済的な豊かさにもかかわらず，日本人は生活の豊かさを実感できていません。この大きな原因のひとつが長い労働時間だといわれています。

● 時短の動き

Q：ところで，若い人はこの長時間労働をどう思っているのでしょうね。

A：最近では，若い人を中心に，より良い条件の職場を求めて転職する人が増えてきています。個人の生活をもっと大事にしようという考え方の表れですね。したがって企業側にとっても，優秀な人材を確保するためには，労働時間を減らし，魅力的な職場にする必要が出てきたわけですね。

Q：この長時間労働の問題に政府はどう対応しているのでしょうか。

● 政府の対応

A：「時短」は政府の政策目標に掲げられています。これに基づいて，1996年までに年間の総労働時間を1800時間まで減らす計画です。そのために，週の法定労働時間を現行の44時間から40時間に短縮する**労働基準法**の改正案が国会を通過，1994年の4月から施行されました。また，国家公務員については，1992年から完全**週休2日制**が実施されています。ほとんどの大企業でも，すでにこの完全週休2日制は実施されています。

Q：しかし，生産性の低い**中小企業**にとっては，この時短を実施するのは難しいのではないですか。

A：確かにそうですね。1993年に労働省が行った調査によれば，現在週40時間以内の労働時間をとっているのは，従業員1000人以上の大企業ではおよそ86％です。しかし，従業員100人未満の中小企業

Economically, Japan has one of the highest standards of living in the world. In 1992 for instance, the Japanese gross domestic product, or GDP, was $28,220 per capita. This is higher than that of the U.S. at $23,120 or France at $22,300 according to the World Bank. Despite this economic prosperity, the Japanese don't feel this wealth in their personal lives. One major factor in this is the long working hours.

Q : How do young people feel about these long working hours?

A : An increasing number of people, mostly younger, are demanding better working conditions and changing jobs accordingly. This is part of the trend toward placing greater value on private lives. Now companies have to create an attractive working environment, with shorter working hours, to secure competent personnel.

Q : How is the government dealing with this problem?

A : Reducing working hours is a government policy goal. They plan to reduce total working hours to 1,800 hours per year by 1996. As the pillar of this policy, an amendment of **the Labor Standards Act** was passed in the Diet, to reduce the officially set working week from the current 44 to 40 hours. The law went into effect in April 1994. Government employees have been on a **five-day week** since 1992. Most large companies have already implemented the five-day week.

Q : But isn't it difficult for **small and mid-sized companies** that have low productivity to do this?

A : Yes, it is. A survey by the Ministry of Labor in 1993 indicated that 86% of large companies with over 1,000 employees have already instituted a 40-hour work week, but only 29% of small and mid-size companies, with under 100 employees, are on this system.

● 産業界の反応

になると，29％程度でしかありません。こうした
ことから政府としては，中小企業に対する時短の
実施を延期する措置をとっています。

Q：労働時間の短縮は日本企業の**国際競争力**を弱め
る，という声も**産業界**では聞かれますが。

A：経営者側では，時短の実施は実質的な賃上げとな
り，生産コストの上昇で競争力を弱めると強く反
発していることも事実です。しかし，時短は時代
のひとつの流れであり，これから労働力人口が減
っていくことを考えれば，時短が進むことを止め
ることはできないのではないでしょうか。結局，
労働時間の長い企業には人は集まりませんからね。

The government has allowed these smaller companies to postpone their reduction in working hours.

Q : But some people in **industry** are saying that the reduction in working hours will weaken the **international competitiveness** of Japanese companies.

A : It's true that managers strongly oppose the new working week, because it means a real raise in wages which increases production costs and lowers competitiveness. But shorter working hours are a historical trend. Considering that the work force will decrease in the future, it seems nearly impossible to halt the reduction in hours. Companies which do not shorten working hours will not be able to attract employees.

14 | 勤労意識の変化

> 新入社員を対象とした調査で，「定年まで同じ会社で働きたい」と答えた人の割合は，1982年では全体の28%でした。10年後の1992年に行われた調査で同じように答えた人は全体の何%だったでしょうか。
>
> ① 6%　　② 16%　　③ 36%

A：若い人を中心に日本人の**勤労意識**もしだいに変わりつつあります。この調査は，日本生産性本部と日本経済青年協議会が行ったもので，クイズの正解は②の16%です。一方，「とりあえずこの会社で働く」「状況しだいで会社を変わる」という人は，1982年には合わせて55%だったのに対して，1992年では71%に達しています。会社を変わってもよいと考える人が若い年代を中心に増えてきているのです。

Q：欧米ではより良い地位を目指して会社を変わり，キャリア・アップするという考え方が一般的ですが，日本ではある企業に就職すると，定年になるまでずっと同じ会社で働く終身雇用制度が定着していますね。このデータは，こうした雇用制度が転換期を迎えていることを示しているのでしょうか。

● 終身雇用は
　転換期か

A：転職する人の数は，景気の好不況に左右されるので一概にはいえませんが，少なくとも日本でも，転職が昔のように「落伍者」というマイナスイメージだけで捉えられる時代ではなくなっていることは確実です。労働省が行っている「雇用動向調査」を見てみますと，過去1年の間に転職をして

The Changing Consciousness of the Japanese Work Force

> In a 1982 survey of new employees, 28% answered that
> they wanted to work at the same company throughout
> their entire career. Ten years later, in 1992, what per-
> centage of employees responded in a similar manner?
>
> ① 6% ② 16% ③ 36%

A : **Ideas about working** have been gradually changing among
young people. According to the survey carried out by the Japan
Productivity Center and the Junior Executive Council of Japan,
the correct answer is number two, 16%. In 1982, 55% of those
surveyed answered that they would work at their company for
the time being, or that they would switch companies based on
the situation. But in 1992, that percentage rose to 71%. So the
number of people who would change companies is increasing,
especially among young people.

Q : In Europe or the United States, changing companies is a common way of climbing the corporate ladder. But the lifetime
employment system is firmly entrenched in Japan. Does this new
data mean that Japanese employment practices have reached a
turning point?

A : Well, the number of people who are changing jobs depends on
business conditions, so it's difficult to generalize. At the very
least, it means that people no longer have a negative image of
switching jobs, and people who change companies are no longer
considered social drop-outs. According to **the Survey on
Employment Trends** by the Ministry of Labor, the percentage

現在の職場にやってきたという人は1983年には6.4%だったのが，1990年には9.6%にまで増えました。ただし景気の後退に伴い，1993年には再び7.5%に下がりました。

Q：転職が一般的な現象になってきたということですか。

A：そうまではいいきれませんが，転職に対する抵抗感は薄れていますね。実際に転職を経験した人にその理由を尋ねた調査でも，「仕事が自分に向いていない」「職場の人間関係が好ましくない」などといった理由を挙げて，自分の都合で転職をした人の割合がここ数年，増加する傾向にあります。また，企業の側も事業多角化のための即戦力として中途採用に積極的になっており，転職しやすい環境が整ってきているともいえます。転職が増えたのは，当面アルバイトを続けながらでも生活していけるぐらいの経済的豊かさが社会基盤として整ったことも背景にあります。

• 昇進についての
意識変化

Q：終身雇用とならんで年功序列，つまり勤続年数が長くなるにつれて地位も給料も上昇していくというシステムが日本の雇用制度の大きな特徴ですが，昇進についての意識はどうでしょうか。

A：昇進については，同期の仲間に後れを取りたくないという，横並び意識は今でも見られますが，一方で，特に昇進にはこだわらないという考えを持つ人も増えているようです。最近では，あらゆる職種の仕事を経験して会社の中で**ゼネラリスト**として昇進していく従来型のほかに，専門知識や技能を身につけた**スペシャリスト**として働きたいという人も大勢出てきていて，これらの人たちの中では昇進にこだわらないとする人の割合が高くなっています。

• 勤労意識変化
の背景

Q：こうした意識の変化の背景には何があるのでしょうか。

of people who had changed jobs in the previous year was 6.4% in 1983. But in 1990, that figure had risen to 9.6%. In 1993 it dropped again to 7.5% because of the economic slowdown.

Q : So is changing jobs gradually becoming more common?

A : Again, that's difficult to determine, but we can say that resistance against it is weaker. People who have actually switched jobs have been surveyed about their reasons. Recently, more and more people are giving personal reasons—for example, they didn't like their job, or their personal relations at the company were uncomfortable.To achieve diversity, companies are hiring people who have changed jobs and have experience. In this way employees can be put to work right away. Therefore the situation is becoming more favorable for changing jobs. Economic prosperity has created a social foundation upon which people can even live on their earnings from part-time jobs.

Q : Most Japanese companies have a seniority system to go along with the lifetime employment system. This means that an employee's salary and position rises according to the number of years worked for that company. How do promotions fit into this new consciousness?

A : Even now, most people don't want to fall behind their colleagues in terms of promotions. But on the other hand, the number of people who are more flexible about promotions is increasing. In the past, the company promoted **generalists**, that is people who had experience in all areas of the company. Recently, however, more people are gaining specialized knowledge or skills and want to work as **specialists.** And the percentage of those who are more flexible about promotions is increasing among this group.

Q : What's behind this shift in consciousness?

A：物質的な豊かさより生活面での豊かさに目を向ける日本人が増え，若い人を中心に価値観の多様化が進んでいることが指摘できます。「何のために働くのか」という質問に対しても，「お金を得るため」と答える人の割合は高いものの，減少する傾向にあり，一方，「自分の才能や能力を発揮するため」と答える人の割合が高まってきています。

Q：日本のサラリーマンといえば，「**会社人間**」「**働き蜂**」などとよくいわれますが，それが変わりつつあるということですか。

A：徐々にではありますが変わりつつあります。新入社員を対象に行った「理想とするサラリーマン像」についての調査では，「会社の中心になって，バリバリ仕事をするタイプ」，あるいは「仕事に忠実で責任感の強いタイプ」を理想像としてあげた人の割合は，10年前の38％から，1992年には21％に低下しています。それに対して，「仕事はそこそこにして，私生活を楽しむタイプ」をあげた人が，3％から12％にまで増えています。

● 私生活重視へ

Q：私生活重視といいますと，今，日本では政府も年間労働時間の短縮に取り組んでいますね。

A：ええ。サービス残業，過労死など，働き過ぎの問題はまだまだ改善されていないものの，労働時間短縮の動きに伴い「会社人間」には否定的で，私生活を重視する傾向が若い世代に浸透しつつあります。

A : Values are changing, especially among young people. Japanese society has already acheived stable economic growth, and people are turning from material prosperity to personal fulfillment. When asked why they work, a large percentage reply that they work to earn money, but that percentage is decreasing. On the other hand, those who reply that they work to display their abilities is increasing.

Q : Japanese workers are often called **"company people"** or **"worker bees."** But this is changing as well.

A : Yes, it is. One survey of new employees asked about their ideal image of employees. The percentage of people replying "someone who works their hardest for the company" or "the type of person who is loyal and has a strong sense of responsibility to his job" dropped from 38% ten years ago to 21% in 1992. And the percentage answering "someone who places emphasis on his personal life over his working life," rose from 3% to 12%.

Q : An example of this emphasis on personal life is the government's efforts to reduce annual working hours.

A : Problems arising from working too much, such as overtime without pay and death from overworking, have not been solved. Younger people are beginning to develop a negative image of "company people" as working hours are reduced. They want to separate their personal lives from their working lives. And the trend of placing emphasis on personal lives is growing stronger.

15 | 変わる就労形態

> 企業には正社員以外にも，パートタイマーやアルバイトといった非正規の雇用者がいます。さて，こうした非正規の雇用者は全体の何％ぐらいいるでしょうか。
>
> ① 5%　② 10%　③ 20%

ポイント

● 雇用形態は
　多様化

A：日本式経営の特徴として説明してきました終身雇用制や年功序列型賃金などは，おもに大企業の，しかも**正社員**を対象としたものです。この章では**非正規雇用者**の状況などについてお話しします。正解は③の20％です。

Q：5人に1人の割合ですか，意外と高いですね。

A：**総務庁**の「**就業構造基本調査**」によりますと，1992年にこうした非正規の雇用者は1054万人で，10年前の1982年より64％も増え，雇用者全体に占める割合は20.1％に達しました。その中身を見ると，**パートタイマー**が11.3％，アルバイトが4.8％，**派遣社員**が0.3％などとなっています。

Q：派遣社員というのは，どんな人たちですか？

A：**人材派遣会社**に登録されていて，そこから一般の会社に派遣されて働く人のことをいいます。ですから実際に働く会社は，1カ所とは限りません。このほかにも，**契約社員**といって個人が直接，企業と期間を設定した雇用契約を結び，一定の仕事

Changing Employment Patterns

> In addition to regular full-time employees, companies hire part-time and temporary employees. From the choices below, choose the correct percentage of total employees occupied by these non-regular employees.
>
> ① 5% ② 10% ③ 20%

A : In Japanese style management, practices such as lifetime employment and the seniority wage system mainly affect only **regular employees** of large companies. In this chapter we will take up conditions of **non-regular employees**. The answer to the quiz is number three, 20%.

Q : That's one out of every five employees, isn't it?

A : A survey of **the Employment Status Survey** by **the Management and Coordination Agency** found the number of casual employees in 1992 was 10.54 million. That was an increase of nearly 64% compared to 1982, over a decade ago. They now make up 20.1% of all the total work force. 11.3% of the work force are **part-time employees** who work on a long-term basis, 4.8% are part-timers, and 0.3% are **temporary employees dispatched by personnel agencies**.

Q : Could you explain more about this last category of temporary workers?

A : Yes. They are employees who register with **personnel agencies** and are sent to companies. They work for several companies for various periods of time. In addition, a new form of **contracted employee** has appeared. These are individuals who are employed on the basis of a contract which sets out the type

ポイント

● 非正規雇用増加の理由

● 勤務形態にも変化

をするといった雇用形態も登場しました。

Q：こうした非正規の雇用者は，なぜ増えたのですか。

A：ひとつには，経済のサービス化，つまりサービス産業の増大に伴って，パートタイムのような労働が必要になったことです。それに女性の社会進出が重なって，パート労働者が増えました。またこのほかにも，ひとつの仕事に拘束されたくないという考え方が強まってきたこと，高齢化社会の到来に伴って定年退職後も働く人が増えたことも，こうした非正規の雇用者が増えた要因です。

Q：女性はどれくらいいるんですか。

A：非正規雇用者の73％が女性で，特にパートは95％が女性です。また仕事の中身ですが，派遣社員のようにコンピューターを操作したり，通訳をしたりと，技能を要求される高度なものも出てきました。昔の非正規雇用者といえば，景気の良いときに工場が男子労働者を臨時的に雇うといったケースが多かったのですが，様変わりしました。さて以上は，雇用形態の多様化についてご説明しましたが，これ以外に**勤務形態**にも変化が起きています。

Q：**フレックスタイム制**なんかがそうですね。

A：そうです。フレックスタイム制は，一定の時間帯を**コアタイム**として決めて，その時間帯は全員を拘束するが，出勤退勤の時間は本人が自由に決められるというものです。

Q：出勤時間を遅くすれば，朝の通勤ラッシュを避けることもできますね。

A：ええ。**運輸省**では，大都市圏の通勤地獄解消のため，このフレックスタイム制を採用するよう企業に働きかけています。この制度は，大企業の研究開発や**情報処理部門**を中心に採用するところが増えており，労働省の調査によると，1990年の時点

of work and term of employment.

Q : Why has the number of these casual employees increased?

A : One reason is the growth of the service industry sector. The growth of this sector has led to an increased demand for part-time employees. Another reason is the growing participation of women in the work force. The desire not to be tied down to one particular job has also been spreading in Japanese society. Furthermore, there has been an increase in the number of people who continue to work after their retirement.

Q : What is the percentage of women among casual employees?

A : Seventy-three percent of casual employees are women. Some 95% of part-time employees who work on a long-term basis are women. Temporary employees like those from personnel agencies usually are required to have high-level specialist skills, such as the use of computers or interpretation. Casual employees in the past often used to be male laborers who were temporarily employed in factories during good business periods. The pattern of casual employment in Japan has changed. Apart from the diversification of **employment patterns, working patterns** have also changed.

Q : You mean the **flextime system?**

A : Yes. Flextime permits flexibility at the beginning and end of the work day, providing that employees work the **core time** on the job.

Q : Starting a little later in the day means you can avoid the morning rush.

A : Yes, that's right. **The Ministry of Transport** is urging companies to adopt flexible working hours in order to ease the horrendous commuter rushes in the large cities. Workplaces which are adopting this sytem are generally those in the research and development sections and **data processing sections** of large

で採用している企業は10％近くに達しています。

Q：「勤務形態の自由化」ともいえますね。こうした動き，ほかにはどんなものが？

A：**「フリータイム制」**といって，フレックスタイム制よりもさらに自由なやり方も登場しました。これは社員自身が勤務時間や出勤時間を自由に設定できます。コアタイムというものもありませんから，日によっては勤務時間が1時間でもいいわけです。この制度は，自由な反面，目に見える実績を上げなければならないという厳しい一面もあります。このほか，まだ珍しいケースですが，自宅にコンピューターの端末やファックスなどの情報機器を置いて会社と電話回線を接続し，出勤せずに仕事をするという**在宅勤務**もあります。

● 勤務自由化の背景

Q：会社は東京にありながら，環境のよい地方に住んで在宅勤務をするというのは，いいですね。勤務形態の自由化の方は，なぜ起きたのでしょうか。

A：働く人の立場からいえば，勤務時間が自由になるということは喜ばしいことです。ですから企業は優秀な人材を集めるために，こうした制度を導入し始めたということがあります。またフレックスタイム制の場合は，これを導入すれば時間外労働を減らすことができるという側面があります。このほか「働き過ぎ」という内外からの批判に応えるため，労働時間短縮の一環として政府がこうした制度の導入を奨励したことも大きな要因でしょう。

Q：なるほど。こういう変化は今後ますます進むのでしょうか。

A：勤務形態の変化は，今後一段と浸透するのではないでしょうか。特にフレックスタイム制については，先ほども触れましたが，政府が導入を奨励し

corporations. According to the 1990 survey by the Ministry of Labor, 10% of corporations had adopted flextime systems.

Q : So there's more freedom in working patterns. Are there any other measures besides making working times more flexible?

A : Yes, there is also the so-called **"free-time system,"** which is much freer than the flextime system. Employees under this sytem are free to set their own work hours, and the times when they start and finish work. Since no core time is required, employees are permitted to work for as little as one hour on a particular day. While employees are free to choose their working hours, they are under pressure to produce visible results. Although still uncommon, it is possible for some employees to work at home and stay in communication with the office by computer or fax. These **"homeworkers"** are able to work at home without having to go to the office at all.

Q : So in this system, for example, you could work at home in comfortable surroundings, without having to commute to the office in Tokyo. Why has this flexibility in working patterns come about?

A : First of all, there is support from employees, because they are able to set their own working hours. Second, there is support from employers. A number of corporations have introduced the flexible working hours system to attract good personnel, and the system also cuts down on the need for employees to work overtime. Another important factor is that the government has encouraged corporations to adopt flextime as a means of shortening working hours and responding to criticism, both at home and abroad, that the Japanese work too much.

Q : Do you think these changes will continue in the future?

A : I think such changes in working patterns will penetrate the work force further. Especially with government encouragement, flextime is sure to increase. Also when the economy slows, compa-

ていますから確実に増えていくと思います。一方,雇用形態の多様化については,不況になると企業は正規の社員以外の人たちを減らしますから,一時的にはその数は減るでしょう。しかし,そうした景気調整型の労働力が増えることは,企業の歓迎するところであり,また,ひとつの職場に拘束されたくないという考え方の若者も増えると思われますので,こうした傾向は今後も続くものと思われます。

nies first cut down on non-full-time workers to save on personnel costs. So in terms of diversification of employment patterns, in the short term I think we're going to see a decrease in the number of casual employees. But I also think we're going to see an increase over the long-term in the number of casual employees, because of the growing number of young people who don't want to be tied to one particular workplace and corporations which like this adjustable work force.

16 | 受難の中高年

従業員を新規学卒者，若年層，中高年層の3つのグループに分けた場合，賃上げを考える際に企業が最も重視するグループはどれでしょう。

① 新規学卒者　② 若年層　③ 中高年層

A：終身雇用と年功序列がゆらぎ始め，中高年のサラリーマンには受難の時代がやってきました。クイズの正解は②の若年層です。1991年に労働省が行ったアンケート調査では，50%以上の企業がこの年齢層を重視すると答えています。10年前の1980年に行われた同様の調査では，60%の企業が**中高年**を重視すると答えていたのと比べてみると大きな様変わりです。

Q：企業は中高年層より若年層を戦略的に重視するようになってきたというわけですね。

● 管理職削減の動き

A：そうなんです。しかも，このところの長期にわたる不況で，ホワイトカラー，特に中高年の**管理職**を削減しようとする企業が増えてきています。まさに中高年層にとって厳しい時代になっているといえますね。

Q：この10年で，中高年層に対する待遇が大きく変化したわけですが，背景にはどんな事情があるのでしょうか。

A：**ホワイトカラー**は，戦後一貫して増え続けてきました。石油危機や円高不況のときには，徹底的な合理化が行われ，**ブルーカラー**と呼ばれる現場労

Struggling Middle-aged and Older Executives

Which group of employees receives highest priority when companies are considering pay raises.

① newly hired employees straight out of college or school ② young employees ③ middle-aged and older employees

A : With the shaky situation of lifetime employment and the seniority system, a time of hardship has arrived for middle-aged and older workers. The correct answer to the quiz is number two, young employees. A survey carried out by the Ministry of Labor in 1991 found that over 50% of companies gave priority to this young employee group. A similar survey in 1980 showed priority was given to **middle-aged and older workers**. There is a major difference here in just over ten years.

Q : Corporations have changed their strategies from emphasizing middle-aged and older employees to the younger employees.

A : That's right. Furthermore, an increasing number of companies are trying to cut back on their office workers, particularly the middle-aged and older employees in **management positions**, because of the protracted recession. These are really hard times for this level of workers.

Q : Companies have dramatically changed the way they treat their middle-aged and older workers over the past ten years. What's behind this change?

A : Well, the number of **white-collar employees**, or office workers, has increased consistently since the end of the Second World War. Companies thoroughly streamlined operations dur-

ポイント

働者は減りました。しかし，このときでさえもホワイトカラーは増え続けました。これは，**製造業**に代わり**サービス産業**の比重が増加する，いわゆる経済のソフト化が進んだためといわれています。しかし，このところの不況で，ホワイトカラーに人余り感が出てきたというわけです。リストラの対象として企業のトップが挙げた中で，いちばん多かったのがホワイトカラーの削減，再配置でした。

Q：それで具体的にはどんな動きが出ていますか。

● 配置転換から
　退職勧告まで

A：まず，会社内の配置転換で，ホワイトカラーをほかの業務に回す方法がとられています。特に，管理職を事務部門から，営業や工場などの現場へ回す配置転換が行われています。また，最近問題になったケースとして，**希望退職**の募集ではなく，指名して退職を勧告する実質的な解雇通知があります。1992年の暮れには，ある大手の音響機器メーカーが，50歳以上の管理職35人に対し退職勧告を行い，大きなニュースになりました。不況の影響が特に厳しいといわれる自動車，電気機械あるいはソフトウエア産業などでは，中高年の社員を中心に**早期退職**の勧告を実施しています。終身雇用制を前提に生活設計をしてきた中高年の世代には大きな衝撃を与えています。

● 中高年管理職
　の削減理由

Q：ホワイトカラーが過剰だから減らそうというのはわかりましたが，その中でも，特に中高年の管理職層が削減の対象になっているのはどうしてなのでしょう。

A：ひとつには生産性の問題があります。特に事務部門で働く中高年の管理職は，高い賃金の割には，営業や生産現場のように直接収益につながっていくわけではありませんからね。人件費というのは

ing the oil crises and the recession caused by the yen's appreciation, and the number of **blue-collar workers**, such as factory workers, decreased. But the number of white-collar workers still continued to increase. This was because the economy was changing, the **service industry** began to overtake the **manufacturing industry**. Now there's a surplus of white-collar workers during this recession. The aspects of restructuring most frequently mentioned by enterprise heads were decreasing and reassignment of white-collar employees.

Q : How are companies actually dealing with the surplus of white-collar workers?

A : First of all, they use in-house transfers, in which white-collar workers are moved to other areas. This is especially prominent in the transferring of managers to areas such as sales and factory sites. As one recent example of the problem, companies are dismissing workers by designation rather than by **voluntary resignation** or **retirement**. At the end of 1992, one large acoustical equipment manufacturer shocked Japan by forcing 35 workers, mostly in management positions, aged 50 and over, to retire. Other industries hard hit by the recession, such as the automobile, electric machinery and software industries have been recommending **early retirement** mainly to their middle-aged and older employees. These policies are really a hard blow to such employees who have planned out their lives, assuming that they would work under the lifetime employment system.

Q : I understand that companies want to reduce the number of white-collar workers because there is a surplus, but why have they targeted the middle-aged and older management?

A : One reason is productivity. Companies have targeted the middle-aged and older office management because they receive a relatively high salary, and their jobs are not directly tied to profits, like those in sales and at factories. Personnel costs are fixed, and

● 企業内失業者の
　増加

固定費用ですから，企業の業績がどうであろうと毎月支払われていきます。さらに，年功序列型賃金で中高年の管理職は，能力や仕事量以上の賃金を受け取っていると見られていますから。

Q：不況で売り上げが低迷している企業としては，なんとかこの**固定費用**を減らしたい。そこでねらわれるのが中高年の管理職層というわけですね。

A：最近では「**企業内失業者**」という言葉をよく耳にします。生産に必要な適正な労働者数と実際の就業者とを比較し，その中で過剰とされる就業者を「企業内失業者」と呼んでいるわけなんですが，この数は現在100万とも200万ともいわれています。このうちの多くがホワイトカラーといわれています。「企業内失業者」がどうしてこんなに増えてしまったかといいますと，終身雇用制度と年功序列型賃金制度という日本企業の大前提があるからなのです。普通のサラリーマンは，いったん入社すれば，何らかの事情がない限りは定年までその会社で働き続け，そして給料は増え続けていきます。実はこの制度は，その会社が成長し続けるということを前提としているわけなのです。しかし，今のように不況が長引き，会社の成長が止まると，会社の中で特に中高年の管理職層が過剰になるという構造があるわけです。

Q：しかし，会社の都合で突然退職を勧告される中高年層にとっては大問題ですね。

A：そうです。このように中高年減らしが続くと，残った社員の会社への信頼感が失われるなど，モラルの低下で，会社の活気が失われる恐れがあります。終身雇用制を否定するようなこうした動きは，日本企業の雇用慣行が根本的に見直される時期にきていることを示しているのかもしれません。

that means companies have to pay them every month, regardless of business performance. In addition, middle-aged and older workers are regarded as receiving more wages, according to the seniority wage system, than their abilities and workloads justify.

Q : Since sales are slumping, companies desperately want to lower their **fixed costs**. That's why they've targeted middle-aged and older managers, isn't it?

A : We've been hearing the phrase **"in-house unemployment"** recently. If we compare the number of workers actually required for production to the number of employees, we'll find there's a surplus of employees, which is referred to as "in-house unemployment". It's estimated that there are between one and two million of these workers now, mainly white-collar workers. The reason why this "in-house unemployment" has reached such high levels is that Japanese companies operate on the premise of the lifetime employment and seniority wage systems. Once an ordinary worker enters a company, he works at that same company until retirement, barring any unusual circumstances, and his salary rises according to the number of years he has worked. But the system is based on the assumption that the company will continue to grow. Right now, the recession is dragging on, companies have stopped growing, and there is a surplus of workers, mostly middle-aged and older managers.

Q : It must be a big problem for middle-aged and older employees who are suddenly urged to retire.

A : Yes, it is. If companies continue to lay off their middle-aged and older workers, the remaining workers will lose their trust in the company. There are some fears that companies may lose their vitality as morale falls. The trend to rejecting lifetime employment may mean that the time has come to reevaluate the base of Japanese employment practices.

17 低い失業率

'80年代後半から始まった未曾有の好景気で，日本の
失業率は2.1%に低下しました。その好景気が去り，
経済不振のまっただ中にあった1993年5月の日本の失
業率は何%だったでしょうか。

① 2.5%　② 4.1%　③ 6.9%

● 日本の失業率

A：日本経済の特色のひとつに，失業率が低いことが
　あげられます。クイズは，不況時の失業率がどの
　程度上がったかを問うものですが，正解は①の
　2.5%でした（総務庁の調べ）。

Q：景気が低迷しているのに2.5%とは，かなり低い数
　字ですね。

A：やはりアメリカでも'90年，'91年と景気が後退し，
　その後ようやく回復のきざしを見せてきました
　が，同じ時期の失業率は6.9%となっています。

● 先進諸国の
　失業率

Q：ほかの先進諸国との比較ではどうですか。

A：'92年の年平均失業率で見ますと，日本が2.2%な
　のに対して，アメリカが7.4%，イギリスが9.9%，
　カナダが11.3%（各国資料による）と，日本の失
　業率がずば抜けて低いことがわかります。またク
　イズでもおわかりのように，景気が変わっても失
　業率の変動はあまりありません。

● 日本の特徴

Q：低水準，小変動ということですね。こうした日本
　の失業率の特徴はどうして出てくるのでしょうか。

A：まず日本独特の雇用形態があげられます。これま

126

Low Unemployment Rate

> Japan's unemployment rate fell to 2.1% due to the unprecedented prosperity which began in the latter half of the 1980s. But then the economy took a downturn. In the midst of this recession in May 1993, what do you suppose the Japanese unemployment rate was?
>
> ① 2.5% ② 4.1% ③ 6.9%

A : One particular feature of the Japanese economy is the low rate of unemployment. The correct answer for the unemployment rate during the recession is number one, 2.5% (Management and Coordination Agency survey).

Q : That's a pretty low figure for a slow economy.

A : Yes. Although the U.S. economy also moved into recession in 1990 and 1991, just recently it has shown signs of recovery and the U.S. **unemployment rate** for the same month was 6.9%.

Q : How does the Japanese figure compare with those of other industrialized nations?

A : Taking the average unemployment rates for 1992, Japan's was 2.2%, that of the United States was 7.4%, Britain's was 9.9% and Canada's was 11.3%. From this comparison you can see that Japan's unemployment rate is incredibly low. As you can tell from the quiz, the unemployment rate is barely affected by fluctuations in the economy.

Q : The unemployment rate is very low and fluctuates little. Why is this?

A : First of all, there's Japan's distinctive employment system. As

ポイント

でにも何度か述べましたように，日本の雇用は，伝統的に終身雇用制度に基づいて行われており，企業経営が多少悪化してもすぐに従業員を解雇するということはありません。労働時間を削減したり，新規採用を控えるといった形で雇用調整を行うので，大量の失業者を出さないですむのです。また，欧米諸国に比べて**自営業者や家族従業者**の割合が高く，雇用されている人の割合が低いことも理由のひとつとして挙げられるでしょう。全就業者に占める雇用労働者の割合を見てみると，アメリカでは91％，イギリスでは86％なのに対して，日本は77％となっています（ＯＥＣＤによる'90年のデータ）。景気後退の時でも，雇用労働者ならば解雇されるところを，自営業者や家族従業者は解雇されずにすむのです。さらに，女性が結婚，出産などを理由に仕事をやめて，そのまま家庭に入ることが多かったことも，失業率を低くしている理由です。つまり求職活動を行わなくなるので，**労働力**としてカウントされなくなるわけです。

Q：前の章でもふれた「企業内失業者」は，失業率の中には入らないのですか。

A：企業内失業者とは，**生産水準**に見合う適正な従業員数と実際の就業者数とを比較して，過剰とされる就業者のことです。日本の全就業者6500万人のうち，実に100万人もの企業内失業者がいるという試算もあります。これらの人たちは，解雇されているわけではありませんから，失業率の中には入っていません。しかし，もし企業内失業者も失業者の中に加えると，日本の実際の失業率は3％台半ばに達するという説もあります。いずれにせよ，日本の表面に表れる失業率は，欧米諸国に比べて非常に低いレベルにあります。

● 日本の失業率の
　見通し

Q：これからも日本の失業率は低い水準を保つことが

we've seen many times to date, employment is based on the lifetime employment system, and companies rarely lay off employees simply because business worsens. They adjust their payroll by cutting working hours and holding off on hiring new employees, so they can get through periods of management difficulty without massive unemployment. Another feature is the higher proportion of **self-employed people** and **people working in family businesses** than in the West. The percentage of people who are employed by others is comparatively low. If we compare the percentages of those employed by others among the total work force, this figure was 91% in the United States, 86% in Britain and 77% in Japan (OECD, 1990). The self-employed and people working in family businesses are not laid off, even when the economy takes a downturn. Also, many women leave their jobs when they get married or have children and stay at home, which is another factor contributing to the low unemployment rate. In other words, these women are not looking for work, so they are not counted as part of the **work force**.

Q : Earlier we touched on "in-house unemployment," but isn't this included in the unemployment rate?

A : In-house unemployment refers to a surplus of employees in proportion to **production level** and number of employees. One estimate found that, out of a total of 65 million employees, 1 million were counted as "in-house unemployed." But these people haven't been laid off, so they aren't included in the unemployment rate. Some people say if you add the number of in-house unemployed to the number of conventionally unemployed, then the unemployment rate would be around 3.5%. However you look at it, Japan's unemployment rate on the surface is much lower than that of Western countries.

Q : Will Japan be able to hold down its low unemployment rate in the

できるのでしょうか。

A：ここ数年，雇用形態が変化するきざしがあります。特に若年層では，ひとつの企業に永久就職するといった意識が薄れ，転職をすることに抵抗を感じない人が増えています。また，企業の方でも従来の終身雇用制度を見直したり，これまでほとんど考えられなかった事実上の指名解雇を行う動きも出てきているので，こうしたことが失業率に影響することはあるかもしれません。

Q：というと，将来日本の失業率が高くなったり，変動の幅が大きくなったりするのでしょうか。

A：確かに緩やかに上昇するすうせいにはあります。1994年7月には，3.0％に上がっています。しかし長い目で見ますと失業率の極端な上昇はありそうもないのです。なぜかというと，日本は出生率の低下に伴い，人口増加率の伸びが鈍化するか，あるいは減少に向かうことが予想されているからです。1992年3月の**雇用政策研究会**（労働省）の報告は，日本の労働力人口は西暦2000年に6697万人に達した後，その後，徐々に減少していくと予測しています。また，働き過ぎといわれる日本でも，労働時間短縮の動きが進んでいます。深刻な**人手不足**をもたらしたバブル景気は過ぎ去ったとはいえ，長期的に見ると人手不足はますます深刻になっていくと考えられます。

future?

A : In the past several years, there have been signs of change in the employment system. Young people especially are less oriented toward staying with one firm for life and are more flexible about changing jobs. Companies as well are revaluating the conventional lifetime employment system and even laying off workers, something that was unthinkable in the past. These factors may have a slight effect on the unemployment rate.

Q : Does this mean that Japan's unemployment rate will rise and there will be more fluctuation in the future?

A : It is true that such a trend is evident. In July 1994 that rate rose to 3%, but in the long term, the unemployment rate probably will not rise sharply. This is because Japan's birthrate is dropping, population growth is slowing, and the population is even predicted to decrease in the future. In March 1992, **the Study Meeting for Employment Policy** of the Labor Ministry reported that the Japanese work force would reach 66,970,000 in the year 2000 and then fall gradually. Although the Japanese are often said to work too much, there is a trend toward reducing working hours. While the **labor shortage** in Japan brought on by the "bubble economy" is now over, in the long term the shortage of labor may become even more serious.

18 | 通勤地獄

> 東京都心の会社に勤めるサラリーマンの平均的な通勤時間は，片道どのくらいでしょうか。
>
> ① 45分　② 1時間15分　③ 1時間45分

● 遠距離通勤者の増加

A：日本のサラリーマンにとって大変なのは，長時間労働に加えて**通勤時間**も長いことです。クイズの正解は，②の1時間15分です。

Q：往復では2時間半になりますね。こうした遠距離通勤の人はどのくらいいるのですか。

A：東京の都区部，つまり23区内で働く人は，1990年の国勢調査で725万人いますが，そのうちの40％あまり，313万人の人がこの地区以外のところから通っています。その人たちの平均通勤時間が，1時間15分なんです。東京の**ベッドタウン**は，どんどん拡がっていまして，こうした遠距離通勤者は5年前と比べて20％ほど増えています。

Q：増えているのはそれだけ，東京近辺で住宅を購入するのが難しくなっているからですね。

A：そうです。このところの**不動産**不況で**地価**は下がったものの，それでも一般のサラリーマンにとっては，東京都内はもちろん，東京近辺の住宅もなかなか手の届かない存在です。住宅を購入する場合，購入可能な価格の範囲は，年収の5倍といわれています。総務庁の1993年家計調査によると，日本のサラリーマンの**年収**は，30代の男子で平均528万円ですから，買うことのできる住宅の価格

132

Commuting Hell

> **What is the average commuting time of one way, for a worker employed in the center of Tokyo?**
>
> ① 45 minutes   ② 1 hour and 15 minutes   ③ 1 hour and 45 minutes

A : The hardest thing for Japanese workers is the long **commuting time** that precedes and follows a long work day. The correct answer is number two, 1 hour and 15 minutes.

Q : That means a two-and-a-half-hour round trip. How many people commute such a long distance?

A : The 1990 national survey found that 7.25 million people work within the 23 wards in Tokyo, and of these, 40% (3.13 million) commute from outside areas. The average commuting time for these people is 1 hour and 15 minutes. The **bedroom communitie**s around Tokyo have been expanding, and the number of long-distance commuters has increased 20% in the past five years.

Q : One reason the number is rising is because it has become quite difficult to buy a house in the Tokyo suburbs.

A : That's right. Although **land prices** have dropped recently because of the **real estate** recession, it's nearly impossible for the average worker to buy a house in the Tokyo area or its suburbs. It is said that a reasonable price for a house is five times a worker's yearly income. According to the survey of households carried out by the Management and Coordination Agency in 1993, the average **annual income** of a male in his thirties is about ¥5.28 million meaning the reasonable price for housing

は2600万円くらいまで。この値段で広さが60m²の
マンションを買おうとしても，東京都心から1時
間以内の**通勤圏**内には見当たりません。

Q：60m²の広さのマンションといっても，4人家族だ
と狭いですね。もう少し広い家が欲しいとなると，
通勤時間はさらに長くなってしまうわけですね。

A：先ほどの313万人のうち，1時間半以上の通勤時間
の人は3分の1。つまり100万人を超える**首都圏**の
サラリーマンが通勤に往復3時間以上かけている
ことになります。

Q：会社での労働時間は8時間。たとえ残業がなくて
も通勤時間を考慮すると，自由な時間はかなり少
なくなりますね。さて遠距離通勤というと，近年
は新幹線での通勤が話題になりますが。

● 通勤圏の拡大

A：新幹線は時速200kmですから，東京から200km離
れたところからでも，1時間ちょっとの通勤時間
で通えることになります。企業によっては新幹線
の料金を交通費として支給するところも出てきま
した。また首都圏の鉄道では，遠距離からの通勤
者のために止まる駅を少なくした快速電車の運行
を増やしているので，通勤圏はこれまでの80km
圏から100km圏に拡大しつつあります。

Q：通勤で大変なのは時間の長さだけではなく，**ラッ
シュアワー**の混雑ぶりがそれに拍車をかけていま
すね。

● ラッシュアワー
の混雑率

A：東京の朝のラッシュアワーは，午前8時前後の1時
間がピークで，この時間帯の混雑率は平均で
200％です。混雑率が200％ですと，立っている人
が新聞を読むこともできず，250％になると身動
きもできなくなるといわれます。'90年の統計によ
ると，最も混む時間帯には首都圏の10路線でこの
250％程度の混雑率になっています。

would be about ¥26 million. Even if a worker were to find a condominium of 60 square meters at that price, he or she still
wouldn't be within a one-hour **commuting distance** of Tokyo.

Q : But a 60-square-meter condominium is small for a family of four.
That is why commutes are getting longer and longer.

A : Of the 3.13 million commuters we mentioned earlier, one-third
commute for over an hour and a half. That means that over 1
million workers working in the **metropolitan area** spend more
than three hours a day commuting.

Q : They work for eight hours a day, and even if they don't have to
work overtime, their free time is greatly diminished by this long
commute. Speaking of long-distance commuting, recently I've
been hearing about people commuting on the Shinkansen bullet
trains.

A : The bullet train runs at 200 kilometers per hour, so if someone
lives 200 kilometers away from Tokyo, they can commute to
their jobs in just over an hour. Some companies are paying the
fares for their employees to commute on bullet trains. Railways
in the Tokyo area have also increased the number of non-stop
express trains for commuters in outlying areas. The commuting
distance, which used to be around 80 kilometers, is expanding to
100 kilometers.

Q : Long commuting times are made even more difficult by the
crowds during **rush hours**.

A : The morning rush hour in Tokyo is the worst for about an hour
around eight o'clock. In this time block, trains are filled, on
average, to 200% of their designated capacity. So if the train is
filled to 200% of its capacity, people who are standing cannot
read a newspaper, and at 250% capacity, people cannot even
move. According to some 1990 statistics, the trains on ten train
routes in the metropolitan area were filled to 250% capacity

● 通勤地獄の解消

Q：まさに**通勤地獄**という状況ですね。電車以外の方法というとマイカー通勤ですが，これも東京の道路の混雑ぶりから見て便利とはいえませんね。

A：東京と近郊の都市を結ぶ高速道路網の整備は進んでいますが，東京に近くなると渋滞が激しく，車での通勤も楽ではありません。ラッシュ時には1時間以上の渋滞を覚悟しなければなりません。首都高速道路の渋滞の状況は，'80年から'90年の10年間に，2倍ほど悪化しています。

Q：東京のサラリーマンにとって，マイカーはほとんど通勤の手段になりえないということになると，通勤地獄解消のための対策は，何か考えられているのでしょうか。

A：JRは苦肉の策として，ラッシュの時間帯には座席を折りたたんで立ち席だけになる車両を導入し，輸送量を増やそうとしています。また政府は時差出勤によって混雑を緩和しようと，民間企業に働きかけています。

Q：でもそうした小手先の対策では，根本的な解決にはならないでしょう。

A：政府の当面の目標は，通勤時間帯でも新聞が読める程度の混雑，混雑率でいえば180％程度に緩和することです。そのために新しい鉄道の整備などに取り組んでいますが，実現には長い時間がかかります。もっと根本的な対策としては，政治や経済の東京への一極集中を緩和しないと，地価の高騰やそれに伴う**遠距離通勤**という問題の解決は難しいのではないでしょうか。そのためにも首都機能の分散といった思い切った手段が必要になってきているといえます。

during the most crowded hours.

Q : These factors combine to create "**commuting hell.**" Other methods of transportation such as private cars aren't convenient because of the jam-packed roads in Tokyo.

A : Expressways connecting Tokyo with its suburbs have been expanded, but the traffic jams are incredible near Tokyo, so it is not easy to commute by car. If you're commuting by car during rush hours, you have to be prepared to add an extra hour to your commute. The number of traffic jams on the Tokyo expressway system doubled between 1980 and 1990.

Q : If private cars are not really an option for workers, what measures is Tokyo trying to eliminate this commuting hell?

A : Well, Japan Railways has introduced railroad cars that have fold-up seats, so that during rush hours they can carry more standing passengers. Also the government has been urging private companies to vary their working hours to relieve some of the congestion.

Q : But these patchwork measures probably won't get to the root of the problem, will they?

A : No, the government's most urgent goal is to relieve the congestion so that trains can operate at about 180% capacity and people can at least read their newspapers. That's why they've begun building new railroads, but it will be some time before these are completed. To get to the root of the problem, government and business will have to move to outlying areas. Otherwise, it will be difficult to solve problems such as outrageous land prices and **long-distance commuting**. Administrative functions will have to be relocated outside Tokyo.

19 会社ぐるみの生活

> 中小企業を対象に行ったあるアンケート調査で，社員旅行を実施していると答えた企業は何％あったでしょうか。
>
> ① 39.9%　② 59.9%　③ 99.9%

● 社員旅行の実態

● 勤務時間外にも
　付き合い

A：**社員旅行**というのは，会社あるいは職場単位で行う慰安旅行のことです。日本ではこの社員旅行がとても盛んで，月刊雑誌「企業実務」が1993年に中小企業231社に対して行ったアンケート調査では，99.9％の企業が，社員旅行を実施していると答えています。

Q：ずいぶん多くの企業が社員旅行を行っているのですね。日本は**企業中心社会**とよくいわれますが，社員同士が一緒に旅行するというのはその典型的な例でしょうね。

A：日本人の働き過ぎはよくいわれることですが，サラリーマンの生活には，就業時間以外にも会社が深くかかわっていることが多いのです。例えば，サラリーマンは，会社がひけた後，同僚や上司と一緒に酒を飲みに行ったりすることがよくあります。ストレス解消ということもあるのですが，こういうときに話題になるのは，ほとんどが仕事のことや会社の人間関係です。

Q：会社を離れてもある意味では仕事は続いているんですね。

A：このほかにも，休日に取引先をゴルフに接待するということもあります。家族から見れば，家庭生

Company-Oriented Life

In a survey of small and medium-sized enterprises what percentage of them actually have company trips or holidays?

① 39.9% ② 59.9% ③ 99.9%

A : **Employee trips** are recreational trips provided by companies for all their workers together or for employees at each workplace. They are quite common in Japanese enterprises and according to a survey by the monthly magazine *Kigyojitsumu*, 231 firms, 99.9% provide such trips for employees.

Q : Quite a lot of companies have company trips, don't they? It is often said that Japan is a **company-oriented society** and the fact that all employees in a company go on a trip together is typical of this.

A : The Japanese are often said to work too much. The company tends to be deeply involved in the lives of their employees even after normal working hours. After a day's work, employees will in many cases go drinking with each other or with their seniors. This is a means of relieving stress. But employees tend to talk about their work or their fellow employees.

Q : You could say they are still working even outside their workplace.

A : Even on their days off, employees often entertain clients by taking them golfing. From their families' point of view, these

ポイント

● 企業一家意識を
　養成

● 住宅も提供

活を犠牲にされることになり，会社中心の生活ということになりますね。

Q：これは総じて，日本のサラリーマンの会社への帰属意識が高いことからくるのでしょうか。

A：日本には，「**企業一家意識**」という独特の概念があります。これは，会社とは社員全体によって支えられているものであり，会社の繁栄は社員の生活の向上につながるという考え方です。この企業一家意識，あるいは会社への高い忠誠心の基盤になっているのが，終身雇用制度や年功序列型賃金などの特徴を持つ日本式経営なのです。

Q：なるほど，会社は一種の共同体といえますね。

A：そうですね。会社以外でのつき合い，先ほどの社員旅行もそうですが，こうしたことはすべて，同じ共同体の中で暮らすもの同士のコミュニケーションを密にし，**連帯感や団結心**を高めようというねらいがあるようです。この共同体の中には，しばしば家族も含まれるんですね。例えば，会社の運動会がそうです。具体的なデータはありませんが，かなり多くの企業が会社主催の**運動会**をやっているようですね。多くの場合，会社が弁当や賞品などを用意し，社員ばかりでなくその家族も参加するのが一般的です。

Q：サラリーマンと企業の関係は，単に労働を供給しその対価として賃金を得る，という関係だけにとどまっているわけではないんですね。

A：これは生活全般にわたっているといえます。例えば，住宅です。企業は住宅を確保し，それを社員に社宅として貸し与えています。これは民間の家賃よりはるかに安いのが普通で，住宅難の大都市で暮らすサラリーマンにとっては大きいことですね。**経済企画庁**が1990年に行った調査によると，従業員499人以下の企業で，**社宅を保有している**

employees' lives center around their company; family-life is sacrificed.

Q : So overall, does this mean many employees have a strong sense of identity with their company?

A : Yes. In Japan there is a **sense of the company being a family**. The company is supported by all of its employees, and because of that, the company's prosperity promotes the lives of its employees. The basis for this view and the high degree of loyalty employees tend to have toward the company has been the system of life-long employment and pay scales based on seniority.

Q : So you could say the company is a type of community?

A : Yes. Those occasions outside of working hours, like drinking together after work or going on a trip together, foster communication between people of the same group. Such activities aim at strengthening a **sense of solidarity and unity**. Sometimes the employees' families are included in this company community, for example, on occasions such as company **athletic meets**. Although there are no specific figures, it appears that many companies hold such athletics meets. The company often provides lunches and prizes. Usually, participation in these events includes not only the employees but also their family members.

Q : So the relationship between salaried workers and their company is not just one of providing labor in exchange for wages?

A : You could say that the company is involved in all aspects of its employees' lives. Another example is the housing which many companies provide to their employees. The rent is usually much lower than that of privately rented accommodation and this is a big plus to employees in large cities, where there is a severe housing shortage. A 1990 survey by **the Economic Planning Agency** found that 80% of companies with under 500 employees

ポイント

のはおよそ80％です。従業員が1000人以上の大企業では，社宅保有率は95％を超えています。

Q：大部分の企業が社宅を持っているということになりますね。

● 福利厚生を充実

A：社員の福利厚生という面から見ますと，企業との結びつきはもっと強くなります。大企業になれば特にそうなのですが，多くの企業が有名な観光地に**保養所**を持っています。このほかにも，買い物や旅行などに際して社員割引などの便宜を図っている企業もありますし，**住宅ローン**や子供の教育ローンを出す企業も多いですね。

Q：入社すると会社の独身寮に住み，結婚すると社宅に移り，休みには会社の保養施設で過ごすとなると，まさに会社ぐるみの生活ということになりますね。しかし，これではどこまでも会社の生活を引きずっていることになり，個人の生活を大事にしたいという若い人には，不満が出てくるのではないでしょうか。

● 多い会社人間

A：そうですね。社員旅行にしても，社員運動会や退社後の付き合いにしても，みんながみんな喜んで参加しているというわけではないようです。みんなが行くからとか，参加しなければ人間関係に悪い影響を及ぼすとかいうことから，しかたなくつき合っているという面もあるようです。ここに経団連（**経済団体連合会**）が1993年に行った興味深い調査があります。あなたにとってほぼ同等の重要度を持つ「会社の事情」と「家族の事情」とが重なった場合，どちらを優先しますか，というのが質問です。例えば，「残業と結婚記念日」や「**社用ゴルフ**と子供の授業参観」などです。これに対して，およそ80％の人が，会社を優先すると答えています。

Q：本当に会社人間が多いのですね。

have **company housing**. For companies with over 1,000 employees, the figure is over 95%.

Q : So the majority of companies have company housing?

A : Yes. By providing for the welfare of their employees, the bonds between the company and employees are further strengthened. Many companies, especially large firms, also own **resorts** in well-known tourist areas. Some firms also offer shopping and travelling discounts to their employees, and many companies also provide **housing loans** and loans to pay for the education of employees' children.

Q : An employee's life revolves around the company. When they enter the company, they live in a company dormitory for single employees. After they get married, they live in company housing. On holidays, they go to company resorts. But isn't there any dissatisfaction among those employees who value their privacy? Wouldn't some young employees dislike the company being involved in every aspect of their life?

A : Not everybody is happy about going on company trips, participating in company athletic meets, or being involved with the company outside of normal working hours. However, most feel they have no other choice, because everybody else is doing the same thing, and if they do not participate, that will upset other people in the workplace. Keidanren, **the Federation of Economic Organizations** carried out an interesting survey in 1993 asking employees whether they would give priority to the company or their family in certain situations of about equal weighting. For example, would they work overtime or go home on their wedding anniversary? Would they play in a **company-organized golf event** or go see their children at school on Parents' Day? Around 80% replied they would give their company priority.

Q : There are a lot of company-oriented individuals, aren't there?

A : 興味深いのは次の設問に対する答えです。「今後はどうなると思いますか」という問いに対して，会社優先派は20％に後退し，家族を優先すると答えた人は30％と，これを上回っています。残りの50％は，どちらともいえないと答えています。

Q : 会社人間はこれからは減っていくというわけですね。

A : そうですね。今の企業のトップの中には，会社こそが自分の人生実現の場であるとか，会社が自分を育ててくれたという人が多いわけですが，これからは，会社は人生の一部分であると考える人が増えてくるのではないでしょうか。

A : The next question is even more interesting. Asked whether they would give priority to their company or their family in the future, 20% said they would give priority to their company. Thirty percent said they would give priority to their family, while 50% said they could not answer one way or the other.

Q : So company-oriented individuals are on the decrease?

A : It appears so. Many in the top echelons of the company feel that the company is their life's stage, or that the company has raised them as people. But in the future there will probably be an increase in the number of people who view the company as only forming one part of their life.

20 | 高い貯蓄率

日本は国際的にも貯蓄率の高い国だといわれています。日本銀行が発表した'91年の統計では，アメリカの貯蓄率は5%でした。それでは同じ時点での日本の貯蓄率は約何%だったでしょうか。

① 6%　② 13%　③ 15%

● 各国の貯蓄率

● 貯蓄大国である
　理由

A：高い**貯蓄率**が日本の経済を支えてきたとよくいわれます。クイズの答えは約15%です。他の先進国を見ると，イギリスは6%，フランス，ドイツはともに13%となっています。ただし，ドイツの統計は旧西ドイツ地域のもので，両ドイツ統一後のデータが出るともっと低くなると予想されています。

Q：**貯蓄大国**日本ということですが，その背景には何があるのでしょうか。

A：さまざまな説があります。まず，1960年代の経済成長のスピードが予想以上に速かったことです。貯蓄率とは，家計の**可処分所得**の中に占める貯蓄の割合です。可処分所得とは，サラリーマンでいえば給与所得から**税金**や**社会保険料**などを除いた**手取りの所得**です。'60年代からの急速な経済成長は日本人に所得の急増をもたらし，貯蓄の余裕を生み出したということです。経済成長とともに日本人の所得は急速に増加しましたが，一方，消費のパターンは急には変わりません。一時的にお金が入れば散財もするでしょうが，月給の形でもらう分にはそれほど増加を実感しませんので，消費

High Rate of Savings

> Japan is said to have a comparatively high rate of savings. According to statistics published by the Bank of Japan for 1991, the savings rate for the United States was 5%. What do you think the savings rate for Japan was in that same year?
>
> ① 6%　② 13%　③ 15%

A : It is said that the high **savings rate** has supported the Japanese economy. The answer is around 15%. Among other industrialized nations, the savings rate in Britain was 6% and in Germany and France it was 13%. The figure for Germany, however, is actually for the former West Germany, so it's expected that the rate for united Germany is lower.

Q : Japan has been called a **savings superpower**, but what's behind this phenomenon?

A : There are several explanations. First of all, the speed of economic growth in the 1960s was much more rapid than expected. The savings rate is the ratio of household savings to **disposable income**. Disposable income, in the case of a salaried worker means the amount of **take-home pay** after **taxes** and **social insurance payments** are deducted. The rapid economic growth in the 1960s led to a rapid increase in Japanese income and this caused the extra margin for savings. In spite of this rapid growth in income, which accompanied the economic growth, the pattern for expenditures did not follow the same trend. A lump sum payment would allow one to be extravagant, but a small increase in salary would not give one the feeling of

行動の変化はゆっくりとしたものとなります。他方，所得は増えているわけですから，その分が貯蓄に回されたということです。もうひとついわれているのは，アメリカやイギリスに比べて人口構成上，平均年齢が低かったということです。

Q：平均年齢が低いと，なぜ貯蓄率が高くなるのですか。

A：貯蓄を取り崩しながら生活する高齢者の割合が低いということですから，平均貯蓄率は高くなります。こうした見方のほかにも，社会保障の水準が低いので人々が老後に備えて貯蓄に励んだとか，住宅価格が高いために貯蓄の目標水準が高いとか，政府がとってきた諸々の貯蓄優遇策を重視する人もいます。結局，これらのうちのどれがというよりは，これらの要因がお互いに作用して，日本の貯蓄率を高いものにしてきたというべきでしょう。

Q：このような高い貯蓄率は，日本経済にどんな影響を及ぼしてきたのでしょうか。

A：貯蓄率が高いということは，長い目で見ると日本経済にとって大きなメリットになってきたといえます。どういうことかというと，日本人が**銀行預金**などの形で行ってきた貯蓄は，経済成長の最も大きなファクターである，**設備投資**の源泉となってきたのです。設備投資は生産能力を高め，しばしば**技術革新**のもととなります。貯蓄率の高さは，設備投資型の経済成長を可能とすることで，長期的な日本経済の強さの要因となっているといえるのです。高度成長期の日本の貯蓄率は伸び続け，1975年にはおよそ23％と，ピークに達しました。その後はすこしずつ低下していて，ここ数年は14％台を推移しています。

Q：ところで景気の変動と貯蓄率との関係はどうなっていますか。

an actual increase; consequently, consumer spending remains flat. On the other hand, the salary itself is actually increasing, so people put the surplus into savings. Another reason is that the average age of the population was younger than that in the United States or Britain.

Q : What is the relationship between the average age of the population being low and the high savings rate?

A : That means the percentage of elderly people living off their savings was lower. Other factors that can be seen are that, since the level of social security was low, people were encouraged to save for their later years. Also, since housing is expensive, the average target for savings is high. Others regard government policies encouraging savings as the most important factor. In the end, all these factors worked together to bring about a high savings rate in Japan.

Q : How has the high savings rate affected the Japanese economy?

A : In the long term, this has been a great boon to the Japanese economy. **Savings in bank accounts** and elsewhere have been a source of **investment in plant and equipment**, a major contributor to economic growth. In turn, such investment raises productivity and becomes the basis for **technological innovation**. It can be said that a high savings rate has made possible economic growth based on investment in plant and equipment, and has become an important factor in the long-term strength of the Japanese economy. The Japanese savings rate continued to rise during the high-growth period, and peaked at around 23% in 1975. Since then it has slowly fallen and in recent years has remained around 14%.

Q : By the way, what's the relationship between fluctuations in the economy and the savings rate?

A：以前ですと，不況になると貯蓄率は低くなるといわれていました。人々は**生活水準**を維持するために，本来貯蓄するお金を消費に回すようになるからです。しかし最近ではこれと逆の現象が起きています。好景気だった'90年は13.5％と貯蓄率は低かったのに，'91年に不況が始まると，一転して14.6％に上昇しています。貯蓄率が高いということは，裏返せば消費が少ないということです。したがって，さらに景気の足を引っ張ることにもつながります。

Q：なぜ変わったのでしょうか。

A：日本人の消費生活が変化してきているのです。例えば，食品，飲料，たばこが消費支出に占める割合は，'70年ではおよそ30％だったのが，'91年には20％に低下しています。反対に，レクレーション，娯楽，教育などへの支出は，'70年の9％から，'91年には11％近くまで上昇しています。

Q：衣食など必需品の割合が減り，娯楽などその気になればいつでも切り詰められる支出が大きくなっているのですね。

A：ですから最近は，景気が拡大すると楽観気分で人びとは**消費性向**を高め，不況になると先行き不安から消費を控え，かえって貯蓄率は上がるという現象が見られるようになりました。

• 今後の貯蓄率

Q：ところで，高い水準を維持してきた日本の貯蓄率も少しずつ低くなってきているようですが，今後も低下し続けるのでしょうか。

A：先ほどもふれましたが，日本の人口構成が比較的若かったことが，貯蓄率の高さの，ひとつの背景となっていたわけです。しかし今後は，急速な高齢化に伴い，若いときに貯めた貯蓄を取り崩しな

A : In the past, it was said that a recession lowered the savings rate because people would spend the money that would be invested in their savings to maintain their **standard of living**. But lately the reverse is true. Although the savings rate was rather low, 13.5%, in 1990, which was a prosperous year, the rate actually rose to 14.6% in 1991 when the recession began. The flip side to a high savings rate is that it lowers consumption, and that in turn puts a drag on the economy.

Q : How did this come about?

A : Japanese consumption patterns have changed. In 1970, for example, 30% of consumption expenditures were for food, drink and cigarettes, but that dropped to 20% in 1991. In contrast, the percentage of expenditures for recreation, entertainment, education and such was 9% in 1970, but rose to nearly 11% in 1991.

Q : The percentage of expenditures on basic necessities such as clothing and food has decreased, and expenditures on entertainment and services, which can be easily reduced if necessary, have been increasing.

A : This is why we've recently seen that as the economy expands, people grow optimistic and their **propensity to consume** increases, and when the economy takes a downturn, people restrict consumption because of uncertainty about the future. And this encourages the tendency to save.

Q : The Japanese savings rate has been maintained at a high level, but it seems to be dropping gradually. Will this trend continue in the future?

A : As I mentioned, previously the Japanese population was relatively young and this was reflected in the high savings rate. In the future, with the rapid aging of the population, it's expected that more people will begin living off the money they saved in their

がら生計をたてる人が増えると予想されます。そのため，国全体の貯蓄率は長期的に低下していく可能性が高いのです。さらに，バブル経済のときに顕著に見られたように，旅行や余暇の楽しみなどのために大胆な消費を行う人も出てきました。こうした消費態度の変化も，日本の貯蓄率を低くしていく一因となるかもしれません。

younger years. This means there's a great probability that the nation's savings rate will decline in the long term. In addition, as we saw during the boom, people are likely to spend great amounts for pleasure and travel. The change in attitudes towards consumption may be one of the factors which will lower the Japanese savings rate.

21 | 変わる消費生活

> ファクシミリ，ＶＴＲ，カラオケ装置，この3つの電気製品の一般家庭への普及率は，それぞれ次のどれでしょうか。
>
> ① 7%　② 18%　③ 75%

A：日本の消費生活は経済成長に伴って多様化，高級化が進みました。クイズは電気製品の**普及率**を問うものですが，正解は**ファクシミリ**が7%，ＶＴＲが75%，**カラオケ装置**が18%でした。このデータは経済企画庁が調査したもので，1993年の数字です。

Q：カラオケ装置がファクシミリより普及率が高いというのは，意外ですね。

A：ファクシミリは，事務所への普及は進んでいますが，一般家庭への普及は始まったばかりです。電気製品の普及については，後ほど紹介することにして，まずは日本の消費水準は本当に高まったのかどうか，**エンゲル係数**から見ていきましょう。

Q：エンゲル係数といえば，**食費**の割合ですよね。

● 各国のエンゲル係数

A：そうです。家計の消費支出の中に占める食費の割合で，消費生活の豊かさを表す数字として昔から使われています。そのエンゲル係数，1990年の各国の統計によると，日本は25.4%なのに対して，アメリカが12.1%，フランスが19.4%，ドイツが21.0%，イギリスが24.5%となっています。

Q：アメリカはなぜこんなに低いのですか。

A：アメリカの場合，家計に占める**医療費**の割合が高

Changing Consumption Patterns

> From the figures below, select the diffusion rates in the
> average household for each of these three appliances:
> facsimiles, video tape recorders and karaoke machines.
>
> ① 7% ② 18% ③ 75%

A : Japanese consumption patterns have diversified and grown more
extravagant along with economic growth. The quiz deals with
the **diffusion rates** of electrical appliances. The correct
answers are, **facsimiles**—7%, video tape recorders—75%, and
karaoke machines—18%. This data was compiled by the Economic Planning Agency in 1993.

Q : I'm surprised that more people have karaoke machines than facsimiles.

A : Most offices now have facsimilies, but they're not as popular in
the average household. We'll talk about the diffusion of electric
appliances later. First, let's look at the **Engel's coefficient**
which shows whether the Japanese standard of living has actually risen or worsened.

Q : The Engel's coefficient refers to the percentage spent on **food
expenditures**, doesn't it?

A : That's right. It shows the percentage of household expenditures
spent on food, which has been used for a long time to express
the substance of consumption patterns. According to the 1990
Engel's coefficient, Japan was rated at 25.4%; the United States,
12.1%; France, 19.4%; Germany, 21.0%; and Britain, 24.5%.

Q : Why is the figure for the United States so low?

A : In the United States the percentage of household expenditures

いので，その分，食費の割合が相対的に低くなっています。また，日本と比べると物価が安いことも，エンゲル係数を下げている要素だということです。ところで日本のエンゲル係数は，1970年は34.1％だったのが，'80年には29.0％，そして'90年には25.4％と下がってきて，やっとヨーロッパ並みになったということです。ちなみにお隣の韓国は，'91年で35.3％です。

● 消費の多様化

Q：エンゲル係数の低下とともに消費の中身も変わってきたと思いますが，その点はいかがですか。

A：ひとつは，「モノからサービスへ」と消費のパターンが変わってきたことです。経済企画庁の調べによると，1980年から1992年の間に，**教育費**が3.6％から4.6％に，またレジャーや習いごとといった**教養娯楽費**も，8.5％から9.8％に増えています。家計の消費支出をサービスとモノとに分けた場合，サービスの割合はだんだん増えて50％に近づいています。もうひとつの傾向は，サービスであれモノであれ，消費の多様化，高級化が進んだことです。

Q：具体的に説明してもらえませんか。

A：まず多様化ですが，**共稼ぎ夫婦**が増えて，それぞれが独自の収入を持つようになったことなどから，消費も自分の好むものを選ぶ個性化，多様化が進みました。例えば乗用車についていえば，1988年の時点で車の種類は国産のものだけでも3000種ほどに増えました。それまでの**少品種大量生産**から**多品種少量生産**に変わったわけです。

● 消費の高級化

Q：高級化の方はどうですか。

A：例えばカラーテレビを例に取りましょう。カラーテレビの普及率は1987年以前からすでに99％を超えていますが，その機能や大きさを見てみますと

taken up by **medical costs** is very high, so the percentage spent on food is correspondingly low. Goods are less expensive than in Japan and this is one factor that lowers the Engel's coefficient. The Engel's coefficient in Japan in 1970 was 34.1%, while it was 29.0% in 1980. When it dropped to 25.4% in 1990, it finally caught up to the living standards of European nations. Japan's neighbor, South Korea, was rated at 35.3% in 1991.

Q : Since the Engel's coefficient dropped, Japanese consumption patterns must have changed, haven't they?

A : Well, one trend is the switch in consumption from goods to services. In the Economic Planning Agency's survey of the years 1980 to 1992, **education expenditures** rose from 3.6% to 4.6%. **Expenditures on educational recreation and entertainment** together increased from 8.5% to 9.8%. If you divide household expenditures between goods and services, the service percentage has gradually increased and is now nearing 50%. Another trend is that consumption in both goods and services is diversifying and becoming more luxurious.

Q : What does that mean in concrete terms?

A : Well, diversification means that as **double-income families** increase, more people have their own personal income. They can buy things that fit their personal taste and that in turn has increased the variety of items consumed. Looking at cars, for example, in 1988, nearly 3,000 varieties of cars were produced for the domestic market alone. So we're seeing a shift from **mass production of a limited variety of goods**, to **limited production of a wide variety of goods**.

Q : What about the increase in luxury?

A : Let's take color TVs for example. According to the Economic Planning Agency, already by 1987, over 99% of Japanese households had color TVs. But if we look at the functions and sizes,

高級化が進んでいることがわかります。1992年の
データによると，2種類の音声が聞こえる**音声多
重放送方式**のカラーテレビが，全体の66%を占め
ているほか，29インチ以上の大型のものが34%も
占めています。

Q：テレビの大きさといえば，以前は14インチから16
インチぐらいが主流でしたよね。

A：そうですね。高級化のほかに，新しい電化製品も
いろいろと普及しています。それが冒頭のクイズ
でご紹介したファクシミリやカラオケ装置です。
これ以外にも，**ワープロ**の普及率は36%，**衛星放
送**の受信装置は21%に達しています。

Q：こうした電化製品の普及率は，外国と比べてどう
なんですか。

A：1993年のデータで日本とアメリカを比べてみます
と，VTRは日本の75%に対してアメリカは80%
と高くなっています。しかしファクシミリは日本
の7%に対してアメリカは2%，ビデオカメラは日
本の26%に対してアメリカは19%と，日本の方が
普及率は高くなっています。さらに衛星放送の受
信装置もアメリカは4%と日本よりかなり低いの
ですが，これはアメリカの場合は，CATV（**有
線テレビ**）が普及しているといった事情もあるの
で，一概に比較はできません。

● バブル崩壊後の
消費

Q：先ほどの消費の高級化，あるいは多様化について
は，バブル経済が崩壊した後，再び変わってきて
いると新聞などには書いてありますが，その点は
いかがですか。

A：そうなんです。バブルのときには値段の高い高級
品がよく売れていましたが，不況に入った後は，
品質の伴わない値段の高いものの売れ行きは大幅
に落ちました。それと先ほど乗用車の種類が3000
種ほどにも増えたといいましたが，車種が多けれ

we can see that consumers are buying more luxurious sets. The latest data for 1992 tells us that 66% of TVs purchased now are models with a **sound multiplex system,** and 34% have 29-inch screens or larger.

Q : Most TVs in the past were about 14 to 16 inches, weren't they?

A : Yes. In addition to the more luxurious items, there's a variety of new electrical appliances on the market. In addition to facsimiles and karaoke machines, 36% of households have **word processors** and 21% have receivers for **satellite broadcasting.**

Q : How do these figures compare to those in foreign countries?

A : If we compare the United States and Japan in 1993, 80% of households in the United States had video tape recorders compared to 75% in Japan. But only 2% had facsimiles compared to 7% in Japan. More people own video cameras in Japan as well, 26% in Japan to 19% in the United States. Only 4% of households in the United States have satellite broadcast receivers, which is much lower than in Japan. But **cable television** is more popular in the United States, so you really cannot generalize.

Q : We were just talking about consumption tending towards more luxury items and diversification, but I've read in the newspaper that these patterns have changed again since the collapse of the bubble economy. What is that all about?

A : During the bubble era, high-priced luxury items sold well, but since Japan entered the recession, sales have fallen off. I just mentioned that there were nearly 3,000 types of domestic cars produced, but production costs are higher when there is more variety. So now automobile manufacturers have begun to

ば生産コストも高くなるので，自動車メーカーは価格の引き下げを目指して，車種の削減やモデルチェンジの頻度を減らし始めています。

Q：多品種少量生産を見直し始めたということですね。

A：ええ。それと商品の種類を少なくするだけではなく，機能の簡素化にも取り組み始めました。ある電気メーカーは，通常はほとんど使われることのない機能をなくすことによって，価格をそれまでの半分にしたビデオカメラを売り出して注目を集めました。

Q：今後はどうなるのでしょうか。

A：**東京商工会議所**は1993年4月，中小企業の経営者を対象に行ったアンケート調査の結果を発表しましたが，それによると，およそ8割の経営者が「電化製品や車に，使わない機能がついている」と答え，およそ6割の人は「モデルチェンジが多すぎる」と答えています。こうしたことから，これまでの行き過ぎた多機能化や多品種化を見直そうという動きは，一段と強まるのではないかと見られます。

decrease the types of cars and the frequency of model changes.

Q : So they've begun revaluating the concept of light production of a mass variety of goods.

A : Right. They are not only reducing the number of types of products, but simplifying their functions. One manufacturer has gained attention by removing some of the functions of its video camera and reducing the price by half.

Q : What do future trends look like?

A : **The Tokyo Chamber of Commerce and Industry** announced the results of a survey of managers of small and medium-sized businesses in April 1993. The survey found that around 80% of managers replied that there are many unused functions in cars and electrical appliances, and about 60% answered that there are too many model changes. So it seems that the excessive number of functions and types of products will be more seriously revaluated in the future.

22 | 家庭像の変化

日本の全世帯のうち，3世代同居の家庭はどのくらいを占めているでしょうか。

① 11%　② 27 %　③ 45%

● 変わる家族構成

A：家族構成や家庭のあり方にも変化が起きています。1991年に総務庁が行った調査によると，**3世代同居の家庭**は，全体の11％でした。

Q：昔は3世代同居が当たり前だったと思うのですが。

A：そうですね。戦前の日本では，「家」を存続させることが非常に重視されていましたから，長男夫婦が家を継いで，両親の世話を見ながら自分の子供を育てるのが一般的でした。こうした3世代同居の家庭は，全体のおよそ40％を占めていました。しかし，今では核家族化が進んで，3世代同居は11％に減り，全体のおよそ60％が**核家族**になっています。

● 核家族化の原因

Q：核家族化が進んだのはどうしてですか。

A：戦後の日本で，家父長が絶大な権限を持つ封建的な「家」のあり方が否定されたこと，それから，工業化に伴い，若者を中心に農村から都市へ多くの人が移り住んだことが原因です。例えば，農業や林業，漁業などいわゆる**第1次産業**で働く人は，1950年には全体の50％以上を占めていましたが，1991年には，全体の6.7％と大きく減少しています。その分，工業やサービス産業で働く人の割合

The Changing Household

> **What percentage of households in Japan had three generations of one family living under one roof in 1991?**
>
> ① 11% ② 27% ③ 45%

A : There are many changes taking place in the composition and patterns of family organization. The survey carried out by the Management and Coordination Agency in 1991 found that 11% of the total were **three-generation families**.

Q : I thought it used to be very common for three generations to live under one roof.

A : Well, before World War II, carrying on the family line was a high priority. It was normal for the eldest son and his wife to inherit the house and look after his parents while bringing up their own children. Consequently, almost 40% of all households had three generations living under one roof. But now the **nuclear family** is more common, comprising about 60% of total households, while three-generation households have declined to 11% of the total.

Q : Why has the nuclear family become more prominent?

A : There are several reasons, but after the war, the Japanese rejected the traditional feudal-like household in which the head of the family had nearly absolute authority. Another reason is that many people, especially young people, moved out of rural areas to the cities as Japan became industrialized. For example, in 1950, over 50% of the work force was involved in **primary industries**: agriculture, forestry and fishing. But by 1991, that figure had plunged to just 6.7%. Now the percentage of people

が増え，それとともに核家族化が進んだわけです。

Q：今，日本の代表的な家庭は，夫婦と子供2人の4人
家族ということになりますか。

● 下がり続ける
出生率

A：そうですね。ただ，最近は子供の数が減ってきて，
1世帯当たりの平均人数は2.99人です。人口1000
人当たり何人の子供が生まれたかでその年の**出生
率**を示しますが，これが日本では急速に下がって
きているのです。1950年には28.1だった出生率が，
1970年には18.8，そして1990年には9.9にまで下
がっています。これは，アメリカやイギリスなど
他の先進国と比べても低い数字です。

Q：出生率がこれほどまでに下がった原因は何ですか。

A：子育てにお金がかかることが原因のひとつに考え
られます。

● 出生率低下の
原因

Q：**経済大国**といわれる日本で，子供を育てることが
そんなに負担なのですか。

A：子供を育てられないほど経済的に困っているとい
うわけではもちろんありません。問題は子育ての
中身です。日本の社会はハイテク化，情報化，国
際化が急速に進んでいます。そういう社会に順応
できるようにするために，教育期間が長くなって
きています。1991年で，高校への進学率は94.6％，
大学への進学率は37.7％になっています。子供2人
の標準世帯で，家計支出に占める教育費の割合は，
1982年の5％から1992年には8％近くに増えていま
す。このほかに，ピアノなど習いごとにかかる費
用を入れれば，この数字はもっと大きくなり，普
通の世帯にとっては大きな負担になっています。

Q：出生率が低下した原因，ほかには？

A：働く女性がずいぶん増えましたが，そうした女性
にとって仕事と子育ての両立が難しいことも原因
になっています。また，ゆとりのある生活を楽し

working in the manufacturing and service industries has increased, and this has encouraged the nuclear family.

Q : Does the typical Japanese family now consist of a husband, wife, and two children?

A : Yes, but with the **birthrate** dropping, average family size is now 2.99 members. The birthrate shows how many children were born per thousand people, and it is falling rapidly in Japan. The birthrate was 28.1 in 1950, 18.8 in 1970 and only 9.9 in 1990. This figure is lower than that of other advanced nations such as the United States and Britain.

Q : Why has the birthrate fallen so drastically?

A : One reason may be that it costs a lot of money to raise a child.

Q : Is raising a child that great of a financial burden in an **economic superpower** like Japan?

A : It is not that people are too strapped financially to raise children. The problem is the care they can provide. Japanese society is rapidly becoming more high-tech, information-oriented and internationalized. And now the number of years of education required to adapt to this society is also increasing. In 1991, 94.6% of students continued on to high school, and 37.7% moved on to university. The percentage of the household budget spent on education in the average family with two children rose from 5% in 1982 to nearly 8% in 1992. If you include extra lessons such as piano lessons, the figure becomes even larger. That has become a burden on the average household.

Q : What other reasons are there for the falling birthrate?

A : The number of working women is rising rapidly and it is very difficult to bring up children and hold a job as well. Some couples are consciously choosing not to have children so that they can

むために意識的に子供をつくらない共稼ぎの夫婦を指すＤＩＮＫＳも一時流行語になりました。

Q：3世代同居から核家族になり，その核家族もさらに小さくなってきているということですね。

● 一人暮らしも
　増加

A：そのとおりです。そしてさらには，1人暮らし世帯も増えています。社会の高齢化が進み，65歳以上の高齢者で，1人暮らしの人は186万5000人もいます。これは高齢者全体のおよそ1割に当たります。また，結婚しない人も増えています。1990年の**国勢調査**によれば，30代前半の男性の未婚率は32.6％，女性は13.9％で，15年前に比べておよそ2倍になっています。

Q：家庭のあり方にどんな変化が起きているのですか。

● 少なくなる
　家族の団らん

A：同じ家庭にいながら家族の生活がバラバラになっていく傾向が見られます。父親は仕事で忙しく，母親も外で働き，子供は学校のあと塾に通うということになれば，家族の生活時間はそれぞれ違うということになります。最近の調査でも，4人に1人の子供は，朝食を子供だけでとっています。また，家族のだんらんのときである夕食時に，両親がそろわない家庭が半数近くあります。今こうした家族が増えてきています。

Q：今後はどんなことが問題になってきそうですか。

A：子供の数が減ってきていることがいちばん大きな問題です。家族のあり方に影響を与えるだけでなく，日本経済にとっても，将来**労働力不足**を招く深刻な問題です。また，高齢者をどう支えていくかも難しい問題です。2025年には，65歳以上の高齢者の数は，全人口の4分の1に達すると予想されています。例えば，1人っ子同士が結婚すれば2人で4人の高齢者を支えることになるわけです。家族や家庭のあり方も当然変わっていきます。

enjoy their free time. These couples are called DINKs, meaning "double income, no kids."

Q : People are moving away from the three-generation family and towards the nuclear family, and even the nuclear family is becoming smaller.

A : That's right, and the number of people living alone is increasing. Japanese society continues to age, and now 1.865 million people over age 65 are living alone. This accounts for about 10% of all elderly people. In addition, the number of unmarried people is rising. A 1990 **national census** indicated that 32.6% of men and 13.9% of women in their early thirties are unmarried. This is twice the number of unmarried people 15 years ago.

Q : How are family patterns changing?

A : Although family members live under the same roof, each member lives a completely separate schedule. The father is busy with work, the mother also works outside the home, children go to cram school after school. A recent survey found that one in four children eats breakfast alone. And nearly half of all families don't eat dinner together, traditionally a time for family gathering. More and more families are falling into this pattern.

Q : What kind of problems will we face in the future?

A : The biggest problem is that the number of children is decreasing. This will affect family patterns and also bring about a **labor shortage** in the future. This has serious implications for the economy. Another difficult problem is how to support the elderly. It's predicted that those over the age of 65 will account for one fourth of the population in 2025. For example, if two only children marry, they will have four elderly people to support. So it's natural that families and family patterns are changing.

23 生活時間の変容

日本人の生活時間帯は年々遅くなる傾向があります。ウィークデーの日に，夜中の1時を過ぎても起きている若者はどのくらいいるでしょうか。地方都市も含めた全国平均の数字です。

①10%　②20%　③30%

A：日本人の**生活時間帯**はどう変化しているのでしょうか，自由時間は増えているのでしょうか。「生活時間の変容」についてご紹介します。クイズの正解は，②の20%です。

Q：5人に1人は，午前1時になっても起きていることになりますね。

A：そうです。この数字は，ＮＨＫが1990年に実施した「国民生活時間調査」によるもので，20代の男性の全国平均です。都会の若者はもっと遅くまで起きています。

Q：テレビも明け方近くまで深夜番組を放送していますからね。

● 増える深夜営業
  の店

A：ええ。それに商店街の店なども，遅くまで営業しているところが増えました。通産省が1988年にまとめた商業統計によると，**コンビニエンスストア**で24時間営業している店は全体の17%，それ以外に，午前0時まで営業しているところが22%もあります。広告代理店，博報堂の生活総合研究所が行った「闇市調査」というおもしろい調査がありますのでご紹介しましょう。

Q：闇市調査とは何ですか。

Changes in Daily Schedules

The daily schedule of the average Japanese tends to grow later year by year. What percentage of young people stay up until at least 1:00 a.m. on weekdays? One of these figures is the national average.

　① 10%　② 20%　③ 30%

A : What do you think about the changes in the **daily schedule** of the average Japanese? Do you think they have more free time? In this chapter we will discuss the changes in everyday schedules. Number two, 20% is the correct answer.

Q : That means one in five people stay up until one o'clock in the morning.

A : That's right. This is the national average for males in their twenties according to a 1990 NHK survey on daily schedules. Young people who live in cities stay up even later.

Q : TV networks broadcast programs until almost dawn.

A : That's right and more stores and restaurants in shopping districts are staying open later too. Business statistics from the Ministry of International Trade and Industry indicated in 1988 that 17% of **convenience stores** operated 24 hours, and that 22% of these stores were open until midnight. An advertising agency, Hakuhodo Institute of Life and Living carried out an interesting survey called the "Midnight Market Survey."

Q : What does that mean?

A：深夜に開いている店を闇市と名づけて，その実態を調査したものです。この調査では，午前0時の時点でどんなものが買えるかによって，商店街の夜の便利さを評価しています。1991年11月の調査結果によると，書店や薬局が開いていたり，レンタカーの店やクリーニング店までもが開いている便利な街は，調査した東京の40の商店街のうち15にも達していました。

Q：深夜だけでなく，朝早く開く店も増えていますね。

A：そうなんです。ゴルフ練習場やテニスコートなど**のスポーツ施設**，また英会話教室といった**カルチャー産業**などでも，午前8時前から営業を始めるところが増えています。

● 生活時間変容
　の要因

Q：こうした生活時間帯の広がりというか，生活時間の多様化というのは，なぜ進んだのでしょうか。

A：共稼ぎ世帯や仕事を持った単身者など，昼間にはお店を利用できない人が増えたことや，コンピューター化の進展で人手が少なくてもお店を開くことが可能になったことなどが指摘できます。

Q：以上は，生活時間帯の変化について見てきたわけですが，生活時間の中身の方はどうなのですか。

● 自由時間は増加

A：欧米の国からは働き過ぎとよく批判されますが，**自由時間**は増えています。冒頭に紹介したＮＨＫの「国民生活時間調査」によると，テレビや行楽，スポーツ，お稽古ごとなどに費やされる自由時間は，1970年には土曜日，日曜日の平均で5時間11分でしたが，1990年には6時間3分に増えました。

Q：自由時間は，この20年の間に1時間近く増えたことになりますね。

A：自由時間が増えた分，睡眠や**家事の時間**が減っています。性別に細かく見てみると，おもしろい結

A : It was a survey concerning stores that are open late at night. It assessed the convenience of shopping districts by what kind of goods or services were available at midnight. According to the survey conducted in November 1991, bookstores, pharmacies, and even laundries and car rental agenies were open at midnight in 15 out of the 40 shopping districts surveyed in Tokyo.

Q : Many stores are opened and many services are available now not only late at night, but also early in the morning.

A : That's right. More **sports facilities**, such as golf driving ranges and tennis courts, and **adult education businesses** like English conversation schools are now open even before eight o'clock in the morning.

Q : What is causing daily schedules to grow longer and more diversified?

A : There has been an increase in the number of people such as dual-income families and working singles, who cannot go to shops during normal daytime hours. Furthermore, shops can be organized with fewer staff members thanks to computerization.

Q : So far we've looked at the changes in daily schedule, but what about the substance of those changes?

A : Although Japanese overwork has been criticized by Western nations, actually our **free time** has been increasing. According to the previously mentioned NHK survey free time on weekends is being used to watch television, go on excursions, and enjoy sports and hobbies. An estimated five hours and eleven minutes was spent on weekends on such activities in 1970, but by 1990, this time had increased to six hours and three minutes.

Q : So the Japanese have nearly one more hour of free time than they did 20 years ago.

A : But the increase in free time has resulted from a reduction in sleeping and **housework time**. The breakdown by sex yields

果になっています。女性の平日の自由時間は，10年前に比べてすべての年代で増加しているのに対して，男性は30代から50代までは逆に減少しています。

Q：なぜなのでしょうか。

A：女性の自由時間が増えたのは，家庭電化製品の技術革新によって家事に取られる時間が減ったためと見られます。一方，中高年の男性は，週休2日制の導入に伴って土曜日の自由時間は増えたものの，平日はその分，残業が増えたことから自由時間が減ったものと見られます。

● 自由時間増加
　の要因

Q：こうした自由時間の増加は，どのような要因によるものでしょうか。

A：まず所得が増えて生活に余裕が出てきたことがあげられます。この10年間で**実質所得**は，1.5倍に増えました。この結果，第21章「変わる消費生活」でもご紹介したように，モノからサービスへ消費が変わりました。従来は料理の材料を買ってきて家で食事をしていたのが，外食をするようになるというのが，その一例です。また労働時間の短縮要求に見られるように，日本人の**勤労観**が変わり，自由時間を増やして生活の豊かさやゆとりに結びつけたいという志向が高まったことも大きな要因でしょう。

Q：さて今後はどうなるのでしょうか。

A：生活の質を高めたい，モノの豊かさより心の豊かさを求めたいという傾向は，今後いっそう強まると思います。しかし睡眠や食事の時間など生理的に必要な時間をこれ以上減らすというわけにはいきませんね。したがって今後一段と自由な時間が増えるかどうかは，労働時間の短縮や**長期休暇制度**の充実など，仕事に拘束される時間をいかに減らすことができるかにかかっているといえます。

very interesting results. Free time for women of all ages on weekdays has risen from ten years ago, but that for men in their thirties through fifties has decreased.

Q : Why is that?

A : It appears that free time for women has increased because less time is required for housework due to technological innovations in household appliances. On the other hand, middle-aged and older men have more free time on weekends thanks to the introduction of the five-day week. But it seems that they now have to put in more overtime on weekdays to cover it.

Q : What's behind the increase of free time?

A : First of all, people have a little more leeway in their lives as a result of the rise in income. **Real income** has increased 1.5 times in the past decade. As we mentioned in Chapter 21, "Changing Consumption Patterns," as a result, consumption is shifting from goods to services. For an example, people used to buy ingredients and prepare meals at home, but now they just eat out. Another reason for the increase in free time is that Japanese **ideas about work** are changing and workers are demanding shorter working hours. People tend to link this free time with the desire for a more fulfilling and comfortable lifestyle.

Q : What will happen in the future?

A : I think that people are going to demand a higher quality of life, and shift from the desire for wealth in material goods to the desire for a more fulfilling life. But it's physiologically impossible to further reduce our sleeping and eating time. So any increase in free time in the future will depend on reducing the number of working hours and realizing an **extended vacation system.**

24 | 高まる教育費負担

日本の小学校は6年制ですが，さて小学6年生のうち，何％の児童が中学受験のために学習塾に通っているでしょうか。

① 18%　② 42%　③ 67%

A：受験戦争の激化に伴い**教育費**の負担は高まっており，**家計**を圧迫する一因となっています。クイズの正解は②の42%です。この調査は**文部省**が1993年に実施したものです。

Q：中学生は，もっと高いのでしょうね。

A：実は，③の67%というのが高校受験を控えた中学3年生の割合で，①の18%は小学3年生の数字です。**学習塾**のほかに**家庭教師**を頼んでいる人もいますから，受験を控えた子供のいる家庭は，教育費の負担が大変です。

- 家計に占める教育費の割合

Q：家計に占める教育費の割合はどのくらいなんですか。

A：1992年末に行われた総務庁の家計調査によると，子供のいない家庭も含めた全家庭の教育費の割合は，全国平均で4.6%です。

Q：意外に低いという感じがしますが。

A：でも第1次石油ショック直後の1974年は，2.6%でしたから，20年ほどの間に倍近くに増えています。しかも家計の収入の伸びは，景気の良し悪しによって浮き沈みがあるわけですが，教育費に関

174

Rising Educational Costs

> Japanese elementary schools go through the sixth grade. What percentage of sixth-grade students study at cram schools to prepare for entrance exams to junior high school?
>
> ① 18%　② 42%　③ 67%

A : With the intensification of competition in education, **educational expenses** are increasing and this puts added strain on the **family budget**. The answer is number two, 42%. This figure comes from a **Ministry of Education** survey in October 1993.

Q : The figure for junior high students must be even higher.

A : Yes, 67% of third-year junior high school students who are preparing for high school entrance exams attend **cram schools**. The figure for third-year elementary school students is 18%. In addition, some people hire **home tutors**, so the education expenditures for chidren with upcoming exams is very high.

Q : What percentage of the household budget is applied to education?

A : Well, the Management and Coordination Agency found in a survey on household accounts that the percentage spent on education, including households without children, was 4.6% at the end of 1992.

Q : That's relatively low.

A : In 1974, immediately after the first oil crisis, education expenses comprised 2.6% of the household budget, but 20 years later that figure has almost doubled. In contrast, household income rises and falls according to the economic cycles, but education

しては景気の影響をあまり受けず，一貫して増加しているのが特徴なんです。

Q：子供のいる家庭の教育費はどうなっているんですか。

A：経済企画庁が1992年6月に調べた別の調査によれば，小学生の子供を持つ家庭の教育費の割合は8.3％，同じく中学生の家庭は10.3％，高校生は11.8％，そして大学生がいる家庭は15.0％にものぼっています。この割合をエンゲル係数になぞらえてエンジェル係数と呼ぶ人もいます。残念ながら外国と比較したデータはないのですが，教育費が1割を超すというのは，重い負担だと思いますね。

● 教育費増大の
　要因

Q：教育費が増えたのは，やはり塾や家庭教師といった受験のための費用が増えたためですか。

A：そうです。教育費の中には，学校に支払う**授業料**や**ＰＴＡ会費**，教科書・参考書代，それに塾や家庭教師などに支払う補習教育費がありますが，この**補習教育費**が教育費全体に占める割合は，1974年の11.3％から1992年の23.8％へと急増しました。

Q：こうした教育費の負担増を招いても，親としては子供をいい学校に入れたいというわけですね。

A：受験戦争のいろいろな弊害は昔から指摘されながらも，**学歴**重視の社会風潮は依然根強く残っていますからね。経済的な面から見れば，教育費というのは**人的資本**への投資という側面を持っています。教育の有無によって，将来の所得が変わってくることもしばしばあるからです。このため母親がパートに出てまで教育費を捻出している家庭もありますからね。その意味では，ほかのサービス的な消費などとは区別して考える必要があるかもしれません。

● 教育費増の
　問題点

Q：今後ますます教育費の負担は，増えていくのでしょうか。

expenses are unaffected by the economy and rise consistently.

Q : What about educational costs for households with children?

A : The Economic Planning Agency found in June 1992 that educational costs comprised 8.3% of the budget for households with children in elementary school, 10.3% for households with junior high students, 11.8% those with for senior high students, and 15.0% for those with university students. Some critics, making a play on Engel's coefficient, refer to this as the "angels coefficient." Unfortunately, we don't have any studies to compare these figures with those of other countries, but I think education fees over 10% of personal income is really a heavy burden.

Q : Have education costs risen because of money spent on cram schools and home tutors to help prepare for entrance exams?

A : Yes. Total expenditures for education include **tuition, PTA member fees**, textbooks, reference materials, and supplementary education such as cram schools and home tutors. The percentage of **supplementary education expenses** to the total costs shot from 11.3% in 1974, to 23.8% in 1992.

Q : But parents want their children to attend good schools despite the increasing costs.

A : Although many faults of the entrance exam wars have been pointed out, the tendency to emphasize a **person's educational background** is strongly rooted. From an economic viewpoint, tuition is an investment in **human capital**, and future income often depends on the kind of education one has received. So some mothers take part-time jobs to earn money for their children's education. In that sense, we have to distinguish these expenses from other types of services.

Q : Do you think education costs will probably continue to rise?

A：学歴重視の社会が変わらない限り，ますます増え
ていくでしょう。しかし，ここで問題なのは，所
得の多い家庭は教育費を多く使うことができるの
で，その分，子供はいい学校に入りやすいという，
所得による格差が出始めていることです。

Q：入学できるかどうかは，家庭の所得より本人の能
力や努力によって決まるのではないですか。

A：もちろん，そのこともあるので一概にはいえませ
んが，でも傾向としては出始めています。日本の
大学でトップといわれる東京大学の調査によれ
ば，1991年4月に入学した学生の家庭の年収は，
平均で1072万円。これは，学生の親とほぼ同じ年
齢層のサラリーマンの年収，約800万円をかなり
上回っています。それに最近の傾向として，学費
の安い国公立の学校より，学費の高い私立の学校
のほうが人気が高くなっています。

Q：これはなぜなのですか。

A：私立の場合，中高一貫教育によっていい大学に入
りやすいということが，人気の大きな理由ではな
いでしょうか。このことに関連して問題なのは，
国の教育予算の割合が減ってきていることです。

Q：教育関係の予算は増えていないんですか。

● 少ない教育予算

A：国の予算に占める文化・教育および科学振興費の
割合は，1970年代の半ばには13％程度あったので
すが，最近では8％を割る状態となっています。
教育費も**行財政改革**の対象となったことから，抑
制されたのです。その結果，国公立学校の施設の
老朽化が進み，これが国公立離れに拍車をかけた
面があります。今後は大学など高等教育の整備を
早急に進める必要があるのではないでしょうか。

A : As long as Japanese society emphasizes educational background, expenses will continue to grow. But the problem is that wealthier households have more to spend on their children's education. So now it is becoming easier for wealthier children to enter good schools.

Q : But isn't whether children are accepted into a school or not more dependent on the student's ability or effort rather than on income?

A : Of course that's true so we can't generalize, but there is a growing trend towards wealthier children having an advantage. The University of Tokyo is considered the most prestigious university in Japan. According to one of their surveys, the average annual income of families with students entering the University of Tokyo in April 1991 was ¥10.72 million This is much higher than the average annual salary of workers of the same age, which is about ¥8 million per year. Recently, the more expensive private schools have become more popular than the less expensive public ones.

Q : Why is that?

A : One big reason is that it's easier to enter a university with a junior and senior secondary education in one institution. Another problem related to this is that the national budget for education is decreasing.

Q : The budget for educational expenses isn't increasing?

A : In the mid-1970s, approximately 13% of the national budget was allocated to culture, education, and promotion of the sciences. But now it's less than 8%. The educational budget has been decreased since it's a target of **administrative fiscal reform**. As a result, public educational facilities are becoming rundown and this spurs a move away from public education. In the future we must quickly improve the secondary education system.

25 | 女性の社会進出

労働市場への参入の度合いを示す指標に，労働力率
があります。これは15歳以上の人口のうち，実際に
働いている人と，働く意志はあるけれど仕事につけ
ないでいる人がどれくらいいるかを表したものです。
総務庁の調査によると，1975年における日本の女性
の労働力率は45.7％でした。それでは1992年には
何％になったでしょうか。

① 40.7％　② 50.7％　③ 60.7％

A：第2部「サラリーマン社会の実態」の最後は「女
　　性の社会進出」についてお話ししましょう。クイ
　　ズの正解は②の50.7％です。半分以上の女性が労
　　働市場に参加しています。

Q：これまで日本では，多くの女性は，結婚・出産を
　　機に仕事をやめて家庭に入るというのが一般的で
　　したよね。

● 女性の社会
　進出の推移

A：そのようなイメージで捉えられがちですが，実は
　　そうでもないのです。1960年代までは，農業，林
　　業，漁業という第1次産業で，家族従業者として
　　多くの女性が家事をしながら働いていて，**労働力
　　率も50％を超えていました**。ところが経済が高度
　　成長する中で，しだいに**第1次産業に従事する人
　　口が減少**し，**第2次，第3次産業**に従事する雇用者
　　の割合の方が大きくなりました。それに伴い第1
　　次産業に従事していた女性の数が減り，都市部で
　　も既婚女性が**専業主婦化**していったのです。しか

Working Women

> The labor force participation rate measures the degree to which the population takes part in the labor market. It includes those in the population over age 15 who are actually working or who want to work but cannot find employment. In a survey by the Management and Coordination Agency 1975, 45.7% of women over age 15 worked outside the home. What percentage of women were working outside the home in 1992?
>
> ① 40.7% ② 50.7% ③ 60.7%

A : The last chapter in this section is about women as working members of society. The correct answer is number two, 50.7%. That means over half of all women in Japan hold jobs.

Q : It has been common so far for Japanese women to quit their jobs to stay at home when they get married or have children.

A : Well, people have held such an image of women, but actually it is not true. Until the 1960s many women worked in family businesses in the primary industries, such as agriculture, forestry, and fisheries. The **labor force participation rate** for women was over 50%. But during the period of high growth the population working in these **primary industries** decreased, while the percentage of laborers employed in the **secondary** and **tertiary industries** increased. With this change, women in the primary industries decreased, and even in cities most married women became **full-time housewives**. But the trend reversed

● 働く女性増加
　の背景

● 各国の女性
　労働力率

　　　しこうした流れは，'70年代中ごろにストップがか
　かり，'80年代になると，外へ勤めに出る女性が増
　え始め，'90年代になって労働力率は再び50％を超
　えたというわけです。

Q：その背景にはどうしたことがあげられるのでしょ
　うか。

A：ひとつには，女性の高学歴化に伴い，「男は仕事，
　女は家庭」という伝統的な考え方が少しずつ薄れ
　てきていること，また，以前に比べて1人の女性
　が産む子供の数が減っていること，家電製品の普
　及等により家事労働時間が軽減され，女性の自由
　時間が増加していることなどが挙げられます。さ
　らに女子雇用率の比較的高い第3次産業のウエー
　トが高くなったことや，パートタイム雇用など，
　既婚女性が就業しやすい雇用機会が増加している
　ことも女性の社会進出の大きな要因でしょう。ま
　た，1986年には，採用や昇進など雇用面での男女
　格差をなくすことを定めた法律「**男女雇用機会均
　等法**」が施行され，女性の活躍する場が広がりま
　した。

Q：欧米諸国と比べるとどうですか。

A：1993年にＩＬＯ（国際労働機関）が発表した各国
　の女性の労働力率を見ますと，日本は50.7％，ア
　メリカは56.0％，イギリスは51.7％，そしてスウ
　ェーデンは79.9％となっています。労働力率その
　ものは，アメリカやイギリスとあまり変わりはあ
　りませんが，これを年齢別にグラフにして見ると，
　日本の女子の労働力率にはある特徴があります。
　25歳から35歳ぐらいの間に，いったん労働力率が
　低下し，その後再び上昇するというM字型のカー
　ブを描いているのです。

Q：結婚・出産の時期にあたりますね。この時期に職

in the middle of the 1970s, and the number of working women began to rise in the 1980s. Now, in the 1990s, over half of all women work outside the home.

Q : What is behind this?

A : One factor is that traditional stereotypes, such as "men work and women stay at home," are gradually breaking down now that more women are continuing on to higher education. Also, women are having fewer children, and with the advent of modern household appliances less time need be spent on housework, so they have more free time. Another important factor is that there are more chances for married women to work, including part-time employment. Tertiary industries employ a relatively high percentage of women. In 1986, **the Equal Employment Opportunity Law between Men and Women** was adopted to eliminate discrimination between men and women for employment and promotions. So now there are more places for women to work.

Q : How does the situation of working women in Japan compare with that in the United States and Europe?

A : Comparing figures between countries in a survey by the International Labor Organization (ILO) in 1993, the labor force participation rate for women is 50.7%, 56% in the United States, 51.7% in Britain, and 79.9% in Sweden. There is not much difference in the figures for Japan, the U.S. and England. This index also shows the age of workers. This is where the patterns of Japanese working women are rather unique. It is at its lowest point between the ages of 25 and 35, and then rises again, so the curve is actually shaped like the letter "M".

Q : That's the age when many women marry and have children. Dur-

を離れる女性が増えるわけですね。

A：実は，日本のようにM字型の労働力率分布を見せる国は先進諸国の中では少ないのです。スウェーデンやアメリカ，フランスでは，こうした現象は見られません。以前M字型を見せていたイギリスでも，現在はほとんどなくなっています。

● 難しい仕事と
育児の両立

Q：日本では，女性が仕事と出産・育児を両立させるのはやはり難しいのでしょうか。

A：1990年に総理府が女性を対象に，「一般的に望ましい就業パターンとは何か」という調査を行ったところ，出産などで一時期家庭に入るけれど子育てがすむと再び働くという，「再就職型」が望ましいと答えた人が64％を占めました。それに対し，就職した後ずっと働き続けるという「継続就業型」が望ましいと答えた人は，4％余りにすぎませんでした。これは，多くの女性が家庭と仕事のバランスを重視しているのと同時に，家庭と仕事の両立の難しさを表しているといえるでしょう。

Q：育児をしながらも仕事を続けたいという女性が，退職しないですむような対策はとられていないのでしょうか。

● 育児休業法の
施行

A：1992年の4月から**育児休業法**が施行され，従業員30人以下の事業所を除いては，女性だけではなく男性も，子供が満1才になるまでの期間，育児休業を取ることができるようになりました。勤続年数が賃金や昇進を決めるひとつの要素になっている日本の雇用形態の中では，出産・育児のために一度仕事をやめざるをえないということは，キャリアを積んでいこうとする女性には不利です。そうした意味で，育児休業法の施行はひとつの前進だといえます。

ing this period the number of women leaving their jobs increases, right?

A : Yes, there are few industrialized nations which show such a pronounced M-curve as Japan does. You don't see these phenomena in Sweden, the United States, or France. Britain used to have an M-curve, but now it has almost disappeared.

Q : It must be difficult for Japanese women to work and rear children at the same time.

A : In 1990, the Prime Minister's Office surveyed women on the most desirable working pattern, and 64% of the pollees replied that they wanted to take leave to have children and then return to work. Only 4% answered that they wanted to work continuously without any leave. Although this shows that many women want to strike a balance between the home and work, it also shows how difficult it is to juggle both.

Q : Are companies now setting up systems so women don't have to quit their jobs to raise their children?

A : **The Child-Care Leave Law** went into effect in April 1992. Under this law, all men and women are entitled to child care leave until the child is one year old. This excludes companies with fewer than thirty employees. In Japan, however, wages and promotions are mainly based on the number of years worked. For women who are trying to build a career, it would be a great disadvantage to leave for childbirth and nursing. In this sense, enactment of the Child-Care Leave Law can be seen as forward progress.

● 一段と進むか
　女性の社会進出

Q：そうすると長い目で見ていくと，日本女性のM字型就業構造もやがてはなくなっていくのでしょうか。

A：これは非常に難しい質問です。というのは，「男は仕事，女は家庭」という考え方が依然として根強いのも事実だからです。例えば，総務庁が行った調査によると，子供のいる家庭で，家事や育児のために費やす時間は，専業主婦で1日に7時間42分，仕事を持つ主婦で4時間39分。それに対して夫は，妻が仕事を持っている場合でもわずか19分という結果が出ています。

Q：家事・育児の負担が，極端に女性にのしかかっているのですね。

A：男性で育児休業を取る人もまだまれですし，**保育施設**の整備の遅れも指摘されています。最近は，結婚する時期を遅らせたり，一生結婚しないで仕事を選ぶ女性が増えたりもしています。また，結婚しても子供を持たずに共働きをする，ＤＩＮＫＳと呼ばれる世帯も出てきました。さらには，ハウス・ワイフをもじって，家事に専念するハウス・ハズバンドという新語も生まれています。このように価値観の多様化が浸透し，男女の役割についての昔ながらの考え方が薄れれば，女性がより社会参加しやすくなっていくのではないでしょうか。

Q : In the long term, will the "M" curve in women's working patterns disappear?

A : That's a very difficult question to answer. One reason is that the idea that "men work and women stay home" is still strongly rooted in Japan. For example, the survey conducted by the Management and Coordination Agency found that in households with children, housewives spend 7 hours and 42 minutes per day on housework and caring for the children. Working mothers spend 4 hours and 39 minutes, while fathers spend only 19 minutes on these activities, even though their spouses have jobs.

Q : So doesn't a disproportionate burden of housework and child-care fall on women?

A : It's very rare for a man to take child-care leave. Furthermore, there aren't many **nursery facilities** in Japan. People are getting married later in life, and more women are electing to stay single and work instead. Also the number of DINKs (double income, no kids) is increasing, too. There's also the new concept of the "househusband," which refers to is men who devote themselves to the home. As values diversify and become more widespread, men's and women's roles will be freed from the old stereotypes, and it will probably become easier for women to hold jobs.

戦後の経済政策
POSTWAR GOVERNMENT
ECONOMIC POLICY

26 | 通産省と産業政策

日本は世界最大のオートバイ生産国です。オートバイメーカーは全部で4社ありますが，この4社は同時に世界のビッグフォーであり，合弁によるものも含めると，世界の総生産台数の80%を占めます。ところで，今からおよそ40年前の1954年に，日本に一体何社のオートバイメーカーがあったでしょうか。

① 23社　② 63社　③ 133社

A：第3部では，戦後の経済政策や日本経済が抱える課題について概括します。まずは，日本の経済成長を陰で支えてきたともいわれる通産省と，その産業政策についてです。ところでクイズの答えですが，大和総研の調べによると，40年前の日本には133社ものオートバイメーカーがありました。

Q：たったの4社へと，どうしてこんなに少なくなってしまったのですか。

• 戦後の産業政策

A：オートバイメーカーの国際競争力を強めるために，通産省の指導のもとに業界の整理統合が進められたためです。このように，日本の戦後の経済発展の過程で，政府は産業界に対して直接，あるいは間接的な介入を行ってきたといわれています。これがいわゆる**産業政策**です。

Q：そして，その中で中心的な役割を果たしたのが通産省だったというわけですね。

A：そうです。特に海外では，そのように理解されています。戦後の発展の中で，具体的な例を挙げながら，順を追って見ていくことにしましょう。ま

The Ministry of International Trade and Industry and Industrial Policy

Japan is the world's largest manufacturer of motorcycles and its four manufacturers are the world's "big four." These four companies, including their overseas joint ventures, produce 80% of the world's motorcycles. How many motorcycle manufacturers were there in Japan in 1954?

① 23 companies ② 63 companies ③ 133 companies

A : In the third part, we are going to summarize postwar economic policy and issues in Japanese economics. First of all, we will consider the Ministry of International Trade and Industry (MITI) and its industrial policies, which are said to have sustained Japanese economic growth. As for the quiz, according to the Daiwa Institute of Research, the correct answer is 133 companies.

Q : Why are there only four now?

A : Under the direction of the Ministry of International Trade and Industry or MITI, the motorcycle industry streamlined and integrated itself to strengthen its international competitiveness. During the period of economic development after the war, the government directly and indirectly intervened in the industry. This is known as **"industrial policy."**

Q : So MITI was the director of this policy?

A : That's right, and that is how it is understood overseas, in particular. Let's give a rundown of the industrial policies throughout the period of post-war economic progress, including some con-

ポイント

● 戦後復興期の
　傾斜生産方式

ず，戦後の**経済復興期**です。この時期，「**傾斜生産方式**」という政策がとられました。経済的な自立基盤を確立するために，石炭や鉄鋼，電力などの**基幹産業**に，原材料や外貨など限られた資源を集中的に投入したのです。これは完全な政府主導で行われました。

Q：それが高度経済成長期につながるわけですね。

● 高度成長期の
　重化学工業化

A：そうです。1960年になると，10年間でＧＮＰを2倍にするという，いわゆる「**所得倍増計画**」が発表されました。このときから日本は**高度経済成長期**に入ったといわれています。この時代の特徴は，産業構造の重化学工業化です。産業界も，海外からの技術の導入や設備投資を積極的に進め，鉄鋼や石油化学，機械産業などが目覚ましい発展を遂げました。この時期，**日本開発銀行**など政府系銀行も，こうした**重化学工業**に対して優先的に資金を供給し，税制面での優遇措置もとられました。

Q：産業界に対する政府の間接的な介入ですね。

● 貿易の自由化

A：そうです。そして日本が先進国の仲間入りするのは，この高度成長の時期です。先進国のクラブであるＯＥＣＤ（**経済協力開発機構**）のメンバーになるために，貿易の自由化が不可避となりました。政府は業種ごとに貿易自由化率の達成目標を設定し，例えば，カラーテレビは1964年に，乗用車については1965年までに，貿易が自由化されています。そして，1972年までに，工業品の貿易についてはほぼ100％自由化されました。この貿易自由化に直面して，輸入品に対する競争力を強化するために，冒頭で紹介したオートバイ業界の整理統

crete examples. We'll start with the **economic recovery period** immediately after the war. The government's policy was called the "**priority production system**." Their objective was to secure a base for economic self-sufficiency. So they concentrated the investment of their limited resources, such as raw materials and foreign currency, in **basic industries**, such as coal, steel, and electricity. This was done completely under government instruction.

Q : And this led to the period of high economic growth?

A : That's right. In 1960, the government unveiled the "**income doubling plan**," the goal of which was to double the GNP within a decade. This is considered the beginning of Japan's **period of high economic growth**. During this period, the heavy chemical industry became the base of the industrial structure. Japanese industry imported foreign technology and invested heavily in plant and equipment. Thus the steel, petrochemical, machine, and other industries achieved remarkable growth. Also during this period government banks like **the Japan Development Bank** gave priority to supplying capital to the **heavy chemical industry**, while the government gave the industry preferential tax treatment.

Q : So that's the indirect intervention on the part of the government.

A : That's right. That was during the high growth period when Japan was becoming one of the most advanced nations. Japan had to liberalize trade to become a member of **the Organization for Economic Cooperation and Development** or OECD, a sort of club for the advanced nations. The government set targets for the trade liberalization of each industry. For example, the market for color televisions was liberalized in 1964, and that for passenger cars in 1965. By 1972, almost 100% of the trade of industrial goods was liberalized. The streamlining and integration of the motorcycle industry was part of the effort to strengthen Japanese competitiveness against imported goods,

193

ポイント

● 知識集約型
産業へのシフト

合も進められたわけです。

Q：政府の強力な指導があったので，133社から4社へ
と大がかりな整理統合が可能だったんですね。

A：この後1971年に，通産省の諮問機関である**産業構
造審議会**が「70年代ビジョン」を発表しました。
重化学工業化の目標は達成されたものの，公害問
題など高度成長のマイナス面が深刻化してきたこ
とから，**知識集約型産業へのシフト**が打ち出され
るわけです。

Q：知識集約型産業といいますと。

A：新技術分野での**高度組み立て産業**，**情報処理産業**，
ファッション産業，**研究開発型産業**などです。

Q：そのときの政府の役割はどうだったのでしょう。

A：政策面で見ますと，半導体やコンピューターなど
先端技術産業に対する金融や税制面での支援措
置，新エネルギーや省エネルギーのための技術開
発に対する援助などがあります。

Q：**半導体産業**では，後発の日本のメーカーが先発の
アメリカのメーカーに追いつき，部分的には追い
越したわけですが，通産省を中心にした官民一体
の協力体制が功を奏したとよくいわれますね。

A：そうですね。政府と産業界の密接な協力関係が打
ち立てられました。政府と民間の共同出資による
研究組合がつくられ，そこでの成果が民間企業に
払い下げられました。戦時経済体制下の名残であ
る中央官庁の統制力が遺憾なく発揮されたという
見方もあります。このへんが，政府の過剰介入と
映り，欧米諸国からの批判につながるのではない
でしょうか。また，政府の提言を受けて，エレク
トロニクスなど**ハイテク産業**が脚光を浴びていた
時期であり，半導体に対する需要が大幅に増えた
ことも，日本側に有利に働いたといえます。

when it was faced with free trade.

Q : With strong government guidance, this streamlining and integration from 133 companies to 4 was possible.

A : In 1971, a MITI advisory organ, **the Industrial Structure Council** announced the "Vision for the 1970s." Japan had achieved a strong heavy chemical industry, but the negative effects of high economic growth, such as pollution, were becoming more serious. So the advisory organ suggested a shift to **knowledge-intensive industry**.

Q : What is knowledge-intensive industry?

A : This includes industries which use new technology, such as the **advanced assembly, information processing, fashion**, and **research and development-related industries**.

Q : What role did the government play at this time?

A : Government policy focused on aid for financing and tax breaks for **pioneer technology industries** such as semiconductors and computers, and also promoted technological development for new forms of energy and energy conservation.

Q : Although Japan had a late start in the **semiconductor industry**, it overtook the United States in some areas. It is often said that this type of public-private cooperation led by MITI was very effective.

A : That's right. The government has a close cooperative relationship with industry. Japan has research laboratories jointly funded by the public and private sectors. Their achievements are passed on to private corporations. Some say this is a perfect example of central government control, a legacy of the wartime economic system. This may appear as excessive intervention, and lead to criticism from the United States and Europe. Also upon government advice, the focus was on **high-tech industries** such as electronics during this period. And the dramatic increase in demand for semiconductors really worked to Japan's benefit.

- 産業調整策の
  推進

- 今後の通産省の
  役割

Q：通産省は常に，日本の産業の発展の後押しをして
きたというわけですね。

A：ところが，'80年代に入るとちょっと様子が違って
きます。1983年に「**特定産業構造改善臨時措置
法**」が制定されます。これは簡単にいうと，石油
化学など国際競争力がなくなった産業に対して，
撤退したり操業を短縮する際は支援しますよ，と
いうことです。不要になった設備の処理や新規分
野に参入するための技術開発などに対し，いろい
ろな面で援助するというものです。例えばエチレ
ンの場合，1983年に620万 t あった年間生産能力
を，プラントを統廃合することで，2年後には470
万 t まで落としました。

Q：これは産業振興策ではなく，産業調整策ですね。

A：しかし，これも政府の産業政策のひとつといえま
す。政府が審議会をつくり，産業界の代表も入れ
てその声を反映させながら将来の産業のあるべき
姿を提言させる。そして，提言されたことを実現
するために，政府が政策面で支援を行うというも
のですね。産業界に対する政府の介入の度合いが
伝統的に少ない欧米諸国から見れば，違和感はあ
るでしょうね。

Q：今後も通産省の役割に変わりはないのでしょうか。

A：経済大国になり，日本の産業界も独自の資金力や
開発力，国際展開力をつけてきました。政府と産
業界の関係も，徐々にですが変質してきています。
21世紀に向けた長期ビジョンでは，単に**経済効率**
の追求だけでなく，国民生活の豊かさや国際協調，
地球環境の保護といったことも考慮しなければな
りません。そういう意味で，日本の産業政策も通
産省の役割も，大きく変質する時代に入ったとい
えます。

Q : So MITI has always backed up the expansion of Japanese industry.

A : Yes, but the 1980s were a little different. **The Temporary Measures Law for the Structural Adjustment of Specific Industries** was adopted in 1983. Simply stated, this law was to aid industries such as petrochemicals, where international competitiveness had weakened. The government said they would help such industries withdraw or cut back on their operations. The goal was to assist these industries in disposing of disused facilities and to support technological development for venturing into new fields. In 1983, for example, the petrochemical industry had an annual production capacity of 6.2 million tons of ethylene. But through the closing and integrating of plants, the yearly production capacity had fallen to 4.7 million tons by 1985.

Q : This was not a policy to promote industry, but to streamline it.

A : This is also an example of government industrial policy. The government created a council with representatives from government and industry to propose future changes for industry and discuss policies aimed at achieving these proposals. This probably seemed curious to western countries, who traditionally had little government intervention in industry.

Q : Will MITI's role change in the future?

A : Japan is now an economic superpower, and its industry has developed the ability to finance, develop, and gain access to international markets by itself. So the relationship between government and industry has gradually changed. The long-term vision for the 21st century is not to simply pursue **economic efficiency**, but also to enrich the Japanese lifestyle, encourage international cooperation, and protect the world environment. So I think we could say that MITI's role and government industrial policy will undergo a major change.

　ＧＮＰ（国民総生産）に占める輸出額の割合を輸出依存度といいますが，1992年の統計によると，旧西ドイツの輸出依存度は33％でした。それでは同じ年の日本の輸出依存度は，どれでしょうか。

　　① 10%　　② 20%　　③ 40%

ポイント

A：日本経済は，「輸出主導型」であるとか「輸出志向が強い」とかよくいわれます。それならば，輸出依存度は当然高いと思われるでしょうが，意外に低く，正解は①の10％です。

Q：旧西ドイツの3分の1以下ですね。

● 各国の輸出
依存度

A：私も調べてみて驚きました。同じ年の各国の輸出依存度を見ると，アメリカは約12％と日本とあまり変わりませんが，フランス，イギリスは23％と，ＥＣ諸国は全般的に高いですね。

Q：なぜなんですか。

A：これは，今や国内市場と同じになったといえるＥＣ（1993年11月 ＥＵ，欧州連合に改組）域内での輸出が多かったためで，ドイツの場合は輸出の6割程度がそうです。

Q：輸出依存度の数字はさほど高くないのに，日本はなぜ「**輸出主導型**」といわれるんですか。

● 輸出主導型と
いわれる理由

A：これまで政府が輸出産業の保護育成に力を入れてきたということもありますが，なんといっても貿易黒字の額が非常に大きいということに行きつく

An Export-Led Economy

> The percentage of export earnings of the gross national product, or GNP, is called export dependency. According to statistics for 1992 the export dependency of the former West Germany was 33%. What was Japan's export dependency for the same year?
>
> ① 10% ② 20% ③ 40%

A : Japan's economy is referred to as being export-controlled or strongly export-oriented. It is natural to think of Japan as being highly export dependent, but the export rate is unexpectedly low. The answer to the quiz is number one, 10%.

Q : That's less than one-third that of the rate for Germany, isn't it?

A : I was also surprised. As to the export dependency of other countries in the same year, the rate for the United States was 12%, which was not much different from the rate for Japan. But the rate for France and Britain was 23%. The EC nations were more dependent on exports than Japan was.

Q : Why is that?

A : It was caused by the large volume of exports within the European Community following the establishment of the European Union in November 1993. This type of trade accounts for 60% of German exports.

Q : Why is Japan often called an **export-led economy**, even though its export dependency figures aren't so high?

A : One reason is that the Japanese government has protected and fostered the export industries. But I think the greatest factor is that Japan's export surplus is huge. According to OECD statis-

と思います。1992年の**貿易収支**をOECDの統計で見てみますと，EC（統計はEC当時のものなのでそのまま使用）全体としての赤字は561億ドル。またアメリカは844億ドルで，合わせると1405億ドル。日本の黒字額は1064億ドルですから，その大半を占めています。こうした大幅な貿易黒字も，円高になれば輸出競争力が弱まって減少するはずなんですが，それがなかなか減らない。そうしたことが，輸出主導あるいは輸出志向が強いといわれるゆえんではないでしょうか。

● 黒字体質の背景

Q：日本経済の黒字体質は，どこからきているのでしょうか。

A：基本的には，日本は**天然資源**に恵まれていないため，原材料を輸入に依存しなければなりません。そのための外貨を稼ぐには輸出を振興することが必要となり，終戦直後から1970年代初めまでは，**輸出振興策**や**輸入規制**による国内産業の保護育成が行われていました。ただし欧米からの批判が強い「集中豪雨的輸出」が始まるのは，1973年の石油危機以降のことです。

Q：石油危機では，日本経済も大きな打撃を受けたと聞いていますが，それがなぜ集中豪雨的輸出に結びついたのですか。

A：'60年代の高度経済成長期に，日本企業は大規模な設備投資を行っていました。それが石油危機によって国内市場が不振となりましたから，各企業は輸出に力を入れたわけです。一部ではダンピング騒ぎさえ起こしました。また石油危機の直前に，日本の通貨は1ドルが360円という**固定相場制**から**変動相場制**に変わりました。その後円高傾向が進みますが，これを克服するために日本企業は巨額の研究開発投資を行った結果，ハイテク化を実現

tics, the **balance of trade** for 1992 showed a deficit of $56.1 billion for the entire European Community, and $84.4 billion for the United States, which adds up to $140.5 billion. This nearly equalled Japan's surplus, which was $106.4 billion. Though this enormous surplus should have decreased with the yen's appreciation, which lowers Japan's export competitiveness, it has not decreased. This is probably why it is still said that Japan is an export-led or export-dependent economy.

Q : Where does this surplus situation in the Japanese economy come from?

A : Basically, since Japan lacks **natural resources**, it has to depend on imports. So Japan has to boost exports to earn foreign currency. From the end of World War II to the beginning of the 1970s, domestic industries were fostered and protected by an **export promotion policy** and **import restrictions**. But it was after the first oil crisis in 1973 that there began the extremely large volume of exports, the so-called "flood export" which the United States and Europe strongly criticized Japan for.

Q : I've heard that the Japanese economy suffered considerable damage from the oil crisis, but what does that have to do with the large volume of exports?

A : During the high growth period of the 1960s, Japanese industry invested heavily in plant and equipment. The domestic market became sluggish due to the oil crisis, so many industries concentrated on exports. Some were even accused of dumping. Immediately before the oil crisis, the Japanese currency switched from a **fixed exchange rate**, pegged at 360 yen to the dollar to a **floating exchange rate**. The yen began appreciating after that and Japanese companies invested enormous amounts in research and development to overcome the situation.

し国際競争力を一段と強めました。それが輸出拡大に結びついたのです。

Q：日本企業はシェア拡大に必死で，シェア競争を海外でも行っているという話がありましたが，そうした体質も黒字の増加に結びついているのでしょうね。

A：そうです。それにもともと日本では，ひとつの業種の中のメーカーの数が欧米に比べると多く，過当競争体質を持っています。例えば各国の主要な乗用車メーカーといえば，アメリカとドイツは3社，フランスは2社なのに対して，日本は9社もあります。

● 輸出主導型経済のメリット

Q：さて，こうした輸出主導型経済がもたらしたプラス面といえば。

A：今お話ししたように**国際競争力**を高めたことでしょう。欧米先進諸国が石油危機以降，経済の活力を失い，失業率も高くなったのに対して，日本は輸出主導で比較的高い成長率を維持できました。円高を克服するための努力が，単なるコストダウンや低価格での輸出に止まらずに，製品の高付加価値化やハイテク化に結びついたことから，技術革新が進み産業構造を高度化することができたわけです。大和総研の調査（1991年）で，主要輸出製品の世界市場でのシェアを，海外にある**合弁会社**の生産分も含めた数字で見てみますと，日本のメーカーのシェアは，オートバイがおよそ80％，ＶＴＲがおよそ70％，カラーテレビがおよそ40％となっています。

Q：こうした日本企業の輸出志向，海外志向といったものが，**貿易摩擦**を生んでしまうわけですね。

● デメリット

A：円高が進んでも，貿易黒字が一向に減りませんから，対外的な摩擦が強まってしまいます。輸出主導型経済のマイナス面でしょう。**貿易不均衡**を是

This led to a flourishing high-tech industry, and increased Japan's international competitiveness.

Q : We talked about how Japanese companies were desperate to expand their share of the market, and competed fiercely overseas to that end. This situation must also have helped boost the surplus.

A : That's right. From the beginning, Japan had more manufacturers in specific industries compared to western nations, so they are extremely competitive. As for passenger car manufacturers, for example, both the United States and Germany have three major campanies, and France has two, while Japan has nine.

Q : Are there any merits in an export-led economy?

A : We have just mentioned raising **international competitiveness**. After the first oil crisis, advanced nations in the West lost their economic vitality and unemployment increased. On the other hand, Japan was able to maintain relatively high growth through exports. Efforts to overcome the strong yen did not stop at reducing costs and lowering prices of exports, but also included increasing the value added to products and developing high technology. This technological revolution strengthened Japan's industrial structure. Looking at Japan's share in world markets of major export products, including those products made overseas through **joint ventures** as shown in a Daiwa Institute of Research survey in 1991, motorcycles comprise 80% of the market; video tape recorders, 70%; and color televisions, 40%.

Q : Inclination to export or expand overseas has led to **trade friction**, hasn't it?

A : Although the yen continues to appreciate, the **trade imbalance** hasn't improved at all and trade friction with other countries has intensified. That's the negative side of an export-led economy.

ポイント

正するためには，**財政政策**や**金融政策**で各国が協調して対策をとることが不可欠ですから，日本だけの責任というわけではありません。しかし日本国内の流通システムなどがネックとなり，輸入が増えない構造があるということは問題でしょう。

Q：ほかにマイナス面といえば何がありますか。

A：輸出競争力の維持のためには，コストダウンなど徹底した経済効率性を追求しますから，どうしても**生産者重視**といいますか，**消費者**の利益を軽視しがちになりますね。

Cooperation on **fiscal** and **monetary policies** by all nations is indispensable to rectifying the trade imbalance, so it is not solely Japan's responsibility. On the other hand, there are still structural problems in the domestic distribution system which block the expansion of imports.

Q : What other demerits are there?

A : If you pursue economic efficiency, such as lowering costs to help maintain international competitiveness, you benefit **producers** but neglect benefits for **consumers.**

28 | 生産者重視の経済成長路線

日本には，公害による健康被害を補償する法律があります。1992年に，大気汚染が原因でぜんそくなどの病気と認定され，補償金が支払われた人は何人いたでしょうか。

① 6000人　② 3万6000人　③ 8万6000人

A：戦後の日本は，生産者寄りの経済成長路線をとってきたために，**大気汚染**をはじめとするさまざまな公害問題を引き起こしました。クイズの答えは，③の8万6000人で，支払われた補償金は960億円余りでした。

Q：**公害**が特にひどかったのは，日本が高度経済成長を続けていたころのことですね。

● 多発する公害

A：ええ。**水銀中毒**による**水俣病**や，工場の排煙による**四日市ぜんそく**などはその代表的なものです。生産を重視するあまり，工場の廃水や廃棄物などによる環境汚染に対する配慮はなされてこなかったといえます。そして公害が発生した後でも，企業側の責任が認められるまでにはかなりの時間がかかりました。例えば，水俣病の場合，地元の学者が，「原因は工場の廃水に含まれる**有機水銀**である」と指摘してから，政府がこれを認めるまでおよそ10年もかかっています。この間，政府は企業寄りの姿勢に終始し，なんの施策も行いませんでした。

● 生産者重視の背景

Q：それほどまでに生産者，つまり企業を重視したその背景は。

Economic Growth Prioritizing Producers

> Japanese law guarantees compensation for health problems caused by pollution. Air pollution has been certified as a cause of asthma and other health problems. How many people were awarded compensation in 1992?
>
> ① 6,000 people   ② 36,000 people   ③ 86,000 people

A : After the war, Japan's policies for economic growth focused on producers and this led to many kinds of pollution such as **air pollution**. The correct answer is number three, 86,000 people and they were paid a total compensation of ¥96 billion.

Q : Damage from **pollution** became more serious throughout Japan during the period of high economic growth.

A : That's right. Some of the more well-known diseases are **Minamata disease** from **mercury poisoning** and **Yokkaichi asthma** from factory smoke. Japan placed so much emphasis on production that it did not really consider the consequences of environmental pollution such as the liquid and solid wastes produced by factories. It took a considerable time for companies to accept responsibility for the pollution even after it was discovered. In the case of Minamata disease, for example, local researchers pinpointed **organic mercury** discharged from factories as the cause. But the government took nearly ten years to acknowledge this fact. The government sided with industry until the end and did little to tackle the problem.

Q : What is the background of the heavy emphasis on producers, in other words, businesses?

A：日本は戦争に負け，焼け野原になりました。戦後の復興は，ゼロからの出発といっても過言ではありません。モノがなかったわけですから，モノを作ることが最優先されました。それが，「企業第一主義」という戦後の日本社会の体質をつくったといえます。それから，日本にはほとんど資源がないわけですから，それを海外から輸入して，製品にして輸出することで外貨を稼ぐことが経済発展の道と考えたわけです。その結果，政府の経済政策も生産者偏重になったというわけです。

Q：このため，先ほどの公害ばかりでなく，いろいろな弊害やひずみも出てきたというわけですね。

A：そうです。企業と地域の住民，あるいは生産者と消費者の利害が対立したときは，多くの場合，企業側の利益が優先されてきました。最近問題になっている化粧品の例を見てみましょう。小売店が安く売ろうとしても，メーカーがそれを許さない。メーカーの意向に反して安く売ろうとすれば，メーカーは製品供給をストップするなどの圧力をかけ，高い価格を維持してきたわけです。

Q：これに対して政府はどうしていたのですか。

A：不公正な取引に対しては，これを監視する政府機関，**公正取引委員会**がありますが，経済成長を優先する通産省の産業政策に押され，これまで十分に機能してきたとはいえません。価格維持を目的にした企業による**生産調整**や，**公共事業**の受注に際しての業者間の談合などは，これまで見逃されがちでした。

• 貿易摩擦が
激化へ

Q：その結果，消費者は高い買い物をさせられてきたわけですね。生産者重視というのは，外国との関係で見るとどうなのでしょうか。

A：日本は**国内需要**をはるかに上回る生産力を持つに至りました。生産大国，輸出大国となり，外国と

A : Japanese towns and cities were destroyed during the war. It is no exaggeration to say that Japan started from zero at the beginning of the reconstruction period. Since they had nothing, they emphasized making products. This created a post-war society which placed industry first. Since Japan had almost no natural resources, it had to import them from overseas. So they tried to build their economy by turning these resources into products, exporting them and earning foreign currency. As a result, the government's economic policy was slanted towards producers.

Q : This resulted in not only pollution, but also other problems.

A : You're right. When there was a conflict of interest between companies and local people, or producers and consumers, the companies won out nearly all the time. Take cosmetics, which has recently become a problem. Even if the retailer tries to sell the goods at a lower price, the manufacturer will not allow it. If the retailer goes against the manufacturer's wish, and sells the product at a lower price, the manufacturer puts pressure on the retailer by cutting off supplies in order to maintain high prices.

Q : What is the government's policy on this?

A : **The Fair Trade Commission** is the government institution which watches for unfair business practices. But it has often been hindered by the Ministry of International Trade and Industry's industrial policy of putting priority on economic growth, so it has not functioned very effectively. It has tended to wink at **production adjustment** for maintaining prices and collaborating when bidding on **public works**.

Q : As a result, consumers are forced to buy items at high prices. How does this policy appear to people overseas?

A : Japan's production capability now surpasses its **domestic demand**. It is a production and exporting superpower, which has

の貿易摩擦も激化してきました。特に，日本製品の主要な輸出先であるアメリカとは，繊維製品に始まり，その後は鉄鋼，カラーテレビ，工作機械，半導体，自動車と，次から次へと貿易摩擦を起こしてきました。

Q：生産者重視が，外国との摩擦を次々と引き起こしたということですね。

A：この黒字を減らすために，政府もさまざまな努力をしてきました。輸入品が入りやすいように，段階的な**関税**引き下げを実施し，今では，工業製品にかかる関税はほぼ100％なくなりました。また，内需拡大策にも取り組んできました。

Q：それでも黒字は減らないんですね。

・生産者重視から
　消費者重視へ

A：そこで問題になってきたのが，日本国内の経済システムです。日本にはさまざまな**規制**が張りめぐらされていますが，これはほとんどが生産者保護のため，といってもいいと思います。例えば，乳製品や小麦粉など多くの製品は，業者が自由に輸入できないことになっています。さまざまな規制があるために業者間の競争は制限され，価格が下がりにくくなっています。これが，外国に比べて日本の物価が高い一因になっていて，**内外価格差**の問題として注目を集めるようになりました。

Q：最近は，規制を緩和しようという動きも出てきているようですが。

A：そうですね。政府はこのところ，生産者重視の政策を改め，消費者重視の政策へとシフトさせていこうとしています。そのため，**規制緩和**を重要な政策課題に挙げています。この規制緩和と内外価格差の問題については，章を改めてお話しします。

intensified trade friction with other nations. Japan's main export target has been the United States. Trade conflict with the U.S. began with textiles, then moved on to steel, color televisions, machine tools, semiconductors, and automobiles.

Q : So the government's prioritizing of producers has triggered trade conflicts.

A : The government has tried a variety of methods to reduce the trade surplus. It gradually lowered **tariffs** to make importing easier. Right now, almost no imported industrial goods are subject to tariffs. The government has also struggled to expand domestic consumption.

Q : But the surplus still hasn't decreased.

A : The problem is in the Japanese economic system. Japan has many **regulations** and most of them protect the producers. For example, there are many items, including dairy products and grains that Japanese dealers cannot import freely. These regulations have limited competition between dealers and producers, so it is difficult to lower prices. This is one of the greatest factors in the high prices in Japan. This **price variance between domestic and overseas markets** has attracted considerable attention.

Q : Deregulation has recently been taking place, hasn't it?

A : The administration is revising the policy of giving priority to producers, and shifting to a policy that serves consumers. This is why **deregulation** is a serious policy issue. We'll take a look at deregulation and differences between prices at home and abroad in another chapter.

29 | 技術立国

技術を輸出することで特許の使用料をどれだけ受け取り，輸入することでどれだけ支払っているかを表したものが，技術貿易収支です。さて1992年の日本の技術貿易の収支は，どれでしょうか。

① 332億ドルの黒字　② 132億ドルの黒字
③ 32億ドルの赤字

ポイント

A：日本製品が海外でシェアを伸ばしている背景には，技術水準の高さがあるといわれます。さて，その技術の実態はどうなのでしょうか。クイズの正解は，③の32億ドルの赤字です。このデータは**日銀の国際収支統計**によるものです。

Q：赤字とは意外ですね。ほかの国はどうなのですか。

● 各国の技術貿易
収支

A：アメリカは129億ドルの黒字なんですが，旧西ドイツは17億ドルの赤字，フランスも7億ドルの赤字，イギリスも1億ドルの赤字なんです。主要国の中ではアメリカだけが黒字国なんです。

Q：最近の日本は，「**技術大国**」というイメージが強いのに，なぜ赤字なのですか。

A：日本の技術で強いのは，応用技術や生産工程での技術革新であって，基礎的な技術や，まったく新しい商品を開発する技術力は，欧米各国に比べてまだ弱いんです。したがって基礎的な分野では，日本がロイヤリティーを支払うケースが多い。こ

Building up a Technological Superpower

> The balance of technological trade is measured by comparing the amount of patent royalties from exporting technology to the amount of royalties paid for importing technology. What was Japan's balance in technological trade in 1992?
>
> ① $33.2 billion surplus   ② $13.2 billion surplus
> ③ $3.2 billion deficit

A : It is sometimes said that the expansion of the market share of Japanese products is supported by their high level of technology. The correct answer is number three, $3.2 billion deficit. This data was compiled from statistics on the **international balance of payments** from **the Bank of Japan**.

Q : I'm surprised to hear that Japan has a deficit. What about other countries?

A : The United States has a $12.9 billion surplus. But the former West Germany has a $1.7 billion deficit, France has a $700 million deficit, and Britain has a $100 million deficit. Among the major nations, the United States is the only industrialized nation with a surplus.

Q : Recently, Japan has been thought of as a **technological superpower,** so why does it have a deficit?

A : Japan is strong in technological innovation of applied technology and the production process. But it is still weaker than the West when it comes to basic technology and the development of completely new products. So in most cases Japan pays royalties for basic technology. It is clear from the regional **balance of tech-**

ポイント

● 日本の技術貿易
収支

● ハイテク製品も
増加

のことは，地域別の**技術貿易収支**を見るとはっきりします。アメリカおよびヨーロッパとの間の収支は，大幅な赤字です。でも日本の技術力は確かに実力をつけていますから，技術貿易の収支も以前に比べると大幅に改善されています。

Q：技術貿易収支のこれまでの経緯はどうなんですか。

A：技術貿易の実態は，輸出と輸入の収支比で表すことが多いのです。1であれば，輸出と輸入が均衡している状態。1以下であれば輸出より輸入の方が多いことになります。この収支比の推移を総務庁の統計で見てみますと，1953年は0.008と戦後最低でした。これはつまり輸出より輸入が100倍以上も多かったわけです。それが1965年には0.1，'75年には0.39，そして'90年には0.91まで上がりました。

Q：輸出と輸入が均衡する状態に近づいているのですね。

A：そのとおりです。それと技術貿易の統計には，過去に結んだ**技術契約**に基づく特許料の受け払いと，新たに契約したものによる受け払いの2種類があるんですが，新たに契約した分の収支比は，1980年代後半以降は1を上回る年が出てきました。

Q：つまり輸出が輸入を上回ったというわけですね。

A：ええ。それにもう一点。技術貿易とは違うんですが，一般の貿易で取り引きされる製品を，技術レベル別にハイテク，ミッドテク，ローテクという3段階に分けてみますと，ローテク製品の貿易収支比が0.6なのに対して，ミッドテク製品は3.0，ハイテク製品は3.5と輸出が輸入を大きく上回っています（1990年ＯＥＣＤ統計）。こうしたデータを見ますと，日本の技術水準は確実に高まっているといえます。

Q：具体的には，どのような技術を輸出し，どのよう

nological trade that Japan has a large deficit with the United States and Europe. But Japanese technological capability is growing stronger, so the deficit in technological trade has been reduced quite a bit.

Q : What is the history of the technological trade balance?

A : The differences between imports and exports show a lot about technological trade. When imports and exports are equal the balance is indicated as 1. If the balance is lower than 1, then there are more imports than exports. According to the statistics of the Management and Coordination Agency regarding the shift in the balance over the years, it was 0.008 in 1953, the lowest since World War II. This meant the volume of imports was more than 100 times the volume of exports. In 1965 it was 0.1, in 1975 it was 0.39, and in 1990 it rose to 0.91.

Q : So now the volume of exports is nearly equal to the volume of imports.

A : That's right. The statistics on technological trade are measured in two ways: receipt and payment of royalties based on **technological contracts** signed in the past and receipt and payment based on new contracts. Since the mid-1980s the figures has exceeded 1 some years.

Q : Japan has had more exports than imports?

A : Yes, and I'd like to add another point. It is not related to technological trade, but general trade products are classified into three categories: high-, middle- and low-level technology. According to 1990 OECD statistics, the balance of low-tech items was 0.6, while that of mid-tech items was 3.0. The balance of high-tech items was the highest at 3.5 (according to OECD statistics for 1990). This means that export figures greatly exceed import figures. These figures show that the level of Japanese technology is definitely rising.

Q : To be concrete what kinds of technology are exported and

ポイント

　　　な技術を輸入しているのですか。

A：総務庁の調査（1991年）で**製造業**を業種別に見て
　　みましょう。技術の輸出が輸入より多い産業は，
　　自動車などの輸送機器や鉄鋼業などで，収支比は
　　それぞれ1.80と1.76です。一方，輸入が輸出より
　　も多いのは電気機械で，収支比は0.65です。

Q：電機業界の技術が，輸入の方が多いというのは意
　　外ですね。

● 技術貿易でも
　摩擦

A：基礎的な研究が弱かったことが，今でも響いてい
　　るということでしょうか。

Q：一般の貿易摩擦と同じく，技術の面でも欧米との
　　間で摩擦が起きているようですね。

A：そうなんです。特にアメリカの企業との間で，**知
　　的所有権**をめぐる訴訟沙汰が相次いでいます。最
　　近のケースでは，日本のカメラメーカーがカメラ
　　の自動焦点技術に関して，米国ハネウェル社から
　　訴えられました。この訴訟では日本のメーカーは，
　　1億2750万ドルもの和解金を支払いました（1992
　　年12月）。また世界最大のコンピューターメーカ
　　ーＩＢＭも，パソコン用ソフトを無断で使用した
　　として1993年の2月，日本の企業を訴えています。
　　アメリカの産業界は近年，**特許料**を収入源のひと
　　つとして位置づけ，知的所有権の保護を企業戦略
　　として重要視するようになりました。

● 技術立国の課題

Q：技術立国を進めている日本の今後の課題といえば
　　何でしょうか。

A：ひとつは，基礎的な研究開発を促進させることで
　　はないでしょうか。今お話しした技術貿易収支の
　　面もそうですし，自然科学分野でのノーベル賞受
　　賞者の少なさを見ても，基礎的な分野での研究開
　　発は十分とはいえません。各国の研究開発費のう

imported?

A : Let's look at the 1991 survey from the Management and Coordination Agency. We can look at the different sectors of the **manufacturing industry** here. Transportation equipment manufacturers such as the automobile industry, and steel industry, export more technology than they import. The respective balances are 1.80, and 1.76. But in electrical machinery, Japan imports more technology than it exports, with a balance of 0.65.

Q : I'm surprised that the electrical machinery industry has a deficit in technology.

A : Basic research in that industry used to be weak, and it may still be affecting the trade of technology.

Q : Just as in general trade, Japan is at odds with the United States and Europe over technological trade.

A : Yes. U.S. companies in particular are filing one suit after another over **intellectual property rights**. In a recent case, the U.S. company Honeywell sued a Japanese camera manufacturer over auto-focus technology. The Japanese company settled out of court for $127.5 million (December 1992). Also IBM, the world's largest computer manufacturer, filed a suit against a Japanese company for unauthorized use of their personal computer software in February 1993. U.S. industry in recent years has secured **patent royalties** as one source of income and regards protecting intellectual property rights as an important business strategy.

Q : What challenges does Japan face as it tries to build up its technology?

A : One is to promote basic research and development and this involves redressing the balance of technological trade. If we look at how few Japanese have won the Nobel Prize in the natural sciences, we can see that Japanese basic research and development is insufficient. Taking a look at the percentage of grants various

217

ち政府が負担している割合を見てみますと，アメリカが44%，ドイツが33%なのに対して，日本の場合は18%と低いのです。技術立国を目指すからには，財政的な支援を強化することが必要ではないでしょうか。

Q：その他には。

A：欧米との技術摩擦を起こさないようにすることはもちろん，今後は発展途上国への**技術移転**をいかに積極的に行うかも大切なことです。また環境問題や省資源，それに新エネルギーの開発など，解決を迫られる地球規模の問題に日本の技術力をどう生かすことができるのか，これも大きな課題といえます。

governments provide for research and development, the United States provides 44%, the former West Germany accounts for 33%, and Japan ranks lowest with only 18%. So if Japan wants to build up its technology, it needs to strengthen financial assistance.

Q : What other issues remain?

A : Of course Japan should try to avoid causing friction over technology with the United States and Europe, but it's also important to think about how actively it will carry out **technology transfer** to developing nations. Japan also has to consider how to make use of its technological capabilities to address pressing global-scale problems such as environmental crises, the protection of natural resources, and the development of new energy sources.

30 | つぶれない銀行

1983年から'92年までの10年間に，アメリカでは1389件の銀行倒産がありました。この間，日本ではどのくらいの銀行倒産があったでしょう。

　① 0件　② 17件　③ 117件

　ちなみに銀行の数は，'91年末でアメリカが1万2000行余り，日本は信用金庫，信用組合を含めても，1000行余りです（アメリカ連邦預金保険公社，日本銀行の調査）。

● 銀行の「不倒神話」

● 戦後の銀行行政

A：この章では戦後の**金融政策**の特徴についてお話ししましょう。まずクイズの答えですが正解は，0件。1件も倒産していません。

Q：日本の銀行が「不倒神話」といわれるほど倒産しないのはなぜですか。

A：それはひとことでいうと，「護送船団方式」といわれるように，行政当局が銀行間の競争を制限するなど，経営基盤の弱い銀行もつぶれないような政策をとってきたからです。

Q：具体的にはどのような政策ですか。

A：それは，第2次世界大戦後にとられた日本の**産業政策，銀行行政**にまでさかのぼります。戦後の日本経済の最重要課題は，いかにして経済的自立を果たし，欧米先進国に並ぶ経済発展を実現するかにありました。これを金融面からサポートしたのが「**低金利政策**」で，企業が低金利で資金調達を行えるようにしたのです。

Failure-proof Banks

> Between 1983 and 1992, 1,389 banks went bankrupt in
> the United States. Guess how many bank failures there
> were during the same period in Japan?
>
> ① 0   ② 17   ③ 117
>
> Incidentally, there were 12,000 banks in the U.S. at the
> end of 1991, and 1,000 banks including credit associa-
> tions and credit unions in Japan (data from Federal
> Deposit Insurance Corporation, the Bank of Japan).

A : In this chapter, we're going to examine the characteristics of
financial policy since World War II. The answer to the quiz is
"zero." No banks failed during that period.

Q : Japanese banks are considered "failure-proof." Why is that?

A : Japanese banks don't fail because of a special administrative policy called the "convoy system," which was set up to protect
banks. For example, government authorities limit competition
between banks, so even banks with weak bases don't fail.

Q : What specific policies protect banks from failure?

A : We have to go back to the Japanese **industrial** and **bank
administration policies** set up following World War II. The
greatest challenge for the postwar Japanese economy was to
gain independence and achieve the same level of economic
development as in Western industrialized nations. A **"cheap-
money policy"** supported this goal on the financial level. Interest rates on savings accounts were kept low so that companies
could procure capital at low interest rates.

●低金利政策が柱

Q：でもそれではお金を借りる側の企業にとっては都合が良かったかもしれませんが，貸す方の銀行にはメリットがあったのでしょうか。

A：銀行の中心業務は，私たち個人から集めた預金を企業に貸し付けることです。この低金利政策のもとでは，銀行にとって貸付資金の仕入れ価格ともいえる**預金金利**も低く抑えられました。そうすることで，銀行は低金利で企業にどんどんお金を貸し付けることができたのです。例えば，10％の金利でお金を借りたい企業があるとします。貸し出しのための経費が2％だとすると，銀行は8％以下の金利で元手となる預金を集めれば儲けは出るわけです。このような場合に**低金利政策**で，預金の金利を5％以下にしなさいという規制がしかれたらどうなりますか。

Q：8引く5で，3％分が銀行の儲けとなります。

A：そうですね。**金利**の規制が敷かれていると，金利を上げることで預金者を獲得するような銀行間の競争が起きることもありません。**資金調達コスト**は低いままに抑えられます。それが銀行の利潤，ひいては経営を安定させることになりました。

Q：企業や銀行には有利だったかもしれませんが，預金者である個人にとっては損な話ですね。

A：そのとおりです。金利規制は企業や銀行には超過利潤をもたらしました。戦後，経済成長を促すことに重点を置いた政策によって，お金を預ける方の立場は軽視されました。日本の金利自由化が欧米と比べて遅れた原因もそのへんにありそうです。

Q：**金利規制**のほかに，銀行を保護する政策としてどのようなものがありますか。

●認可と指導で
　銀行を保護

A：銀行同士の競争を避けるためのさまざまな政策がとられました。例えば，銀行業を始めるには大蔵

Q : This cheap-money policy may have been advantageous for companies, but how did it benefit the lending banks?

A : The main function of banks is to gather money from individuals, and then lend it to corporations. Under this policy, the **deposit rate** through which capital for lending is accumulated, could be kept low. With low interest rates, banks can lend out large amounts to companies at lower rates. For example, say a company wants to take out a loan at 10%. Assuming the loan process requires 2% of that interest, the bank can profit if it pays savings accounts a rate lower than 8%. If interest rates for savings are restricted to 5% under the **low-interest policy**, what does that mean for the bank?

Q : Well, eight minus five is three, so the bank gets a 3% profit.

A : That's right. Since the **interest rates** are regulated, banks can't compete to gain customers by raising interest rates on savings. So the cost of **capital procurement** is held down. A bank makes a profit and business is stabilized.

Q : The policy of keeping down interest rates may have benefited corporations and banks, but wasn't it disadvantageous to the individual saver?

A : Yes, it was. The regulation of interest rates brought excessive profits to banks and corporations. But postwar policy prioritized economic growth, and neglected the individual depositor. This is one reason why interest rate liberalization has been lagging behind the West.

Q : Other than **interest rate regulation**, how does government policy support banks?

A : Various policies have been adopted to avoid competition between banks. For example, it is extremely difficult to obtain a bank

大臣の免許が必要なのですが，免許の取得は厳しく制限され，戦後は新しい銀行はほとんどできませんでした。また，すでにある銀行が新しい店舗を創設するにも大蔵大臣の認可が必要です。さらに，行政当局が銀行の資産内容をチェックし，経営に対して口出しする場合があります。

Q：当局がそのような政策をとっても倒産しそうな銀行が出てきた場合はどうするのですか。

A：経営が危なくなった銀行については，倒産を避けるために，経営内容が健全な銀行によって**救済合併**させるように指導してきました。また政府機関から人材を送り込む場合もあります。

Q：しかし，経営の危ない銀行を救済合併する方の銀行にとって，何かメリットはあるのですか。

A：先ほど述べましたように，銀行の新規店舗の開設や店舗の拡大には厳しい制限があります。合併する方の銀行は，合併される銀行の店舗とその業務をそのまま引く継ぐことができますので，**店舗網**の拡大をねらう銀行にとっては大きなメリットになったわけです。

Q：ところで，日本でもいよいよ金利の自由化が最終段階に入りましたね。

● 金利の自由化が
及ぼす影響

A：そうですね。欧米諸国では'60～'70年代初頭から預金金利の自由化が進められ，'80年代には多くの国ですでに完全自由化となりました。一方，日本の預金金利の自由化は，'79年にごく一部で始まりましたが，1,000万円以下の個人向けの預金の**金利自由化**がスタートしたのは，'89年になってからでした。しかし'94年10月からは普通預金の規制もはずされ，日本でも預金金利は完全に自由化されました。

Q：これからは銀行間の競争が激しくなることが予想されますが，今後も日本の銀行は倒産しないとい

charter required to enter the banking industry from the Finance Minister. Not one new bank has been established since the end of World War II. Banks must also obtain authorization from the minister to establish new branches. In some cases, government authorities also check bank assets and become involved in bank management.

Q : What does the government do, if a bank is about to go under despite such measures to prevent failure?

A : If a bank looks like it might fail, it is instructed to merge in a so-called **"relief merger"** with a sound bank before the situation becomes serious. Also government agencies sometimes send personnel to private banks.

Q : How does a sound bank benefit by merging with a bank with poor management?

A : As I mentioned previously, the opening of new branches and expanding of existing branches is severely restricted. A bank which acquires an unsound bank gains all of that bank's branches and accounts. So the acquisition is actually a great merit for the bank which is trying to expand its **branch network**.

Q : By the way, Japan is now in the final stages of liberalizing its interest rates, isn't it?

A : Yes, the West began liberalizing interest rates on savings at the beginning of the 1960s and 1970s. By the early 1980s, most countries had completely liberalized interest rates. On the other hand, Japan began liberalization an a very small scale only in 1979. **Liberalization of interest rates** on individual savings under ten million yen started in 1989. Interest rates for ordinary savings accounts had been regulated, but were liberalized completely in October 1994.

Q : That means competition between banks will increase. Will Japanese banks still be failure-proof?

えるのでしょうか。

A：1993年10月には，経営の破綻した**信用金庫**が解体されました。店舗や**営業権**，従業員が6つの**金融機関**に引き取られたのです。これは戦後初めてのケースで，事実上の倒産といえるでしょう。こうしたケースは今後増えていく可能性があります。

Q：これまでのように，経営の危ない銀行を，経営の健全な銀行が吸収合併するということにはならないのですか。

A：それは難しくなっています。救済する方の銀行にとっての最大のメリット，つまり店舗網の拡大や規模の拡大といったメリットがなくなってきているからです。そのいちばんの大きな要因が「金利の自由化」なのです。いままでは規制で金利が低く抑えられていたため，銀行は低コストで資金を調達できました。しかし，金利が自由化されれば，預金を獲得するための銀行同士の競争が激しくなり，金利は上昇します。預金を集めようとすればするほど預金全体の平均金利は高くなります。そのため，銀行の経営方針を「**預金量重視**」から「**利ざや**（貸出金利と預金金利の差）**重視**」へと転換することが必要となってきているのです。店舗網の拡大や規模の拡大が収益拡大につながらなくなるわけです。

A : In October 1993, a **credit association** which had gone bankrupt was broken up. Its branches, **trade rights,** and employees were divided among six **financial institutions.** This is considered the first real bank failure in postwar history, but the number of such cases may increase in the future.

Q : Will sound banks with good management continue to acquire unsound banks as they have in the past?

A : This has become a more difficult problem. The greatest merit for the acquiring institution used to be that it could expand its branch network, but that will no longer be necessary. The greatest factor is the liberalization of interest rates. Since interest rates have been kept low, banks have been able to procure capital at a low cost. But once liberalized, banks compete fiercely to obtain savings accounts and therefore will increase interest rates. The more accounts they compete for, the higher the overall interest rates will rise. Therefore, bank management policy should shift from an emphasis on the **amount of savings** to an emphasis on **profit margin,** which is the difference between what they pay for accounts and what they can charge for loans. Expansion of business no longer means expansion of profit.

31 一億総中流

総理府は毎年，国民生活に関する世論調査を行っていますが，1992年5月に行われた調査で，「生活程度が中」と答えた人は何％いたでしょうか。

　① 50%　② 70%　③ 90%

A：普通の日本人は，自分の生活水準についてどう考えているのでしょうか。まずはクイズの答えです。正解は，③の90％です。「自分の生活は中流だ」と答えた人が，90％を超えたのは1970年のことで，それ以来この数字はほとんど変わっていません。「**一億総中流**」という言葉がいわれるゆえんです。

Q：日本は，本当に経済的に平等な社会を実現したのでしょうか。

● 主観的中流意識

A：そうはいえません。この調査での質問は，「世間一般から見て，お宅の生活程度はどのくらいか」という極めて主観的なもので，年間の収入や保有する資産を基礎にしたものではありません。それから，回答の選択肢も，「上」，「中の上」，「中の中」，「中の下」，それに「下」と，5つのうち3つが中流に分類されるので，中流と答える人はどうしても多くなってしまいます。

Q：それでは，日本では実際には，貧富の差がかなりあるということですか。

A：そうともいえません。第1章でお話ししたように，日本では，社長と新入社員の給料の差は，他の国に比べるとずっと少ないのです。それから，**耐久**

228

Middle-class Consciousness in Japanese Society

> The Prime Minister's Office conducts a public opinion poll every year on peoples' lifestyles. What percentage of the pollees replied that they belong to the middle class in the May 1992 survey?
>
> ① 50% ② 70% ③ 90%

A : What does the average Japanese think about his or her standard of living? The answer is number three, 90%. In 1970, over 90% of Japanese considered themselves to be in the middle class, and the figures have changed little since then. That's why it is said that **all Japanese are middle class.**

Q : Is it then possible to say that Japan has achieved economic equality?

A : I don't think so. The survey asked how the pollees compared their standard of living with the general public, so the answers were extremely subjective. It was not based on yearly income or assets value. The choices in the answer to the survey were upper, upper-middle, middle, lower-middle, and lower. Three out of five of the answers are classified as the middle class, so many people simply answered they belong to this category.

Q : Does that mean there is actually a large gap between the rich and poor in Japan?

A : Not necessarily. As we mentioned in Chapter 1, the salary difference between new employees and company presidents is much smaller than in other countries. Looking at the diffusion of

消費財の普及率を見てみますと，カラーテレビや電気冷蔵庫が，ほとんどすべての家庭にあります。また，乗用車は78％以上，ルームエアコンもおよそ70％の家庭に普及しています。

Q：自分の生活が中流と考える人が多いのもうなずけますね。ずっと以前からこうなのですか。

● 中流意識の形成

A：そうではありません。戦前の日本では，高等教育を受けたエリートサラリーマンと，教育をそれほど受けてない一般の労働者の受け取る所得には，かなりの差がありました。

Q：その差がだんだんと小さくなってきたわけですね。

A：所得格差が縮小する最初の動きが見られたのは戦時中のことです。戦時中の人手不足で，ホワイトカラーとブルーカラー労働者の**賃金格差**が縮まったといわれています。それから，自分の生活を中流と考える人が90％を超えたのは1970年のことだといいましたが，これは日本が高度経済成長を達成しつつあったときですね。ちょうど高度成長の果実が行きわたり始めたころです。

Q：つまり，多くの人が世間並みに耐久消費財をそろえ，ある程度の豊かさを実感することで，中流意識が形成されていったわけですね。

A：そうです。この「中流」というのは，相対的な生活水準を問題にしているのであって，絶対的な豊かさを問題にしているわけではありません。ですから，日本でいう中流というのはいわゆる中産階級のことではありません。この**中流意識**の実態をもう少し詳しく見てみますと，その時々の経済の動きを反映して，その中身に微妙な変化が見られます。

● 中流意識の
　実態は

Q：それはどういうことですか。

A：'60年代から'70年代にかけての傾向としては，「中の中」と考える人の比率が緩やかに上昇し，逆に，「中の下」と考える人の比率が減りました。

durable goods, we see that almost all Japanese households have color televisions and electric refrigetrators. Over 78% of households own cars, and about 70% own air conditioners.

Q : These figures back up the idea that many Japanese consider their lifestyles to be middle class. Has this always been true?

A : Well, before World War II, there was a great difference in income between highly educated, elite workers and less educated laborers.

Q : So that gap has gradually narrowed?

A : It's said the gap began to narrow during the war. Since Japan experienced a labor shortage at that time, the **difference in salaries** between white and blue-collar workers shrank. As we've mentioned before, it was in 1970 that over 90% of the population began to think of themselves as middle class. This was almost at the height of the high economic growth period, when the benefits of that period became more prevalent.

Q : In short, many people were then able to buy durable goods and began to feel their nation's prosperity to a certain extent. That's how "middle class" consciousness appeared.

A : That's right. In Japan, "middle class" refers to the relative standard of living. It is not an issue of absolute prosperity. That's why "middle class" does not refer to rank in society. If we look closely at the pattern of **middle-class consciousness**, we see that it fluctuates slightly according to the economic conditions.

Q : How is that?

A : Well, from the 1960s to the 1970s, the percentage of people who considered themselves to be in the "middle of the middle" gradually increased, while those who considered themselves to be in

生活が改善されたという実感が，こうした意識の変化につながっていったと思われます。ところが，'80年代に入ると，この逆のことが起こります。自分の生活程度を「中の中」と考える人は，'79年には60.6％でしたが，'92年には53.6％に減っています。逆に，「中の下」と考える人は，'79年の22.2％から'92年には26.2％に増えています。

Q：これは何を意味しているのでしょうか。

● 資産を持つ人と持たない人

A：戦後，日本では，給与所得は一貫して上昇し続けました。しかし，**不動産や株**など資産の価値は，それを上回る勢いで上がりました。つまり，資産を持つ人と，持たない人との格差は広がっていったわけです。そして1987年，大都市の地価や株価が大きく上昇しました。いわゆるバブルの発生です。東京で，普通のサラリーマンが一戸建ての家を買うことは，ほぼ不可能になりました。この年の調査で，自分の生活程度を「中の下」と考える人の比率は，23年ぶりに30％を超えました。

Q：資産を持つ人と持たない人との間の不平等感が強まったわけですね。

A：家計経済研究所が1992年に行った調査によると，「中の中」と答えた人と「中の下」と答えた人との間の所得には，わずかの違いしかありませんでしたが，住宅の床面積では大きな違いが見られました。「中の下」と答えた人では50m²以下の人が多いのに対して，「中の中」と答えた人では75m²あたりが中心になっています。

Q：資産の面で格差が出てきたということですね。

A：そうです。バブルで地価が大きく上昇する前に住宅を購入した人や，相続で住宅を得た人は，生活面でゆとりがあると考えるのに対して，そうでない人は，不平等感から自分の生活程度は，「中の

the "lower middle" a decreased. It appears that the improvement in lifestyle led to a change in consciousness. But in the 1980s, the opposite phenomenon occurred. In 1979, the percentage of the population who considered themselves "middle-middle" was 60.6%, but that figure fell to 53.6% in 1992. Those who considered themselves "lower-middle" rose from 22.2% in 1979 to 26.2% in 1992.

Q : What do all these figures mean?

A : After the war, wages rose consistently in Japan. But **asset values** such as of **real estate** and **stocks** surpassed the relative growth in wages. This meant that the gap between people with assets and those without assets widened. Then in 1987, land and stock prices in large cities soared. This was the beginning of the speculative "bubble economy." It became almost impossible for the average worker to buy a **detached house** in Tokyo. According to a survey conducted in the same year, the percentage of people who considered their lifestyles "lower-middle" surpassed 30% for the first time in 23 years.

Q : The feeling of inequality between those who had assets and those who didn't must have grown.

A : A survey by the Institute for Household Economy found that there was only a slight difference in income between those who replied that they were "middle-middle" and those who replied that they were "lower-middle." But there was a large difference in the floor area of their homes. Most of the people who consider themselves "lower-middle" had homes with floor space of less than 50 square meters, while those who thought they were "middle-middle" had homes with a floor space of around 75 square meters.

Q : So the gap lies in their assets.

A : That's right. People who were able to buy homes before the land prices soared during the bubble economy and people who inherited their homes felt they had more leeway in their lifestyles.

ポイント

「中」には至っていないと考えたのではないでしょうか。なお，同じ調査で，「中の上」と答えた人は10.4％でしたが，この層の人たちは「中の中」と比べると所得面でもかなり高く，貯蓄も多く，住宅の床面積も120m²程度が中心になっています。

Q：一口に中流といっても，その中身を見るとかなりの幅があるようですね。

● 年間所得の実態

A：最後にひとつ，客観的な数字をあげておきます。勤労者世帯の1年間の所得に関して，総理府が1992年に行った調査です。**年間所得**を，500万円未満と，500万円以上1000万円未満，それに1000万円以上，と3つに分けた場合，500万円未満の人がおよそ17％，500万円から1000万円までの人がおよそ58％，そして1000万円以上の人が25％でした。「一億総中流」といわれる日本ですが，この数字を見て，あなたはどう考えますか。

But those who didn't have homes felt an inequality, and thus didn't think they had reached "middle-middle" status. Among the pollees, 10.4% replied that they were "upper-middle," but compared to the "middle-middle," their income was much higher, they had more savings, and the area of their homes was about 120 square meters.

Q : Within that one phrase "middle class," there are a fair variety of meanings.

A : In conclusion, I'd like to throw out some figures that speak for themselves. The Prime Minister's Office conducted a survey in 1992 on the **annual income** of workers' households. Annual income fell into three brackets: below ¥5 million (17%), between ¥5 million and ¥10 million (58%), and above ¥10 million (25%). Japan is said to have a large middle-class population. Now that you have seen the figures, what do you think?

32 | 経済のソフト化，サービス化

国勢調査によりますと，サービス業など第3次産業に
従事する人の割合は，終戦直後の1947年には23％で
した。さて45年後の1992年は何％でしょうか。

① 40％　② 60％　③ 80％

A：日本の**産業構造**は，経済成長とともに第3次産業
　　の従事者が増え続け，いわゆる経済のソフト化，
　　サービス化が進んでいます。クイズの正解は，②
　　の60％です。

Q：3倍近くに増えたわけですね。本論に入る前に，
　　第3次産業とは具体的にどんな産業なのか，説明
　　してもらえませんか。

● 第3次産業とは

A：**第3次産業**には，**商業**や**金融・保険業**，**不動産業**，
　　それに**サービス業**などがあります。このうちサー
　　ビス業というのは，フィットネスクラブなどの健
　　康産業から，ＯＡ機器の操作を行う人を派遣する
　　人材派遣業，それに高齢化社会の到来に伴って増
　　えてきた有料老人ホームまで，多種多様です。こ
　　のサービス業に従事する人の増え方は，特に激し
　　いですね。なお**第1次産業**は，農林水産業。**第2次
　　産業**は製造業や建設業，鉱業などです。

Q：第3次産業が増える一方で，第1次産業の方は減っ

The Expansion of the Service-Oriented Economy

> A national population survey found that in 1947, immediately after World War II, the percentage of the work force employed in tertiary industries such as the service industry was 23%. What was that figure in 1992, 45 years after the previous survey?
>
> ① 40% ② 60% ③ 80%

A : Within the **industrial structure** of Japan under economic growth, the number of employees in tertiary industries has increased. As a result, the economy tends to be more oriented toward software and services. The correct answer is number two, 60%.

Q : That means the number has nearly tripled. Before we turn to the main topic what exactly are tertiary industries?

A : **Tertiary industries** include **trading, finance and insurance, real estate** and **service industries.** And the service industry refers to a wide variety of businesses, such as the health industry like sports clubs, temporary agencies which dispatch personnel to operate office equipment, and even private nursing homes which are increasing in number as the population in Japan grows older. The number of people employed in the service industry has risen dramatically. **Primary industries** include agriculture, forestry, and fishing industries. **Secondary industries** refer to areas such as the manufacturing, construction, and mining industries.

Q : If the tertiary industry has continued to expand, primary indus-

てきたのですね。

A : その通り。先ほどの統計によると第1次産業の従事者は、1947年のときには53％と過半数を超えていたのに、'92年には6.4％にまで激減しました。第3次産業、特にその中のサービス業に従事する人の割合が高くなったことは、経済のソフト化、サービス化が進んだひとつの表れなのですね。

● 経済のソフト化、
　サービス化とは

Q : 経済のソフト化、サービス化という言葉は、今ひとつはっきりしないのですが。

A : このふたつの言葉は同じような意味に使われることもあるので、それぞれの言葉を厳密に定義するのは難しいのですが、簡単にいえば、産業構造の変化に伴い、経済の比重がモノ中心からサービス中心へと変化していくことですね。このことは、第3次産業の従事者が増えることだけを意味するのではありません。第1次産業の農林水産業や第2次産業の製造業などでも、**情報管理**や**マーケティング**といったサービスやソフトに関連した仕事が増えています。さらに生活の質的な向上や心の豊かさといった、モノだけでは測れない面が重視されるようになることをソフト化ということもあります。

Q : 具体的な例を挙げてもらえませんか。

A : 例えば、従来は家事労働でやっていたハウスクリーニングや、個人の輸入代行といった時間節約型のサービス、それにパソコン通信の普及に伴うネットワークの提供といった新しいサービスが次々と生まれています。また製造業のソニーが、アメリカの映画会社であるコロンビア・ピクチャーズを買収して、ハードとソフトの両方を手がけようとしているのも、その具体化の一例です。

● ソフト化社会の
　特徴

Q : ソフト化社会の特徴を一言でいえば。

A : モノ中心の**ハード社会**では、モノをいかに決めら

238

try must have shrunk.

A : That's right. The statistics used in the quiz showed that in 1947 the majority of the population, 53%, was engaged in primary industry, but that percentage has shrunk to 6.4% in 1992. On the other hand, the tertiary industry, especially the service industry, is now employing a large percentage of the population. This is one sign of how important a role the software and service industries have come to play in the economy.

Q : What exactly does that mean?

A : Since these two terms are sometimes used in almost the same way, it is difficult to define them precisely, but to put it simply, structure has undergone a change, and the economy has shifted from a product-oriented to a service-oriented economy. This trend is not limited to the tertiary industry, however. Even in the primary industries of agriculture, forestry and fisheries, and the secondary industry of manufacturing, there is more emphasis on software-related areas such as **information management control** and **marketing**. By the word "software" is meant the areas where goods are less important than the improvement in the quality of life.

Q : Can you give me a concrete example?

A : Well, there are all kinds of new services being offered, such as house-cleaning services, previously done by housekeepers and private import business agencies offering services that save time. There are also services offered through networks of personal computers. One concrete example of this attempt to combine so-called hardware and software is manufacturer Sony's purchase of Columbia Pictures, an American movie studio.

Q : What are some of the characteristics of this new economy?

A : In the **goods-oriented economy**, the most important thing is

れたように正確に作るかが重要視されていましたが、**ソフト化社会**になると、そうしたことは当たり前のことで、デザインや色のいいもの、つまりセンスの良さが大切になってきます。

Q：こうした傾向は外国でも進んでいるのでしょうか。

A：'91年のデータで比べてみますと、第3次産業に従事する人の割合は、日本が59％なのに対して、アメリカは73％、イギリスは70％、フランスが66％と、いずれも日本より高くなっています。ちなみに韓国は48％です。イギリスの経済学者が唱えた法則によると、経済が発展すればするほど産業の中心は、第1次産業から第2次産業、そして第3次産業へと移っていくということです。この点で、日本の産業構造のソフト化、サービス化はまだ欧米並みには達していないといえそうです。

Q：このようにソフト化、サービス化が進んだ背景は？

A：この背景には、第21章「変わる消費生活」でもお話ししましたが、国民の生活水準の向上に伴い、モノがほぼ充足されたことでモノ離れが起きました。そして、ほかの人とは一味違うものを求める「ぜいたく志向」が強まるなど、国民のニーズも多様化しました。また核家族化や女性の社会進出などで、家事労働を代行するようなサービスに対する需要が高まったこと。さらには余暇時間の増大や都市化の進展によって生活様式が変わったことなどが挙げられます。

Q：こうした傾向は今後ますます強まるのでしょうか。

A：そうだと思います。いま急激に情報化が進んで、パソコンや携帯電話が普及したり、テレビ会議で出張をしなくても意見交換ができます。経済のソフト化、サービス化には、情報が重要な役割を果たしますから、情報化が進めば進むほど、経済のソフト化、サービス化も進むものと見られます。

● ソフト化が
　進んだ背景

to make goods precisely according to the standards. But in the **service-oriented economy,** high-quality goods are a matter of course, so design, color, fashion and taste are emphasized.

Q : Is this trend becoming more prominent in other countries, too?

A : Yes. If we compare 1991 data, we find that the tertiary industry employs 59% of the work force in Japan, as against 73% in the United States, 70% in Britain, and 66% in France. All these countries have larger service industries than Japan. And in South Korea, 48% of the work force is engaged in the tertiary industry. A British economist said that as a rule, as the economy grows, the work force shifts from primary to secondary to tertiary industries. Considering this rule, the Japanese industrial structure is not yet on a par with that of Europe and the United States.

Q : What's behind this shift?

A : As we mentioned at the beginning of Chapter 21 "Changing Consumption Patterns," as the national standard of living rises and desire for goods is satisfied, the public becomes less focused on general goods and demand more luxurious items which suit individual tastes. The needs of the people have diversified. The trend toward the nuclear family and the increase in the number of working female family members increases the demand for services offering such things as housecare. One other factor is the change in lifestyle with the increase of free time and growth of cities.

Q : Will this trend keep growing in the future?

A : I think so. Right now, the emphasis on information is growing rapidly. Personal computers and cellular phones are becoming more popular. People are now able to teleconference and exchange opinions without actually taking a business trip. As information becomes even more essential, the economy will become increasingly service and software-oriented.

33 | 張りめぐらされた規制

日本では，デパートや大型スーパーが新しい店を出すとき，いろいろな規制をクリアーしなければなりません。さて次の3つの項目のうち，大型店が新しく店を開くときに，規制の対象になっていないのはどれでしょうか。

　① 閉店時刻　② 店員の人数　③ 売り場面積

A：日本は，行政による**規制**や指導が大変多い国だといわれ，いま規制緩和の必要性が叫ばれています。クイズの正解は②の「店員の人数」で，閉店時刻や売り場面積については，「**大規模小売店舗法**」という法律によって規制されています。

Q：閉店時刻や売り場面積が，なぜ規制の対象になっているのですか。

A：この法律のねらいは，大型店の開店が周辺の小さな小売業者に与える影響を少なくしようというものなので，そのために閉店時刻などを規制するわけです。しかし結果として大型店の新規開店を難しくしてしまい，消費者に不利な結果をもたらします。

● 規制の実態は

Q：一体そうした規制の数は，どのくらいあるのですか。

A：総務庁の調べによると，こうした規制，政府機関による許認可の数は，1993年3月末で1万1402件にのぼっており，前の年より460件増えています。

● 規制の多い理由

Q：**規制緩和**が必要だと叫ばれていながら，かえって増えているんですか。なぜこんなに規制が多いのですか。

242

Widespread Regulation Network

> When a department store or a large supermarket opens
> a new store, they are required to pass many kinds of
> regulations. Which of the following items is not regu-
> lated in the case of large-scale stores?
>
> ① closing time ② number of employees
> ③ store floorage

A : It is said that Japan has many administrative **regulations** and
guidelines for stores. That is why there are so many people call-
ing for deregulation. The answer to the quiz is number two, the
number of employees, but actually the other two matters are
restricted by **the Large-scale Retail Store Law.**

Q : Why are the closing time and the store floorage regulated?

A : The purpose of the law is to reduce the effect of large stores on
small retailers nearby. That's why business hours and such are
controlled. But as a result, it is extremely difficult to open new
large stores, and that in turn is detrimental to the consumer.

Q : How many kinds of regulations are there?

A : The Management and Coordination Agency reported that as of
March 1993, there were precisely 11,402 government permits
and licenses, 460 more than in the previous year.

Q : Despite calls for **deregulation**, the number of restrictions are
actually increasing. Why are there so many regulations?

A：これまでにも説明してきましたが，戦後の荒廃から立ち直るために日本は，消費者よりも生産者を重視する政策をとってきました。そして，そのために**食糧管理制度**や**金利規制**，**事業の免許制**などいろいろな規制をしてきました。これが現在でも旧態依然として残っているために，規制が多いのです。規制の中にはもちろん必要なものもあります。例えば工場の廃水などを放置しておけば，深刻な公害が発生しますし，国民の健康を守るための医薬品製造に関する規制など，社会的な意味合いを持った規制があります。しかし経済的な規制の中には，廃止した方がよいものが多いですね。

Q：それはどんなものですか。

A：例えばタクシー料金は認可制で，なおかつ「同一地域同一運賃」という原則がとられており，たとえ業者が値下げ申請をしても，運輸省は長い間これを認めませんでした。また，酒屋や米屋は免許制になっていて，新規に開業するのは容易ではありません。

● 規制のマイナス面

Q：規制がもたらすマイナス面をまとめるとどういうことになりますか。

A：ひとつは，生産者を保護するために価格を維持しようとするため，消費者には安いものが手に入らない。また規制によって業界への新規参入を阻害すると，競争によってもたらされるはずの技術革新など経済の活性化が促されない，などといったマイナスがあります。

● 動き出した
　規制緩和

Q：最近になって規制緩和の動きが活発になったのは，なぜですか。

A：ひとつは**外圧**があります。欧米の企業が日本に進出しようとしても，さまざまな規制があるために

A : As mentioned in the previous chapters, since the Second World War, the Japanese government has attached greater importance to producers than to consumers in order to rebuild industry. The **food control system, regulations of interest rates,** and **business licensing system** were all part of this industrial policy. Since this old structure still remains, the number of regulations has increased. Of course some of the restrictions are necessary, for example, regulations which affect society. If we allow factories to discharge their liquid wastes freely, it will cause serious pollution, and we have regulations with social repercussions such as those on medicine to protect public health. But there are many economic restrictions which should be abolished.

Q : Which ones should be discarded?

A : For instance, the taxi business used to abide by the "same fare for the same region" policy, which means that fares are licensed. Taxi companies have not been allowed to lower fares. Even though taxi companies have made application for a reduction of fares, the authorizing Ministry of Transport has not granted permission. Similarly, liquor shops and rice shops require licenses and it is quite difficult to open new shops.

Q : In sum, what are the disadvantages of having so many regulations?

A : For one thing, prices are artificially maintained to protect manufacturers, meaning higher prices for the consumers. And when regulations block new entries into an industry, this dampens economic vitality such as technological innovations produced by competition.

Q : Why has the movement for deregulation become so active recently?

A : **Pressure from abroad** is one factor. Even though Western companies are trying to penetrate the Japanese market, it is

進出しにくい。その一方で日本の貿易黒字だけは，ますます増える。そうした状況に欧米各国は不満を強めています。それで日本政府としても，なんとかしないといけなくなってきたわけです。

Q：どうも日本という国は，外圧がないと動かないところがありますね。

A：残念ながら，そのとおりですね。ただし，これだけ注目されるようになった背景には，外圧だけではなく私たち消費者の不満もあります。それは，これだけ円高になって円の**購買力**は強まっているにもかかわらず，私たち消費者には豊かさの実感がない。なぜそうなのかというと，外国に比べて日本の物価が割高であるという問題，すなわち内外価格差の問題があるわけです。こうした内外価格差を生むのは，張りめぐらされている規制にあるのではないかと不満が高まったのです。

Q：規制緩和の具体的な取り組みを教えてください。

● 政府の規制
　緩和策

A：細川内閣当時の首相の私的諮問機関である**経済改革研究会**は，1993年12月，経済改革に関する報告書をまとめましたが，その中で規制緩和を積極的に進める方針を打ち出しました。この方針の中では，「経済的な規制については原則自由で，規制は例外的なものとする。また社会的な規制についても必要最小限に抑える」という考えを打ち出しています。また政府も，規制緩和に乗り出しました。1994年2月に決めた行政改革大綱では，600項目以上の規制の廃止や縮小を打ち出し，タクシー料金の多様化など，一部についてはすでに実施しました。

Q：タクシー料金の値下げ申請を認めたという動きですね。

A：そうです。先ほども触れましたが，タクシー料金について運輸省は，たとえ業者から値下げの申請が

very difficult because of the various regulations. On the contrary, Japanese export surpluses to these nations are increasing. Therefore, Western nations are growing increasingly discontent with the status quo, so the Japanese government has to do something.

Q : It seems that the Japanese government will not act without pressure from overseas.

A : Unfortunately, that is true. But in the background of this focal issue is the fact that the pressure comes not only from abroad but also from consumer dissatisfaction. Despite the yen's extreme appreciation and its strong **purchasing power**, Japanese consumers do not feel their own prosperity. This is because prices in Japan are much higher than prices abroad. People suspect this price disparity is caused by the widespread network of regulations.

Q : How is deregulation being undertaken?

A : **The Advisory Group for Economic Structural Reform**, a private advisory panel to former Prime Minister Morihiro Hosokawa, compiled a report on economic reform in December 1993 which urged aggressive plans for deregulation. The council recommended the abolishment of economic regulations, in principle, and the minimization of social restrictions. The government has since launched a campaign to promote deregulation. Over 600 regulations were to be either abolished or eased in the package of fundamental administrative reforms set out in February 1994, and some of these have already been enacted, including allowing fare competition among taxis.

Q : This must mean the government has finally approved the lowering of taxi fares.

A : That is correct. As we just noted, in the past, the Ministry of Transport would not have approved applications by taxi compa-

● 規制緩和の
　今後の動き

出てきても，これまではそれを認めませんでした。しかし1993年11月，京都のタクシー会社から出ていた値下げ申請を初めて認可し，京都市とその周辺では，料金の違うタクシーが走り始めました。

Q：こうした規制緩和は，今後，本格的に進むのでしょうか。

A：規制緩和をしなければならないという流れはできてはいるものの，どこまで実現するかというと難しいですね。ひとつには，権限を持つ官僚がなかなかその権限を手放したがらないことがあります。それと，規制が緩和されれば，業種によってはそれだけ新しい企業の参入が増えることも予想されますので，既得権を持っている企業や業界団体が反対する可能性もあります。しかし日本経済がこれからさらに飛躍するためには，民間企業に活力を与える「規制の緩和」は必要であり，その流れは一段と進むものと見られます。

248

nies to lower fares, even if they were submitted. But in November 1993, a Kyoto taxi company was granted permission to lower fares, so there is now a difference in fares among taxis in the Kyoto region.

Q : Will this deregulation program be fully implemented?

A : Although the trend is for compulsory deregulation, it is difficult to know how far to go. One problem is that bureaucrats do not want to relinquish power. If regulations are eased or abolished, more new companies are sure to gain access to various industries. And companies and industrial associations with vested interests may oppose this movement. But deregulation is necessary to reinvigorate the private sector and promote further economic progress. Therefore many feel that deregulation will continue for the forseeable future.

34 | 内外価格差

東京の物価はニューヨークに比べてどのくらい高い
でしょうか。

　　① 30%　　② 50%　　③ 70%

ポイント

● 拡大する内外
価格差

A：東京の物価は世界一高いといわれています。この
章では，最近話題になっている**内外価格差**の問題
を取り上げます。答えは，**①**の30%です。経済企
画庁の調査によると，1992年の東京の**物価**は，ニ
ューヨークに比べ平均で31%高く，コメや牛肉，
ビール，ガソリン，映画の入場料などは2倍から4
倍も高くなっています。

Q：昔から日本の物価は高かったというわけではない
のでしょう。

A：そうなんです。例えば，20年前の1972年には，逆
に日本の物価の方がニューヨークよりも30%も安
かったんです。

Q：どうして日本の物価水準の方が逆に高くなってし
まったのですか。

● 円高が最大要因

A：**円高**が最大の要因と考えられています。事実，内
外価格差が拡大したのは，円高が急激に進み始め
た1985年の**プラザ合意**以降のことですから。それ
以前は，1978年の円高の一時期を除いて，日本の
物価はアメリカよりも安かったのです。

Q：どうして円高が原因なのですか。

A：円高になれば，ドルベースで見た品物の値段は上
昇することになります。ここで，国内で生産され

The Price Gap between Japan and Abroad

How much higher are prices in Tokyo compared to New York City?

① 30% ② 50% ③ 70%

A : Prices in Tokyo are said to be the world's highest. In this chapter we will discuss the **disparity between domestic and foreign prices.** The correct answer is number one, 30%. The Economic Planning Agency reported Tokyo **commodity prices** in 1992 were an average of 31% higher than New York prices. But prices on rice, beef, beer, gasoline and movie tickets were two to four times higher.

Q : Have prices in Japan always been high?

A : Well, 20 years ago in 1972, prices in Japan were 30% lower than New York prices.

Q : Why have Japanese prices become so inflated?

A : The biggest factor is the **appreciation of the yen**. The disparity in prices in Japan and abroad widened after 1985, when the yen began to appreciate rapidly due to **the Plaza Accord.** Before that, excepting 1978, when a temporary appreciation of the yen occurred, prices in Japan were cheaper than those in the United States.

Q : How does the yen appreciation affect prices?

A : When the yen appreciates, dollar-based prices on goods go up. There is now competition in the marketplace between domestic

● 政府の規制に
　問題

ているものと，海外で生産されて輸入されたものとの間で競争が働けば，輸入品の方が円高で安くなった分だけ競争力がありますから，国内の物価水準は下がるはずです。しかし，前章でお話ししたように，さまざまな規制が新規参入を制限しているため，この競争が働かないことがあるわけです。

　例えば，安い輸入品を取り扱う業者が少ない，いないということになると，消費者の手に届かないことから，同じ品物について日本と海外で価格差が大きく開いてしまいます。そして，円高がさらに動きを助長するというわけです。

Q：しかし，円高になって海外から安い輸入品が入ってきて，物価が下がることはないのですか。

A：それは当然あります。例えば，円高で原油の輸入価格が下がり，それを燃料にして発電している電気の料金が下がったという例はあります。しかし全部が全部そうなるわけではありません。ここにも規制の問題が出てきます。流通やサービスといった非製造業部門は，規制で保護されている分野が多いうえ，生産性を上げる必要性があまりありませんでした。さらに，サービスは輸入することができないので，国内での供給が限られ，厳しい競争にさらされていないこともあります。また，日本では食料品が特に割高です。これは，政府の農産物輸入規制や価格に対する規制が働いているからです。

　例えば，小麦を例にとってみましょう。日本の小麦の生産コストはアメリカのおよそ8倍です。しかし，安いアメリカの小麦も日本にくれば同じ値段になります。小麦耕作農家を保護するために，食糧管理制度のもとで政府は，安く輸入した小麦を国内価格と同じ価格にして卸しているからです。1985年のプラザ合意以降，円高が急速に進

products and products manufactured abroad which are then imported. Imported goods are cheaper due to the yen's appreciation, meaning that domestic price levels should be lower. However, as we saw in the earlier chapters, such open economic competition does not work well, because various kinds of regulations prevent new access to the market.

For example, if few enterprises handle inexpensive imported goods, these products do not reach consumers. Therefore the gap in prices for identical items in Japan and abroad grows wider. This is further affected by the strengthening of the yen.

Q : However, the strong yen allows lower-priced products to be imported from overseas so prices should go down.

A : That is true to some degree. For example, the yen's appreciation reduces the import price of crude oil. Oil is used to produce power, and then electricity prices drop. But this doesn't apply across the board. At this point we have to consider government regulations. The non-manufacturing sector, such as distribution and services, is not forced to raise its productivity because it is protected by regulations. Furthermore, since services cannot be imported, such firms do not face any international competition. Prices of food products are especially inflated in Japan because of government regulations on agricultural imports and prices.

Wheat, for example, costs eight times more to produce in Japan than in the United States. But if U.S. wheat is imported to Japan, it is sold at the domestic price, due to the government food control system implemented to protect Japanese wheat farmers. The government wholesales the inexpensive imported wheat at the same price as domestically produced wheat. Since the Plaza Accord went into effect in 1985, the yen has grown rapidly stronger, and prices on imports have fallen dramatically. Even though the wholesale prices of items which are not regulated by the government have dropped, those which are regu-

み，輸入物価は大幅に下落しました。これに伴い，政府の規制を受けていない品目の卸売物価は下がりました。しかし，規制を受けている品目の卸売物価はまったく下がりませんでした。政府の規制も内外価格差を生む原因のひとつであることを示しています。

Q：東京で買う輸入品の背広やワンピースなどの衣料品，それにハンドバッグなども，外国よりかなり高いといわれていますね。

A：これは，消費者のブランド志向が影響しているためと考えられます。輸入業者が消費者のブランド志向を利用して，値段を高めに設定しているからです。高いから高級品なのであって，安ければ誰でも買うことができ，ブランドの意味がなくなるというわけです。

Q：香水や口紅など化粧品も同じ理由から高いのですか。

● 販売制度にも一因

A：これについては，化粧品や医薬品，出版物など特定の商品の**販売制度**も影響しているといえます。これらの商品については，メーカーが販売価格を指定できるという決まりがあり，商品の自由な競争を妨げています。この制度に関して最近話題になったのがコンパクトディスクです。日本ではこの制度に縛られて安売りできないことから，香港やシンガポールに輸出されたコンパクトディスクを日本に逆輸入して安売りするディスカウントショップが出てきているということです。

● 内外価格差対策

Q：この内外価格差をなくすためにはどのような対策が考えられますか。

A：基本的には，**市場メカニズム**が完全に働けば内外価格差は生じないはずです。今，政府が進めようとしているのは，規制の緩和です。競争がなかったり，それが制限されていることから，価格も下がらないのです。競争できるような環境を整えて

lated haven't. This demonstrates that government regulations are one source of the disparity between Japanese and foreign prices.

Q : I've also heard that imported clothing such as men's suits, women's dresses and handbags are much more expensive in Japan than in foreign countries.

A : This is more due to the effect of consumer's preferences for brand-name items rather than government regulations. Importers take advantage of this affinity for brand items and set high prices. They are luxury items because they are expensive, and consumers wouldn't like these brands if everyone could buy them.

Q : Is this true of cosmetics such as perfumes and lipsticks?

A : These prices are also affected by the **retail system** for particular items, including cosmetics, medicine and published materials. Manufacturers are allowed to designate retail prices on these products. And this prevents open competition. One item sold under this system which recently is being debated is compact disks. CDs cannot be sold inexpensively because of this system, so there are now discount stores which reimport compact disks of Japanese origin from Singapore or Hong Kong to sell at discounted prices in Japan.

Q : What measures are there to eliminate the disparity in prices?

A : Basically, if the **market mechanisms** are fully functioning, there shouldn't be any disparity in prices between Japan and abroad. The government is trying to push for deregulation. Prices won't fall if there is no competition, or if it is limited. We thus need an environment which promotes competition. Also,

いくことが必要です。また，貿易の対象にならないサービス業などでは，価格差が縮まるということはありません。しかし，海外の業者の新規参入や，国内で新たに同様のサービスを提供する業者が登場することで競争が促され，価格差の縮まるケースも出てきています。もともと生産性が低いこの部門では，規制による保護もあり，生産性が上がっていないケースが多いわけです。このためにも規制緩和が重要になってきますね。

price disparity won't be narrowed through international transactions in the non-manufacturing sector, because it isn't a trade item. Foreign firms in the service industry have gotten new access to the market and by competing with domestic firms the price gap has closed to some degree. Still this sector has always had low productivity, both because it has been protected by government regulations and because it is difficult to raise productivity. This is why deregulation is important.

> ヨーロッパでは，一般大衆向け乗用車のモデルチェンジは8〜10年ごとに行われていますが，日本では何年ごとに行われているでしょうか。
>
> ① 2年　② 4年　③ 8年

ポイント

● 頻繁なモデル
　チェンジ

A：日本は資源の少ない国でありながら，製品のモデルチェンジは欧米諸国より頻繁です。今回は資源消費型生産についてお話しします。まずはクイズの答えですが，正解は②の4年です。車の種類によって差はありますが，日本では一般大衆向けの乗用車はどのメーカーも，4年ごとにフルモデルチェンジをし，2年ごとにマイナーチェンジをするというサイクルが定着してきました。アメリカでも5年から6年ですから，日本の自動車はモデルチェンジするのが非常にはやいといえます。

Q：自動車以外の製品も，そうなのですか。

A：家電製品のモデルチェンジはもっとはやいですね。通産省の調査によりますと，テレビで12〜13カ月，ビデオデッキでは9〜10カ月と，わずか1年前後で，新しい機能をつけたり，デザインを変えたりした新製品が発売されています。

● モデルチェンジ
　の理由

Q：日本ではどうしてこんなにモデルチェンジが頻繁に行われるのでしょうか。

A：まず，日本の「シェア至上主義」の経営方針が挙げられます。日本の製造業の経営陣は，市場での自社製品のシェアを拡大することを常に第1目標

Resource Consumption Production

> The models of European passenger cars are changed about every 8 to 10 years. At what interval does the model of the average Japanese car change?
>
> ① every 2 years ② every 4 years ③ every 8 years

A : While Japan is poor in resources, Japanese companies change product models more often than Western companies. In this chapter we will take up resource consumption products. The correct answer is number two, models are revised every 4 years. Of course the interval depends upon the type of car, but almost all Japanese passenger car manufacturers fully redesign their models every 4 years, and make minor changes every 2 years. Models are generally changed every 5 to 6 years in the United States. So the appearance of new model Japanese autos is quite rapid.

Q : What about products besides cars?

A : Well, **home appliances** are redesigned even more often. A survey by the Ministry of International Trade and Industry indicates that models of televisions are changed every 12 to 13 months, and video recorders every 9 to 10 months. So even within one year, new functions are added, designs are changed, and new products are put on the market.

Q : Why are **model changes** so frequent in Japan?

A : One reason is the Japanese management philosophy, which pursues market share at all costs. The management of Japanese manufacturers constantly revises models to attract consumers

と考えてきました。それで，消費者を自社製品に引き付けるための手段として，モデルチェンジを繰り返してきたのです。モデルチェンジをするためには開発費がかさみます。しかし，日本の企業は，モデルチェンジをしないで市場でのシェアを失うことよりも，多少開発費がかさんでも，モデルチェンジを行うことを選択してきたのです。それに加えて，日本人特有の性質も理由のひとつにあげられるかもしれません。日本人はもともと，ちょっとした工夫を加えて**付加価値**をつけるという作業がたいへん得意なのです。

Q：開発が進み，便利な機能がつくのはよいことですが，一方で，せっかく購入した製品がすぐ旧モデルになってしまいますね。

• 見直しの動き

A：そういうこともあって，最近行き過ぎたモデルチェンジを改めようとする動きがあります。自動車業界でモデルチェンジ期間がすこしずつ延びる傾向にありますし，家電メーカーでもワープロ，コードレス電話などを手始めとして，今まで半年に1回新製品を売り出していたのを1年に1回にする方向にあります。こうした見直しの直接の原因は，このところの不況でメーカーの収益が落ち込み，**研究費や開発費**を削減したいこと，また欧米のメーカーから競争上不公平だとの声が強かったことがあります。さらに大きな要因として，消費者側の声があります。最近行われた消費者に対するアンケート調査でも，モデルチェンジを繰り返すたびに増える機能を使いこなせないといった不満が目立っています。

Q：モデルチェンジがあまりにも頻繁に行われると，使い捨て文化につながりませんか。

A：たしかに過度に消費者を刺激することによって，まだ使えるものを捨てさせ，真新しいものを買い

to their products. The costs of developing new models add up, but even if development costs increase Japanese companies would rather pay the price of development than lose their share of the market. So they have elected to change products frequently. The particular characteristics of the Japanese people could be considered a factor as well. Japanese people have always been good at innovating and adding **extra value** to a product.

Q : It's fine to encourage development and add convenient functions, but that also means that products quickly become out-of-date after they've been purchased.

A : That is one reason why there has been a recent movement to redress the past practice of overly frequent model changes. Japanese auto manufacturers now tend to change their models more gradually. Manufacturers of home appliances, word processors, cordless telephones and other products are leaning toward changing their models once a year instead of every six months. There are several direct causes for this reconsideration. One is that Japanese manufacturers want to slash **R and D costs** because of declining profits induced by the recession. Another is that more foreign companies are complaining that this results in unfair competition. In addition, consumers are dissatisfied. One recent consumer survey found that consumers are unhappy with the frequent model changes because they can't make effective use of all the new functions.

Q : Don't frequent model changes result in throwing away things after limited use?

A : It's true that consumers are overly stimulated, and are encouraged to throw out items which are still usable, and buy new mod-

に走らせるという側面があります。新製品が安い値段でどんどん出てくるので，家庭用電気製品を修理することも少なくなりました。省資源の観点から見ても問題ですね。

● リサイクルの
取り組み

Q：資源を再利用する，リサイクルの取り組みはどうなんですか。

A：例えば日本では，自動車は重量ベースで75％程度再利用されていて，リサイクルに関していえば，比較的進んだ商品です。また古紙回収率も，'91年度で50.9％（環境庁の調査），と先進国の中では，オランダにつぐ高い水準となっています。しかし総体的に見ると，残念ながら欧米に比べて日本は，まだまだ**リサイクル問題**，ひいては**環境問題**に対して意識が低く，リサイクルへの取り組みもあまり進んだ国だとはいえないようです。

Q：具体的にいうとどういうところにそれが表れているでしょうか。

A：たとえば古紙に関していえば，**再生紙**を普段の業務に使用している企業の数は限られています。また，ヨーロッパでは洗って再利用することのできるガラスびんが主流であるのに，日本では流通や持ち運びには便利だけれども再資源化が難しいアルミ缶の割合が増えています。

Q：日本は資源が少ない国ですし，2度にわたる石油ショックを経験していますから，省エネや，リサイクルについての意識は高いのではないかと思っていましたが。

A：たしかに，節約は日本人の美徳であったし，エネルギー枯渇への危機意識が高まったこともあります。しかし，バブル経済といわれたこの間までの景気拡大でそうした危機感が薄れ，さらに，円高に伴う**1次産品価格**の下落で，**廃棄物**の回収，再利用への意欲がそがれました。そして不況になると今

els. New products are marketed at low prices, so hardly anyone repairs home appliances and such goods anymore. This is also a strain on resources.

Q : What about efforts to recycle and reprocess resources?

A : In Japan, 75% of the body weight of automobiles is now recycled. So recycling methods for cars are advanced. In 1991, 50.9% of all used paper was collected for recycling (Environment Agency survey). Among the industrialized nations, this high percentage is nearly on par with Holland. However, unfortunately, in general Japanese are far less conscious of **recycling** and **environmental issues** than their western counterparts. As a result, Japan is not very advanced in terms of recycling.

Q : What do you mean specifically?

A : For example, only a limited number of companies use **recycled paper** in their daily rountine. Also, bottles, which can be washed and reused, are very common in Europe; however, in Japan, the use of aluminium cans, which are difficult to recycle, is on the rise because they are easy to transport.

Q : Japan has few natural resources and has experienced oil crises twice, so you would think Japanese would be quite conscious about recycling.

A : It's true that frugality is a Japanese virtue. They have been concerned about exhausting resources in the past. But with the recent economic expansion, people have neglected this. People have also lost interest in collecting **waste products** and recycling because of the yen's appreciation and the decline in the prices of **primary goods**. And now that Japan has entered a

● まだ甘い法規制

度は，**再資源製品**の価格が低迷し，これらを扱う業者が不振に陥ってしまうということで，思ったほどリサイクルが進んでいるとはいえないようです。

Q：リサイクルを進めるための法律の整備についてはどうなんですか。

A：日本では，1991年を「リサイクル元年」と位置づけ，「**再生資源の利用の促進に関する法律**」いわゆるリサイクル法が施行されて，資源リサイクル促進のために事業者，消費者，国，および地方公共団体などがそれぞれの部門で果たすべき義務および，役割を方向づけました。ただし，これはあくまで努力義務の明文化にとどまっています。ヨーロッパでは自動車メーカーに対してリサイクルを義務づけたり，飲料容器としてのアルミ缶の生産販売を禁止している国もありますから，それらに比べると，日本の資源再利用に関する法規制はまだ甘いようですね。

recession, the price of **recycled products** is stagnant, and few businesses are interested in becoming involved in the field. So recycling is not as advanced as you would think.

Q : Are there any laws to encourage recycling?

A : Japan designated 1991 as the year to promote recycling. **The Law for the Promotion of Utilization of Recycled Resources** was adopted. This law described the duties of entrepreneurs, consumers, national and regional public organizations, and the roles they should play in boosting the recycling of resources. But at best, this law only stipulates that effort should be expended towards this end. European auto manufacturers are required to recycle, and some countries have even prohibited the sale and production of aluminium cans as drink containers. So by comparison, Japanese laws are rather too weak to enforce the use of recycled resources.

36 | 急がれる社会資本の整備

> 国民1人当たりの公園の面積は，ドイツのボンが
> 37.4m²，ロンドンが25.6m²，ニューヨークが23.0m²
> です。では東京は次の3つのうちのどれでしょうか。
>
> ① 2.6m²　② 10.6m²　③ 20.6m²

ポイント

A：**社会資本**といってもさまざまですが，クイズはそのひとつ，公園の広さに関するものです。正解は，①の2.6m²です。

Q：ロンドンやニューヨークの10分の1程度ですね。なぜこんなに大きな違いがあるのですか。

A：ひとつは，日本の国土が第2次世界大戦により壊滅的な打撃を受け，ほとんど一からつくり直さなければならなかったという事情がありました。もうひとつは，高度経済成長の過程で社会資本の整備は，産業関連のものに重点が置かれ，公園など生活関連のものは後回しにされてしまったからです。

● 社会資本とは

Q：話を戻して恐縮ですが，社会資本とはどういうものか，あらためて説明してもらえませんか。

A：社会資本というのは，道路や港湾，ダム，それに公園や教育施設など公共的な施設やサービスのことを指します。これらを整備することは**営利事業**では成り立ちにくいものが多く，主に国などが**公共投資**として整備します。その範囲は広く，経済の発展段階によっても，必要とされる社会資本の中身は違ってきます。

Insufficient Social Capital

> The public park area per capita in Bonn, Germany, is 37.4 square meters, 25.6 square meters in London, and 23 square meters in New York. What is the area per capita in Tokyo?
>
> ① 2.6 square meters   ② 10.6 square meters
> ③ 20.6 square meters

A : There are several kinds of what may be called **social capital** and the per capita area of parks is one of them. The correct answer to the question is number one, 2.6 square meters.

Q : That's about one-tenth of the public park area in London and New York. Why is there such a great difference?

A : One reason is that World War II delivered a devastating blow to the Japanese islands. Japan had to rebuild nearly from square one. Another reason is that during the era of high economic growth, industrial social capital was given priority, so facilities for the benefit of the public, such as parks, took a backseat to economic development.

Q : I'm going back to the beginning, but could you explain once more what social capital is?

A : Social capital refers to public facilities and services such as roads, ports, dams, parks, and educational facilities. In most cases, it is difficult to make a **profitable business** by building social capital, so mainly it is the government which constructs most of these facilities through **public works investment**. The range of investment is quite wide, and the form of social capital that is required depends on the stage of economic development.

Q：具体的にいいますと。

A：先ほども少し触れましたが，例えば工業化を進めている段階では，**工業用水**の確保や製品を運ぶための港湾や道路といった，生産に関連するものの整備が必要ですね。しかし工業化が一段落すれば，**上下水道**や教育施設，住宅，それに公園など生活関連の社会資本の整備が求められます。

Q：公園の整備状況が欧米よりも遅れていることは伺いましたが，それ以外の社会資本の整備状況はどうなんですか。

● 整備されている
　生産関連

A：総じていえば，生産，産業関連の社会資本の整備状況は，欧米の水準に近づいたが，生活関連のものの整備は，まだまだ遅れているといえます。産業関連のもので，ひとつ例を挙げれば，1年間にどのくらいの航空貨物を輸送したかを調べた**国際民間航空機関（ICAO）**の1989年のデータがあります。それによると日本は54億ton-km（1tのものを1km運ぶ単位）で，フランスの39億ton-kmやイギリスの23億ton-kmを上回っています。ただしアメリカの場合は国土が広いこともあって174億ton-kmと飛び抜けて多くなっています。

Q：生活関連の社会資本で，公園以外のものはどうなんですか。

● 遅れている生活
　関連

A：「**うさぎ小屋**」といわれたことのある住宅について見れば，1人当たりの面積は，日本は25.0m²で，61.8m²のアメリカとは比較になりませんが，イギリスの35.2m²や旧西ドイツの37.2m²と比べても，見劣りがします。また下水道の普及にしても，日本は44％にとどまり，イギリスの95％，旧西ドイツの91％，アメリカの73％に比べて大きく

Q : Could you be more specific?

A : We touched briefly on this earlier, but let's take industrialization as an example. In the early stages, production-related facilities like securing a **water supply for industry**, and roads and ports for transporting products are required. But once industrialization has the necessary facilities, then social capital to enrich the public lifestyle is required, including such things as **waterworks, sewers**, educational facilities, housing and public parks.

Q : We now know that the area of public parks is smaller than that in the United States and Europe, but what about other types of social capital?

A : In general, social capital related to production and industry is nearly on the same level as western standards, but that related to the public lifestyle lags far behind. One example of social capital related to industry is data compiled by **the International Civil Aviation Organization** (1989) concerning the annual volume of aircraft cargo. This data is measured in ton-kilometers, a unit which means one ton carried one kilometer. It showed that Japan transported 5.4 billion ton-kilometers, surpassing France with its 3.9 billion ton-kilometers and Britain with its 2.3 billion ton-kilometers. And partly because of its geographical size, America transports more than 17.4 billion ton-kilometers.

Q : What other conditions of social capital improve public lifestyle other than parks?

A : Looking at Japanese houses, once referred to as **"rabbit hutches,"** floor area per capita is only 25.0 square meters. This figure cannot even be compared to the United States where the average is 61.8 square meters. And it is still much smaller than the 35.2 square meters in Britain, and the 37.2 square meters in the former West Germany. In addition, only 44% of houses are connected to public sewage systems, which is much lower than the

● 社会資本整備
　の課題

　　　　　　　引き離されています。

Q：生活大国を目指そうとしている日本にとって，生活関連の社会資本の整備は急務といえそうですね。

A：そのとおりです。総理府が1990年に実施した世論調査によると，55％と半数以上の人が，身近なところにある道路の整備状況に不満があると答え，40％前後の人が，**レクレーション施設**や**福祉施設**の整備状況に不満があると答えています。

Q：それでは日本は，こうした社会資本を今後どのように整備していこうとしているのですか。

A：通産大臣の諮問機関である**産業構造審議会**は，1993年11月，産業構造の改革に関する中間報告書をまとめましたが，その中で「社会資本の整備は，社会の高齢化が深刻にならない'90年代にできるだけ拡充すること」を求めています。そして具体的には，高齢者向け**公営住宅**の建設など高齢化社会に備えた対策や，コンピューターのネットワークづくりといった情報化関係など，生活関連分野の整備を重点的に行うよう提言しています。

Q：社会資本の整備は内需拡大にもつながるので，貿易黒字の解消を求める欧米各国の要求にも応えることになりますね。さて整備を進めるにあたっての課題といえば。

A：これまでは，施設すなわちハードの整備に重点が置かれてきましたが，今後は，ソフト面の整備に力を入れることが必要だと思います。

Q：大きなホールを造ったのはいいが，それを十分に使いこなすことができないという話をよく耳にしますものね。

● 民間活用で
　ソフトの整備を

A：ええ。もうひとつ大事なことは，ソフト面での整備を進める際に，**民間部門**の活力をどう利用して

rate in Britain (95%), the former West Germany (91%), and the United States (73%).

Q : For Japan, which is trying to improve the quality of people's lives, increasing this type of social capital is the most urgent task.

A : That's right. A survey by the Prime Minister's Office in 1990 indicated that 55% of the population is dissatisfied with the road conditions in their neighborhoods. And around 40% felt that the **recreation** and **welfare facilities** were unsatisfactory.

Q : How will Japan build up this social capital in the future?

A : **The Industrial Structure Council,** which is an advisory organ to MITI, compiled a midterm report on industrial structure reform in November 1993. The report advised that social capital should be expanded as much as possible during the 1990s, before society faces the serious problems as the average age of the population increases. To be specific, the council suggested that Japan give priority to lifestyle-related investment, such as **public housing** for the elderly and the creation of a computer network to expand the information industry.

Q : Building social capital will cause domestic demand to expand, so this will help respond to western demands that Japan slash the trade surplus. So what are the challenges facing such improvement?

A : Until recently, Japan has emphasized hard social capital, such as facilities. But in the future, it will have to make efforts to learn how to fully utilize these facilities.

Q : It has often been said that it's fine to build great facilities, such as concert halls, but people don't know how to take full advantage of them.

A : Yes, and another important item is how to utilize the vitality of the **private sector** in this development. Japan's **industrial**

いくかです。これまでの**産業基盤**の整備は政府主導で行われてきましたが，政府は生活関連分野の整備はあまり得意ではない。そこで民間のノウハウをいかに生かすかが重要になってきます。最後にもう一言つけ加えるならば，生活関連に重点を置くことは必要なのですが，だからといって産業関連の整備を怠ってはいけません。アメリカでは，道路や橋のメインテナンスを怠ったために閉鎖される道路や橋が出てきてしまい，それが経済の成長の足を引っ張ったといわれています。高齢化社会が到来すれば，公共投資の財源は今よりも苦しくなるし，施設の維持補修も増えてきます。その意味では，公共投資の配分の適正化をはかり，効率的な整備をすることが一段と必要になってくるでしょう。

foundation has been built under the direction of the government. But the government is not skilled at fortifying lifestyle-related social capital. This is why it is vital to tap the skills of the private sector. In conclusion, I want to add that it's important to give priority to social capital to enrich the national lifestyle, but that does not mean that we can slack off on investing in industrial social capital. The United States has neglected to maintain its roads and bridges, so many have been closed down. This has shackled economic growth. With the rise in the average age of the population, budget resources for public investment will be tightened and more facilities will require maintenance and repair. So in this sense, it will become even more important to allocate public works investment properly, and continue to improve existing facilities efficiently.

37 | 低い食糧自給率

日本の穀物自給率は低いといわれますが，1992年の
自給率は何％だったでしょうか。

① 29%　② 49%　③ 79%

A：アメリカは世界最大の農産物輸出国ですが，日本
は世界最大の農産物輸入国です。さて，クイズの
正解は，①の29%です。

Q：それにしても低いですね。

● 各国の穀物
自給率

A：他の国の数字を見ると，アメリカは180%，イギ
リスは110%，旧西ドイツは95%になっており，
日本の自給率の低さが目立ちます。また，ＯＥＣ
Ｄの調査によると，穀物のほかに，肉や野菜，魚
や乳製品なども含めた**食用農産物**の自給率で見て
も65%と，かなり低いといえますね。ほぼ100%
自給しているコメや，ほかのわずかな農産物を除
けば，かなりの部分を輸入に頼っています。乳製
品や卵の自給率は，85%からほぼ100%になって
いますが，これも，**飼料用穀物**のほとんどを輸入
に頼っていることを考えれば，自給率が高いとは
とてもいえません。

● 食糧自給率が
低い理由

Q：なぜ，日本の食糧自給率はこんなに低いのでしょ
うか。

A：ふたつのことが指摘できます。ひとつは，1960年
代から始まった高度経済成長による急速な**工業化**
です。農産物を作るよりは工業製品を作るのに適
した産業構造に転換していったわけですね。この

Japan's Low Rate of Self-sufficiency in Food Products

> **Japan is said to produce little of the grain it consumes. What percentage of Japan's grain supply was grown domestically in 1992?**
>
> ① 29%　② 49%　③ 79%

A : The United States is the world's largest exporter of agricultural products and Japan is the world's largest importer. The correct answer to the quiz is number one, 29%.

Q : That's very low, isn't it?

A : Yes it is. Compared to the United States with 180%, Britain at 110% and former West Germany at 95%, the figure for Japan seems extremely low. According to an OECD survey, the supply of total **agricultural foodstuffs** is quite low as well, at around 65%. These include meat, vegetables, fish and dairy products as well as grain. Excluding rice, for which Japan is nearly 100% self-sufficient, and a few other agricultural products, Japan has to rely heavily on imports. Japan supplies 85% to 100% of its own dairy products and eggs. But when you consider that it has to import almost all of the **grain for animal feed**, that figure doesn't seem so high.

Q : Why does Japan produce so little of its food supply?

A : There are two major reasons. One is the rapid **industrializion** which began in the high growth period in the 1960s. Japan converted its industrial structure to one suited to producing industrial goods rather than agricultural goods. There was a huge flow

過程で，労働力として農村から都市へ人口が急激に流入し，農業離れが進みました。全労働人口に占める農業人口の割合は，1950年の45％から，1990年には3％にまで落ちています。当然，農産物の輸入は増え，その分だけ食糧の自給率は下がりました。もうひとつは，コメの消費の落ち込みです。日本人の生活スタイルが西洋化し，食生活が多様化するとともに，コメ離れが進んだためです。例えば，高度経済成長が始まった1960年代の初めには，日本人1人当たりの年間のコメ消費量は120kgだったのに対し，今ではおよそ70kgにまで落ちています。

● コメの消費と
　食糧自給率

Q：コメの消費が減ることと食糧の**自給率**が下がることと，どういう関係があるのですか。

A：コメの消費が減れば，ほかの穀物の消費が増えますね。しかし，これらの農産物の自給率はもともと低く，ほとんどが輸入です。例えば，1992年の自給率は，小麦が12％，大豆が4％，といったところです。消費が増えた分だけ輸入が増えることになります。食糧全体の自給率はそれだけ下がるわけです。

Q：ところで，食糧のほとんどを輸入に頼りながら，コメだけは自給を維持してきたということですが，これはどうしてなのですか。

A：コメの100％自給というのは，政策的に維持されてきたといってもいいと思います。なんといってもコメは日本人の主食ですし，コメに対する愛着もあります。実際，高度成長が始まる前までは，日本人のカロリー摂取量の60〜70％は，コメでまかなわれてきました。コメの自給を維持する制度として，**食糧管理制度**があります。政府がコメを生産農家から買い上げ，それを消費者に売り渡すものです。

● 食糧管理制度の
　問題点

276

of labor into the cities from agricultural areas, and the population tended to move away from agriculture. The percentage of the labor force employed in agriculture dropped from 45% in 1950 to 3% in 1990. When agricultural imports rose, Japan's self-sufficiency in food declined correspondingly. The other reason is the fall in rice consumption. The Japanese lifestyle has become westernized, leading to a more diverse diet and a movement away from rice. For example, at the start of the 1960s, annual rice consumption per capita was 120 kilograms, but now average consumption has dropped to around 70 kilograms.

Q : Is there a relationship between the decline in rice consumption and the decrease in food **self-sufficiency rate**?

A : If the rice consumption falls, consumption of other grains rises. But Japan has never produced a large volume of these other agricultural products, so most of them are imported. In 1992, for example, Japan produced only 12% of its wheat and 4% of its soybeans. An increase in consumption, therefore, results in a rise in imports, which causes a drop in net self-sufficiency.

Q : By the way, why has Japan maintained self-sufficiency in rice, when it depends so heavily on imports for almost all its other food supplies?

A : For a long time, the aim of government policy was total self-sufficiency in rice. Rice is the staple of the Japanese people, so they are very sensitive about rice. Prior to the high growth period, rice provided 60% to 70% of the caloric intake of the Japanese people. Japan established a **food control system** to maintain self-sufficiency in rice. The government buys rice from producers and then sells it to consumers.

Q：この制度はいつできたのですか。

A：これは戦時中につくられたもので，もともとはコメの安定供給を目指すものでした。この制度は，戦後まもなくの食糧難の時代には，米価を安定させ，物価を安定させるのに貢献しました。しかしその後増産が続き，コメ余りの状態になりました。コメが余っている状態でも，政府は農家からコメを高く買ってきたわけですから，食糧管理制度は，いまや農家の収入を保障するという意味合いの方が強くなってしまいました。

Q：コメの消費が低下しているのにコメの生産農家を保護するというのは，理屈に合わないのではないですか。

A：そうですね。現在，日本のコメは国際価格に比べて数倍高くなっています。というのも，日本には零細農家が多く，効率的な大規模経営ができないため，どうしてもコスト高になってしまうからです。それと，政策的に保護されているために，農家の間で生産性を上げようという刺激となるものが失われているという側面もあります。

Q：ところで，輸入を認めず100％自給を維持してきたコメも，ついに部分自由化をせざるを得なくなりましたね。

● 市場開放と
日本の農業

A：そうなんです。1993年の暮れに決着した**ガットのウルグアイラウンド交渉**で，日本はコメ市場の部分開放に合意しました。こうした中で，日本のコメ作りも，国際的な競争のもとで生産性を上げなければならないところまできています。

Q：日本のコメが国際競争に負けて衰退し，食糧の自給率がさらに下がる心配はありませんか。

A：これについてはふたつの見方があります。ひとつは，安い外国の農産物が無制限に入ってくると，

Q : When was this system introduced?

A : The system was created during the war, so its original purpose was to secure a stable rice supply. The system helped maintain stable supplies and consumer prices during the food crisis immediately after the war. But soon rice production increased, and resulted in a surplus. The government still bought rice from farmers at a high price even though there was a surplus. So the system came to mean an income guarantee for rice farmers.

Q : But isn't it irrational to protect rice farmers even though rice consumption is falling?

A : No, it's not. The price of rice is several times higher than international prices. Most Japanese rice farmers produce on a small scale, so they can't operate as efficiently as large-scale farmers. This pushes up costs. Also, rice farmers have lost their incentive to boost productivity because they are protected by the government.

Q : Although Japan has been 100% self-sufficient in rice, Japan at last had to partially liberalize its rice market.

A : As you know, Japan agreed to partially liberalize its rice market at **the Uruguay Round of the GATT negotiations** at the end of 1993. The time has come for Japan to boost productivity based on international competition.

Q : But if Japan loses out in international competition in the rice market, won't the rice farmers be weakened, and produce even less of Japan's rice supply?

A : Well, there are two arguments. One is the food security argument. These people believe that if imports of inexpensive agri-

ポイント

日本の農業は壊滅状態になるというものです。そうなれば，何か事が起こった場合に，食糧の調達が困難になり，安全保障上問題だというものです。食糧安保論ともいえるもので，こうした立場をとる人は，市場を全面的に開放して，農産物を無制限に輸入することには反対しています。もうひとつは，これとはまったく逆のもので，外国との競争にさらされれば，日本の農業は生産性が上がり，近代的な産業へ脱皮していくというものです。この一例として，オレンジの輸入自由化により，日本のみかん農家の生産性が上がったことを指摘する人がいます。しかしそれ以前に問題なのは，農家の深刻な後継者不足です。1993年，高校を卒業して農業を継いだ人は，全国でわずか1700人余りでした。農業は生産性が低く，ほかの産業に比べると収入も低いために，若い人を引き付ける魅力がないのです。アメリカやイギリスも工業国なのに，食糧の自給をしています。これは，**農業人口は減ったけれども生産性が高くなっているから**です。今，日本の農業は大きな曲がり角に来ています。食糧の自給率を上げるためには，どうしたら生産性を上げ，農業を魅力的なものにできるかを考えなければならないと思います。そうしなければ，後継者も育たないわけですから。

cultural products are completely unrestricted, they will destroy Japanese farmers. Then if a crisis occurs, it will be difficult to procure food, leading to a security problem. The opposing argument is that Japanese farmers will boost productivity through international competition, and transform themselves into a modern industry. One supporting argument for this is that some Japanese tangerine farmers increased productivity when orange imports were liberalized. But even before all this, there is a serious shortage of labor and successors in the farming industry. In 1993 only 1,700 high school graduates went into farming in Japan. Productivity is low, and wages are lower than in other industries, so young people are not attracted to farming. The United States and Britain are able to maintain self-sufficiency in food even though they are industrial nations. This is because they have been able to boost productivity, even though the **agricultural population** has decreased. Japanese agriculture is now at a crossroads. They will have to think about how to boost productivity and make farming more attractive to young people in order to raise self-sufficiency. If they don't, they won't be able to find successors.

38 産業公害から生活公害へ

ある国際会議がまとめた報告書によると，過去90万年の間の地球の平均気温の変化の幅は，いちばん変化が大きかったときでも，およそ2万年かけて5℃程度でした。最近，二酸化炭素などの増加による「地球温暖化」が問題になっていますが，さて今の状態をこのまま放置しておくと地球全体の平均気温は21世紀末までにどのように変化すると，この報告書は予測しているでしょうか。

① 100年程度では地球全体の平均気温に変化はない。

② 平均気温が3℃上昇することがありうる。

③ 平均気温が6℃上昇することがありうる。

ポイント

A：今や環境汚染は地球的規模になりました。クイズに出てきた報告書は，国連環境計画と世界気象機関が共同で開いているIPCC「**気候変動に関する政府間会議**」が，1990年8月にまとめたものです。正解は②の3℃上昇です。

Q：3℃気温が上がると，どういう影響が出るのですか。
A：北極や南極の氷が解けて，地球の海水面が65cmも上昇してしまうということです。

From Industrial Pollution to Household Pollution

Research on changes in average global temperatures over the past 900,000 years has been reported at an international conference. The greatest change in a specified period was reported to be a five degree Centigrade fluctuation during a 20,000-year period. Among the causes mentioned for "global warming," is the increase in the concentration of carbon dioxide and other gases in the atmosphere. By how much did the report predict the average global temperature would change by the end of the 21st century if no action is taken?

① There will be no change in the average global temperature over a mere 100-year period.
② The average temperature could rise by three degrees Celsius.
③ The average temperature could rise by six degrees Celsius.

A : Environmental pollution has developed into a global issue. The figures used in the quiz were reported in August 1990 at **the Intergovernment Panel on Climate Change** (IPCC), organized by the United Nations Environment Program and the World Meteorological Organization. The answer is number two, the average temperature could rise by three degrees Celsius.

Q : How will that affect us?

A : The ice caps at the North and South Poles will melt and the level of the oceans of the world will rise 65 centimeters.

283

● 日本の公害の
　歴史

Q：そうなると低い陸地では埋没するところも出てく
　るでしょうね。さて経済発展と環境問題というのは
　常に背中合わせですが，日本の場合，環境問題は
　どのようなプロセスをたどってきたのでしょうか。

A：東洋の奇跡とも呼ばれた日本の高度経済成長は，
　国民の所得を高め，快適な生活を可能にしました。
　しかしその反面で，多くのひずみをもたらしまし
　た。すなわち「公害」です。1960年代の終わりご
　ろから1970年代の初めごろ，そろそろ高度経済成
　長が終わりを告げるころですが，気がつくと日本
　列島は工場からでる黒い煙と，魚も住めない汚れ
　た水でいっぱいになっていました。

Q：深刻な公害病が発生し，裁判に持ち込まれたケー
　スもありましたね。

A：そうです。世界的に有名になってしまった水俣病
　も，そのひとつです。工場廃水に含まれる有機水
　銀が魚類を介して人体に入り，四肢の麻痺や言語
　障害など重い中毒症状をひき起こしたもので，国
　から水俣病であると認定された人だけでも2000人
　を超えました。ほかにも**カドミウム中毒**や大気汚
　染によるぜんそくなど，全国各地で深刻な公害病
　が発生しました。

Q：そうしたひどい公害も，今ではだいぶ改善された
　ようですが。

A：公害問題に対しては，規制の強化，企業による公
　害防止のための投資あるいは低公害化のための技
　術開発など，さまざまな対策がとられました。ま
　た1970年代の石油ショックをきっかけに，鉄鋼や
　石油化学など重化学工業中心だった産業構造が，
　エレクトロニクスやサービス産業中心へと変化し
　たこともあって，公害源となっていた工場が減り，

Q : In that case, low-lying areas will be submerged. Economic development and environmental issues have always been inseparable. How did environmental problems develop in Japan?

A : Japan's rapid economic growth has been called the "Oriental miracle." This growth raised the level of national income and made it possible for the Japanese people to live a comfortable life. On the other hand, the development distorted Japanese society in many ways. One problem is pollution. From the end of the 1960s until the beginning of the 1970s, at the end of the high growth period, people finally noticed that black smoke from factories had covered the islands, and that water ecosystems were so dirty fish could not live there.

Q : Pollution also caused several serious illnesses, and several cases were brought to court.

A : That's right. Minamata disease is one of such cases. Factory waste water containing a high concentration of organic mercury contaminated fish, which were then ingested by humans. It caused a terrible poisoning, which led to such problems as paralysis of the limbs and speech impediments. More than 2,000 people have been officially recognized by the government as having Minamata disease. There are other serious diseases in various parts of the country, such as **cadmium poisoning** and asthma caused by air pollution.

Q : Serious pollution seems to have been dealt with.

A : Well, it's true that various measures have been taken to reduce pollution. The government has established tight regulations, and companies have invested in pollution prevention systems or developed low-pollution technology. Since the oil crisis in the 1970s, the industrial structure, based on the heavy industries such as steel and petrochemicals, has shifted to a focus on service and high-technology industries. The horrible pollution of the

● 産業公害から
　生活公害へ

● 変わる公害対策

かつてのような深刻な産業公害はやわらいだといえます。ところがその後，従来とは異なった次元での環境汚染が問題になってきました。

Q：といいますと。

A：従来の公害といえば，工場からの**煤煙**や**廃水**などが主な原因でしたが，その後問題になったのは，一般家庭から出されるゴミや汚水，それに自動車の排気ガスなど生活公害ともいえるものです。例えば廃棄物の場合，工場や事業所から出る産業廃棄物は1年間に4億 t 近く（1990年度）と多いことは多いのですが，一般の家庭からも5000万 t を超えるゴミが出ており，その種類が多様なこともあって処理はやっかいです。

Q：私たちにも責任があるということですね。

A：そうなんです。現在問題になっている環境汚染は，ゴミの問題にしろ，**地球温暖化**にしろ，なにか特定の大きな公害の発生源があって，それを取り除いて時間がたてば状況が改善されるというかつての産業公害とは違って，私たちの生活のあちこちにその原因が潜んでいるのです。より快適な生活を求めた結果，使い捨てのプラスチックの容器が増えてゴミになる，自動車に乗ると二**酸化窒素**が排出されて**酸性雨**を降らせる。しかも，その雨は国境を越えてよその国の人の頭の上にも降るといった具合です。

Q：ということは，対策の方も従来とは変わらなければいけませんね。

A：そうです。初期のころの対策は，公害が激しい地域だけを対象に，しかも工場など特定の排出源に注目して煤煙や汚水の排出基準を設けて規制するものでした。しかしそれでは，工場の数が増えてしまえば環境は悪化するし，自動車の**排気ガス**による汚染も防ぐことはできません。このため，そ

past has been eased somewhat. But following that, environmental pollution has become apparent in a different dimension.

Q : What is that?

A : **Black smoke** and **waste water** from factories was once the main cause of pollution. But these days the problems also include garbage and sewerage from ordinary households, automobile exhaust and other such things from our daily lives. Waste products from factories and industry, for example, amounted to approximately 400 million tons in 1990. Household waste amounted to 50 million tons. Household garbage is difficult to dispose of because of its variety.

Q : We have to take responsibility for that, too.

A : That's right. The current environmental issues, whether garbage or **global warming**, come from a variety of factors in our lifestyle. These problems are different from industrial pollution, which will disappear once the source has been remedied. Now the source is our lifestyle. Our demand for a more comfortable lifestyle has resulted in disposable plastic containers, which increase the volume of garbage. And the **nitrogen dioxide** produced by our cars causes **acid rain**. Moreover, that acid rain cannot be stopped at national borders.

Q : That means that measures should be different from those of the past.

A : That's right. Earlier measures focused on only severely damaged areas, regulating specifically only effluent and emission standards of factories. But these measures could not prevent the circumstances from growing worse nor could they eliminate **exhaust gas** pollution. Thereafter, the government extended measures to cover the entire nation and to regulate emissions

の後の公害対策は，対象地域を全国に広げるとともに，規制物質も自動車の排気ガスなどに対象を広げました。また一定の地域における汚染物質の総量を規制する総量規制という新しい手法も導入しました。さらに環境に影響を及ぼす恐れのある大規模な事業を行うときには，事前に**環境アセスメント**，つまり環境影響評価を行うなど環境汚染を未然に防ぐ手だてもとられるようになりました。

● 地球規模の
　汚染へ

Q：ところで冒頭のクイズにもあったように，今や環境汚染は地球規模にまで広がってきたということですね。

A：そのいちばん象徴的な例が，二酸化炭素の増加に伴う地球温暖化の問題なんですね。環境汚染が地球規模になれば，国際的な取り組みが不可欠です。その意味で注目されるのは，1992年6月にブラジルで開かれた初めての**地球サミット（環境と開発に関する国連会議）**です。

● 地球サミットの
　成果と課題

Q：では最後に地球サミットの成果と課題について説明してください。

A：地球サミットでは，「各国は自国の資源を開発する権利を有すると同時に，他国の環境に損害を与えないようにする責任がある」という原則を盛り込んだ**リオ宣言**を採択。またこの宣言を実行するための行動計画「**アジェンダ21**」も採択しました。地球温暖化の対策としては，二酸化炭素の排出量を1990年レベルに戻すことを目指した「**気候変動枠組み条約**」にも150以上の参加国が署名しました。しかしこうした成果があった一方で，**環境保全**に重点を置く先進国と経済開発を重視する発展途上国との立場の違いは依然として大きく，今後はこうした立場の違いを克服しながら，参加各国がいかに行動計画を実行に移していくかが課題といえます。

as well. Gross volume controls were established for specific areas to regulate the gross volume of contaminants. Furthermore, when one wants to start up a major business that might have a negative effect on the environment, they must to submit an **environmental assessment** showing what measures they intend to take to prevent pollution from occurring.

Q : You mentioned earlier that environmental pollution has become globalized.

A : The most characteristic instance of this is the problem of the rise in global temperatures resulting from the increase in the amount of **carbon dioxide.** Such global issues require international cooperation. That is why **the Earth Summit (the United Nations Conference on Environment and Development)** held in Brazil in June 1992 drew such attention.

Q : In closing, could you explain the results and continuing issues addressed at the summit?

A : The nations at the Earth Summit issued **the Rio Declaration,** the principle of which states that every nation has the right to develop its own resources but at the same time has a responsibility to avoid damaging the environment of other nations. **"Agenda 21"** was also adopted as a means of carrying out the declaration. More than 150 participating nations signed a treaty, agreeing to **the Framework Convention on Climate Change,** which aims at reducing the amount of carbon dioxide emissions to the levels of the year 1990. Despite such results, there is still a big gap between advanced nations which give priority to **environmental protection** and developing nations which give priority to economic development. It remains to be seen how well participating nations will actually overcome this difference in implementing "Agenda 21."

情報化社会の到来とともに日本では，コンピュータ
ーによって新聞の記事や統計データなどの検索サー
ビスを行う民間のデータベース・サービス業が増え
ています。1991年に通産省が行った調査によると，
東京には全国の40％に当たる179の事業所がありまし
た。さてクイズは，これらの東京の事業所が上げて
いる売上高は，日本全体の何％を占めているでしょ
うか。

　① 63%　② 83%　③ 93%

- 東京への一極
  集中

A：東京への**一極集中**はますます進み，さまざまな弊
　害をもたらしています。クイズは，情報について
　も東京への集中がいかに進んでいるかを示すもの
　で，正解は②の83％です。東京は，日本の政治，
　経済の中心地であり，最近では国際都市としての
　様相も強めています。このため情報も東京に集中
　していることから，**データベース・サービス業**と
　いった業種が，成立しやすい環境にあることを示
　しています。

Q：東京への集中度を示すデータとして，ほかにはど
　んなものがありますか。

A：まず人口の集中度ですが，東京都およびそれに隣
　接する3県を首都圏ととらえて見てみますと，面
　積は日本全体のわずか3.1％にもかかわらず，人口
　は3188万人と4分の1を占めています。また**事業所**
　の数だけを見ると，東京は全国の10％程度で人口
　比に見合っていますが，大企業の**本社**の数を見て

Centralization

> With the advent of the information society in Japan, private database services which provide newspaper articles and searches for statistical data are growing. In a 1991 survey, the Ministry of International Trade and Industry found that 179 offices or 40% of all database offices were located in Tokyo. What percentage of nationwide accounts do the net sales of these offices in Tokyo amount to?
>
>   ① 63%   ② 83%   ③ 93%

A : **Concentration** in Tokyo has grown stronger and the result has been detrimental. The quiz shows just how completely information is concentrated in Tokyo. The answer is number two, 83%. Tokyo is the heart of the Japanese government and economy, and it has been growing more international recently. This is why information is centered in Tokyo, and this is also why it is a good environment to set up businesses in the **database service industry**.

Q : What other data show the high centralization in Tokyo?

A : First of all, there is the population. Tokyo and its three neighboring prefectures are considered the greater metropolitan area, in land area only 3.1% of the Japanese archipelago. But 31.88 million people, one-quarter of the total population, live in this area. About 10% of all **corporate offices** are located here, which is roughly in correspondence with the population. But

みますと，**上場企業**1641社のうち968社と，大企業の本社の59%が東京に集中しています。

● 各国の状況は

Q：外国の場合はどうなんですか。

A：東京のように政治もビジネスもと，いろいろなものが集中している都市は，あまりないようです。たとえばアメリカの場合は，政治の中心地がワシントンなのに対して，商業，金融の中心はニューヨークと分かれていますよね。**中央官庁**の分散が進んでいるのは，旧西ドイツです。議会や大統領府はボン，最高裁判所はカールスルーエ，中央銀行はフランクフルト，産業関係の官庁はハンブルクとミュンヘンなどと分散しています。

● 東京への集中は
　いつから

Q：東京への一極集中はいつごろから起きたのですか。

A：最近始まったことではなく，近世以降，東京（江戸）が日本の政治的，経済的中心になったことから起きています。一極集中は，ある程度までは経済的に効率的であるというメリットがありました。しかし，特に1980年代後半になって，過度の集中が地価の急激な上昇をもたらすようになると，一極集中の弊害の面が強く意識されはじめたのです。

Q：第18章「通勤地獄」のテーマのときに触れましたが，地価の急騰によって東京のサラリーマンが家を持つことは，ますます難しくなりましたね。

A：そうです。そのために東京のサラリーマンは，長距離通勤を余儀なくされているわけです。そのほかにも，**自治体**が**公共用地**を取得することが難しくなったり，企業がオフィスを確保することも難しくなるなど，経済面でも弊害が出てきました。

Q：ではその対策ですが，地方分散は進んでいるんですか。

when we look at the number of **headquarters** of major businesses, the statistics show that 968 of the 1,641 **listed corporations**, or 59%, are headquartered in Tokyo.

Q : What about cities in other countries?

A : There do not seem to be many cities like Tokyo where both government and business are centered. In the United States, for example, Washington is the heart of the government, but trade and finance companies are centered in New York. And the former West Germany has made progress in distributing the **central government offices** to regional areas. The Parliament and President's Office is located in Bonn, the Supreme Court is in Karlsruhe, the Bundesbank (Central Bank) in Frankfurt, and the government offices related to industry are in Hamburg and Munich.

Q : When did this over concentration in Tokyo begin?

A : The population concentration is no recent phenomenon, but followed the centralization of political and business activities in Tokyo (Edo) at the advent of the modern period. It was advantageous for quite some time for businesses to concentrate in Tokyo both for reasons of economics and efficiency. But since the latter half of the 1980s, the extreme concentration of population has rapidly pushed up land prices, and people have become more aware of the problems of overconcentration.

Q : As we mentioned previously in Chapter 18 "Commuting Hell," soaring land prices have made it more difficult for the average worker to own his own home in Tokyo, haven't they?

A : Yes, that's true. And because of this, many workers are forced to commute long distances. In addition, there are economic disadvantages. For example, **local governments** have problems obtaining **land for public works projects**, and companies have a hard time finding office space.

Q : Are any measures being taken to promote decentralization?

● 進まぬ地方分散

A：結論を先にいってしまえば，全然進んでいません。首都を東京から他のところに移すべきだという遷都論は，早くは1960年代からありました。そして地価高騰が問題になった後の1992年には，**国土庁の首都機能移転問題懇談会**が中間報告をまとめ，新首都建設の提言を行いました。しかし，どこに建設すべきかという肝心な点は決まりませんでした。

Q：遷都とまではいかなくても，先ほどのドイツのように，中央官庁の一部を分散させるという方法がありますが。

A：しかしこの首都機能の一部移転について中央官庁は，総論では賛成だが，実際にどの機関を移転させるかという各論の段階になると，反対意見が出てまとまりません。

Q：民間企業の対応はどうですか。

A：高度経済成長を達成した1960年代後半から1970年代にかけて，民間企業は公害問題を解決するため，あるいは低賃金労働者を求めるため，都心にあった工場を周辺地域や地方に移転させるケースがありました。しかし民間企業にとって本社は，情報の収集，官庁の許認可，営業活動の効率の点からいって，東京にある方が基本的に有利なため，中央官庁が地方に移転するなど大きな変化がない限り，東京を離れることはなさそうです。

● 今後の見通しは

Q：さて，地方への分散の，今後の見通しはどうなるのでしょうか。

A：遷都や中央官庁の移転がなかなか難しいとなれば，現実的に可能な対策のひとつとして，地方自治体へ権限を委譲する方法があると思います。首相の諮問機関である**第3次臨時行政改革推進審議会**は，1993年10月にまとめた最終答申案の中で，**地方分権**の推進を掲げました。これを受けて政府も，1年後をメドに，まず地方分権への手順など

A : In short, decentralization has not been carried out. Suggestions to move the capital out of Tokyo were made as early as the 1960s. In 1992 when overinflated land prices had become a serious problem, **the Round-table Committee on the Issue of Capital Relocation** formed by **the National Land Agency** proposed building a new capital in their mid-term report. But there is no specific plan about where to build it.

Q : However, even if the capital itself were not moved, some of the metropolitan government offices could be dispersed to different areas, as in Germany.

A : Overall, all central government organs are in agreement that metropolitan offices should be decentralized. But they are at odds on a practical level as to which offices should be moved.

Q : What about the reaction from private companies?

A : Towards the end of the high-growth period, from the late 1960s to the early 1970s, some corporations moved their plants to outlying areas to help reduce pollution and lower labor costs. But it is advantageous for private companies to be headquartered in Tokyo to gather information, to obtain government permits, and to make their sales more efficient. They won't be able to leave Tokyo unless central government offices move outside of Tokyo.

Q : What are the prospects for decentralization?

A : As long as it seems difficult to actually move the capital or central government offices to outlying areas, a more realistic solution would be to transfer more power to local governments. **The Third Provisional Council for Promotion of Administrative Reform**, an advisory body to the Prime Minister, in its final report in October 1993, proposed just such a **transfer of power to local governments**. In response, a year later the govern-

を盛り込んだ「地方分権大綱」を策定し，その後，地方分権推進に関する基本的な法律の制定を目指すことになりました。またこのほかの対策としては，時間はかかりますが，空港や通信施設など地方の基盤整備を進めることによって，地方への分散がしやすくなるような条件を整えることが重要だと思います。

ment began to work out an outline for the transfer of power, including suggestions for how to prepare for such a transfer. They then tried to establish a basic law for promoting the decentralization of power. Other measures, although they may take time, are necessary to develop the necessary infrastructure such as airports and communications networks which would faciliate a move to outlying areas.

40 | 高齢化社会への対応

> 65歳以上の高齢者が日本の全人口の中で占める割合
> は，1993年には13.5%でしたが，およそ30年後の
> 2025年には，この割合は何%になると予測されてい
> ますか。
>
> ① 16%　② 21%　③ 26%

A：日本は世界一の長寿国です。経済成長の果実が社
会に行きわたり，国民生活も豊かになってきまし
た。そして，それとともにやってきたのが，社会
の高齢化によるさまざまな問題です。さてクイズ
の答えですが，正解は③の26%です。

● 急速な高齢化の
要因

Q：4人に1人が老人というわけですか。大変な高齢化
社会になるわけですね。どうしてこんなに高齢化
が急速に進んでいるのでしょうか。

A：ひとつは，医学の進歩によって**平均寿命**が長くな
ったことです。厚生省の1992年のデータで見ると，
日本人の平均寿命は，女性が82.2歳，男性が76.1
歳で，男女ともに世界一です。それともうひとつ
の理由として，出生率の低下が挙げられます。1
人の女性が一生に何人の子供を産むかを示すのが
合計特殊出生率ですが，日本では1992年には1.50
まで下がっています。生まれる子供が少なくなり，
長生きする人が増えれば，当然，高齢者の割合は
増えていくことになります。

Q：人口の高齢化は日本だけの問題なのですか。

● 先進国の現状

A：これは先進工業国共通の問題です。むしろ社会の
高齢化という意味では，ヨーロッパの国々の方が

An Aging Society

> In 1993, 13.5% of the Japanese population was over 65
> years old. Thirty years from now in the year 2025, what
> percentage of the population will be over 65 years old?
>
> ① 16%   ② 21%   ③ 26%

A : The Japanese have the longest life-expectancy rate in the world.
    Economic growth has brought prosperity but also the problems
    of a graying population. The correct answer is number three,
    26%.

Q : Does that mean one in every four people will be a senior citizen?
    That's a very high average age for a society. Why is the age of
    the population rising so rapidly?

A : One reason is that advances in medical care have lengthened the
    average life-span of the Japanese. According to the data from
    1992 (the Ministry of Health and Welfare) the Japanese have the
    longest life-span in the world, with women at 82.2 years and men
    at 76.1 years. Another reason is the dropping **total fertility
    rate**, which shows how many children a woman has during her
    lifetime. This birthrate has fallen to below 1.50 in 1992, so while
    fewer children are being born, more people are living to an
    advanced age. Naturally, the average age of the population is ris-
    ing.

Q : Is this problem limited to Japan?

A : No, all industrialized nations face this problem. In fact, Euro-
    peans now have a higher average age than the Japanese. Let's

進んでいます。例えば，60歳以上の老人の全人口に占める割合を比べてみますと，1991年の時点で，スウェーデンがトップで22.8%，ノルウェーやベルギー，イタリア，イギリスとみな20%を上回っていますが，日本は17.2%で，世界で19位です（アメリカ商務省）。しかし，問題なのは，日本の人口の高齢化が異常な速さで進んでいるということです。

Q：どのくらいの速さなのですか。

A：全人口の中で65歳以上の高齢者の数が，7%以上を占める社会を**高齢化社会**といい，これが14%を超える社会を**高齢社会**と呼んでいます。この65歳以上の老人の割合が，7%からその2倍の14%になるのに，フランスでは115年，スウェーデンでは85年，イギリスでは45年かかりました。しかし，日本はわずか24年でそうなると予測されています。冒頭でご紹介したように，1993年の時点で13.5%でしたから，日本は今，高齢社会の入り口に立っているといえます。

● 高齢化社会の
  問題点

Q：高齢者が増えてくると，どんな問題が出てきますか。

A：いちばん大きな問題は，高齢者の生活をどう支えていくかということでしょう。高齢者が増え続ける一方で，15歳から65歳までのいわゆる**生産年齢人口**は，相対的に減り続けます。当然，社会の負担は増えます。

● 年金の負担増

Q：**年金**など**社会保障**の負担のことですね。

A：ええ。例えば，サラリーマンの多くが加入している**厚生年金**ですが，その受給者の数は，1977年のおよそ330万人から，わずか14年後の1991年には1055万人と，3倍以上に増えています。受給者の数は，今後さらに増えていきます。これは働く人の負担が増えていくことを意味します。

compare data for the percentages of the population over 60 in 1991. Sweden was on top with 22.8%, followed by Norway, Belgium, Italy and Britain which were all over 20%. In contrast, Japan was 19th in the world at 17.2% (U.S. Department of Commerce). But Japan's problem is that the age of its population is rising very rapidly.

Q : How fast is it rising?

A : When the population over 65 years old comprises over 7% of the total, the society is called an **aging society**. When that percentage surpasses 14%, it is called an **aged society**. In France it took 115 years for the population over 65 years of age to double from 7% to 14%. It took 85 years in Sweden and 45 years in Britain.But this process is likely to take only 24 years in Japan. As mentioned at the beginning of this chapter, in 1993 the figure for Japan stood at 13.5%, meaning that Japan is at the threshold of becoming an aged society.

Q : What problems arise with an aging population?

A : The greatest problem is supporting the senior citizens. As the number of senior citizens increases, the **productive population,** aged 15 to 65, correspondingly decreases. So naturally the burden on society is greater.

Q : You must be referring to the burden of **social insurance**, such as **pensions**.

A : That's right. For example, many employees subscribe to **employees' welfare pension**. The number of recipients has tripled in only 14 years, from 3.3 million in 1977 to 10.55 million in 1991. The number of recipients is continuing to grow. This means the burden on working people will increase.

Q：このままでは年金がパンクするとの不安も一部でささやかれていますね。

A：現在，サラリーマンは**年金の原資**として，平均で自分の給料のおよそ7％を**保険料**として支払っています。しかしこのまま受給者の数が増えていくと，サラリーマンの負担率もはね上がり，2025年にはおよそ17％になると予測されています。**厚生省**では，厚生年金の支給開始年齢を，現行の60歳から65歳に引き上げざるを得ないとしています。平均寿命がのび，高齢化がさらに進むと，年金以外にもいろいろな問題が出てきます。

Q：といいますと。

● 寝たきり老人問題

A：例えば，寝たきりや痴呆老人の問題です。1985年には，寝たきりと痴呆性の老人の数は合わせて120万人でした。これが厚生省の試算では，2010年には，300万人に達すると予測されています。**老人医療費**は，この間に9倍にはね上がるものと予測されています。

Q：医療費ばかりでなく，そういう人たちの世話も大変ですね。

A：これが非常に大きな問題になっています。負担が大きくなり過ぎて支えきれず，家族が崩壊するという悲劇も起こっています。さらに，家族が小さくなり，今，1家族の平均人数は3人を割っています。老人夫婦だけの世帯や，老人1人きりの世帯も急速に増えています。もう家族だけでは支えきれない問題になっているのです。

Q：高齢者を社会全体で支えていけるように，制度を整えていかなければなりませんね。

● 老人の生きがいの問題

A：そうですね。このほかに，老人の生きがいの問題も出てきています。日本人の大多数を占めるサラリーマンの例を見てみましょう。戦後の工業化，都市化に伴い，サラリーマンの数は急激に増えました。

Q : There is concern among some people that unless measures are taken, the pension system will fail.

A : Right now, salaried workers pay into the **pension fund** about 7% of their income through their **insurance fees**. If the situation continues as it is, workers will end up paying about 17% of their income by 2025. **The Ministry of Health and Welfare** is saying that it has no choice but to raise the recipient age from age 60 to 65. The average life-span is still increasing, and as people grow older they start to suffer from more problems in addition to those associated with pensions.

Q : For example?

A : Many senior citizens suffer from immobility or senile dementia. In 1985, for example, 1.2 million senior citizens were either immobile or suffering from senile dementia. The Ministry of Health and Welfare estimates that this number will rise to 3 million by 2010. **Medical costs for the elderly** are predicted to multiply by nine times during this period.

Q : It is not only a matter of medical expense. It will be very difficult to take care of these people.

A : Yes, how to care for senior citizens is a difficult issue. In some cases the burden becomes so great it can cause the family to collapse. In addition, the family unit is shrinking, with the average family now consisting of less than three people. The number of elderly couples and senior citizens living alone is soaring. So this has become a problem which cannot be solved solely within the family.

Q : We have to build a system in which senior citizens will be supported by the entire society.

A : That's right. We also have to think about helping elderly people find a reason to live. Let's take salaried workers, who account for a substantial proportion of the population. The number of such employees grew rapidly with post-war industrialization and

今では，働く人のおよそ80％がサラリーマンです。現在，30人以上を雇用する企業のおよそ80％で，定年は60歳もしくはそれ以上にのびています。しかし，サラリーマンというのは，ずっと仕事をし続けてきて，ある日定年を迎えると，その次の日から行き場がなくなるというケースが多いのです。毎日が日曜日みたいになるのですが，今まで会社中心の生活をしていたことを考えれば，新たに趣味や生きがいを見つけるのは大変なわけです。

Q：人生80年の時代といわれているわけですから，60歳で社会から完全に引退してしまうというわけにはいかないですよね。

● 定年延長へ

A：そこで労働省では，65歳まで定年を延長するよう企業に働きかけるための法改正を進めています。現行の「**高齢者雇用安定法**」では，60歳定年を事業主の努力義務と定めていますが，この目的はほぼ達成されたとして，さらに65歳まで継続して雇用するよう企業に求めていくというものです。

urbanization. At present, approximately 80% of the work force consists of salaried workers. Over 80% of companies which employ over 30 workers have a retirement age of either 60 years or above. But such employees work their whole lives, and when they retire, they don't know what to do with themselves. Every day becomes a holiday for them, and considering that their entire lives have been company-centered, they find it hard to find new hobbies and new reasons for living.

Q : People now live until they are 80 years old, so they really can't afford to completely withdraw from society at age 60.

A : The Ministry of Labor is now proceeding with legal reforms which would recommend companies to extend employment to age 65. **The Law Concerning Stabilizations of Employment of Older Persons** says that companies should employ workers until retirement age at 60. This target has very nearly been achieved, and now they are demanding that companies keep workers on until they reach age 65.

日本経済と国際社会
THE JAPANESE ECONOMY AND
INTERNATIONAL SOCIETY

41 | 貿易摩擦と市場開放

> 1993年のアメリカの貿易収支の赤字は，およそ1160億ドルでした。さて，この貿易赤字のうち対日赤字は何％を占めているでしょうか。
>
> ① 20%　② 35%　③ 50%

- 貿易赤字の
  時代も

A：第4部は，国際社会の中での日本経済を取り上げます。その中で最大の問題は**貿易摩擦**，とりわけアメリカとの摩擦でしょう。クイズの正解は③の50%，正確にいいますと51.2%です。

Q：アメリカの貿易赤字の半分以上が，対日赤字なんですね。

A：したがってアメリカの日本に対する不満は強く，日米貿易摩擦は深刻です。

Q：そもそも日本の**貿易黒字**が問題になったのは，いつごろなんですか。

A：日本自体，戦後しばらくは**貿易赤字**に悩まされていました。日本の**貿易収支**が黒字になったのは，1960年代の半ばになってからのことです。そして黒字額が急速にふくらみ，深刻な貿易摩擦を生むようになったのが，'80年代の半ばですね。ただし個別商品については，アメリカとの間で'60年代から次々と貿易摩擦が起きていましたが。

- 日米貿易摩擦の
  原因

Q：冒頭のクイズでも明らかなように，日本の貿易摩擦といえば，最大の相手国はアメリカですが，なぜこれほどまでに対米黒字がふくらんだのですか。

A：基本的には，日本が**輸出主導型，輸出依存型の経済**であることと，アメリカが輸入品に対して極め

Trade Friction and Market Liberalization

> In 1993, the U.S. trade deficit amounted to $116 billion.
> What percentage does its deficit with Japan account
> for?
>
>   ① 20%   ② 35%   ③ 50%

A : In this fourth section, we are going to take up the Japanese economy within the international community. The greatest problem in
this area is **trade friction**, particularly with the United States. The
correct answer is number three, it is 51.2% to be exact.

Q : The U.S. trade deficit with Japan accounts for over half of its total
trade deficit.

A : That's right. So there is strong dissatisfaction with Japan, and U.S.-
Japan trade friction is severe.

Q : When did Japan's **trade surplus** first become a problem?

A : Japan itself suffered a **trade deficit** after World War II. The **balance of trade** turned into a surplus around the mid-1960s. It was
not until the mid-1980s, however, that the trade surplus rapidly bur-
geoned and trade friction became serious. Conflict over individual
products, however, had already occurred in the 1960s.

Q : As the figures in the quiz show, whenever we consider trade friction
Japan's biggest trade problem lies with the United States. Why is its
surplus with the United States so large?

A : There are several explanations, but basically, Japan has an **export-
driven, export-dependent economy**. The U.S. has been quite tol-

て寛大な国であることが原因と考えられます。それともちろん日本の国際競争力が強くなったことも輸出を急増させる結果をもたらしました。また日本の貯蓄率が高いことも原因のひとつだという見方もあります。といいますのは，日本で貯蓄された資金が，国内の投資にすべて使われることなく海外に流出しますと，海外で投資や消費に使われます。特にアメリカの場合は消費志向が強いために，これが輸入拡大につながり，貿易赤字の増大に結びつくというわけです。

● 日本の対米政策

Q：強まるアメリカの黒字削減要求に対して，日本がとってきた対策は。

A：アメリカとの間で貿易摩擦の対象になったものを整理しておきますと，'60年代が繊維製品，'70年代が鉄鋼や家庭電化製品，'80年代に入って自動車，半導体と変わってきました。日本がとってきた対策は，自動車までは輸出の自主規制が中心でした。しかしそれにもかかわらず対日赤字は増えたことから，アメリカの要求は厳しくなりました。例えば自動車の例をとれば，輸出を減らす方策として日本車の現地生産が行われるようになったにもかかわらず，現地生産の日本車が増えてくると，今度はそれを米国車と認定するためには，一定の比率以上の米国産部品の使用が必要との要求を出してきました。

Q：輸出の規制だけではなく，日本はもっと輸入を増やすべきだという要求も強まっていますが。

A：ええ。この要求に応えて日本は，1988年には牛肉やオレンジなどの農産物の輸入自由化，1993年の年末には，ガットのウルグアイラウンドで主食であるコメの部分輸入化にも応じました。

Q：それでもアメリカの対日赤字は減るどころか，増えたんですね。

erant toward imported goods. Of course, Japan has strengthened its international competitiveness, and that has led to an increase in exports. Some people believe Japan's high savings rate is another factor. That is, the capital saved in Japan is not only used for domestic investment, it flows overseas and is spent in investment and consumption. On the other hand, the United States has a high consumption rate, so this increases imports from overseas, which in turn expands the trade deficit.

Q : America has been making stronger demands for reducing this surplus, but what kind of policy has Japan taken?

A : Let's look at some of the sources of tension so far. In the 1960s the target was textiles, in the 1970s, it was steel and home appliances, in the 1980s it was cars and semiconductors. Japan's main policy through problems over automobiles had been to voluntarily restrict exports. But even this has not stopped the U.S. deficit with Japan from rising. The United States has made stronger demands. Take cars as an example. When Japanese built more factories in the United States to reduce exports, the factories were required to use a certain percentage of U.S.-made parts for the automobiles to be certified as American-made cars.

Q : The United States has not only demanded that Japan restrict exports, but also that Japan increase imports as well.

A : Yes, in response to this demand, Japan opened up its market for agricultural products such as oranges and beef in 1988. At the Uruguay Round of GATT at the end of 1993, Japan agreed to partially liberalize its rice market.

Q : But instead of decreasing the deficit, that actually increased the deficit, didn't it?

● 日米構造協議から
　包括経済協議へ

A：そこで登場したのが「**日米構造協議**」で，1989年
9月から始まりました。企業系列や規制などの日
本の制度や慣行が，市場の閉鎖性の原因ではない
かということで，日本経済のシステムまでが協議
の対象になったわけです。

Q：話し合いの成果はあったのですか。

A：日本が公共投資を上積みすることなど，いくつか
の合意はなされましたが，「構造」という言葉の捉
え方に日米間でギャップがあったため，話がかみ
合わない面もあり，大きな成果にはつながりませ
んでした。この後アメリカ政府では，どうも構造
協議では貿易不均衡の是正につながらないとの見
方が強くなったために，日米間の交渉は1993年7
月から再び，個別分野を重視した「**日米包括協議**」
に形を変えました。

Q：新しい協議の進捗状況は，どうなのですか。

A：アメリカは，不公正な貿易国に対して一方的に制
裁を発動することができる**包括通商法スーパー
301条**という強い手段を背景に，日本との交渉を
行いました。その結果，日米は1994年10月，政府
機関による**電気通信機器**や**医療機器**の購入という
政府調達と保険の分野では合意に達しました。し
かし最も市場規模の大きい自動車および自動車部
品の分野については合意に達せず，アメリカ側は
自動車の補修部品について，一般のスーパー301
条による制裁手続きを開始する方針を決めました。

Q：スーパー301条による制裁発動という最悪の事態
は免れたものの，今後も厳しい交渉が続けられる
ことになるわけですね。

A：そうです。包括協議の最大の焦点は，日本市場の
開放度を測るための客観基準を設定するかどうか
という点にありましたが，日米が歩み寄って合意
した政府調達分野でも，合意内容に客観基準が盛

A : Well, **the U.S.-Japan Structural Impediments Initiative** started in September 1989. During these talks, the United States said that Japan's market was closed due to practices such as the keiretsu system and government regulations. The whole Japanese economic system came under a microscope during these talks.

Q : Did the negotiations produce results?

A : The two parties came to agreements on several points, such as Japan raising investments in public works. But there is a perception gap between the United States and Japan on the word "structure." So they ended up talking in circles and were unable to produce significant results. The United States began to insist that the Structural Impediments Initiative would not redress the trade imbalance. So negotiations between Japan and the United States evolved into **the U.S.-Japan Framework Talks** on bilateral trade in July 1993.

Q : How are the new negotiations proceeding?

A : The United States has negotiated with Japan over **Super 301 Provisions of the Omnibus Trade and Competitiveness Act.** Sanctions can be put into effect unilaterally by the United States under Super 301. As a result, as of October 1994, agreements on **government procurements** (including **telecommunications equipment** and **medical equipment**) and insurance have been reached. But they have not reached agreement on cars and car parts, the biggest market. Therefore the U.S. decided to start procedures to implement Super 301.

Q : The worst case scenario, the full activation of Super 301, has thus far been avoided, but tough negotiations will continue for the foreseeable future.

A : Yes. The Omnibus Trade and Competitiveness Act focused on objective criteria for measuring how wide the Japanese market is open. Although the two nations concluded an agreement on government supply, they have different interpretations about the objective cri-

ポイント

● 黒字削減の目標

り込まれたかどうかについて日米に解釈の違いが
あり，今後に問題を残しそうです。

Q：日本は大幅な貿易黒字を今後どうするのでしょうか。

A：大幅な貿易黒字に対する不満はアメリカだけでは
ないこともあって，日本としてはなんらかの対策
をとらざるをえない立場に立たされています。
1994年3月末には市場開放策を盛り込んだ「**対外
経済改革要綱**」を発表しました。この要綱では，
ＧＤＰ（国内総生産）に対する黒字の比率を，
1992年度は3.4％だったのを，1994年度には2.8％
程度に縮小することや，外国企業の進出を阻んで
いる規制を廃止することなどを打ち出しています。

　　以上は日米摩擦を中心にご紹介しましたが，最
後にその他の地域についてひとこと。このところ
日本の貿易黒字が，ＮＩＥＳやＡＳＥＡＮなどア
ジア向けが増えていて，'92年以降は対米黒字を上
回っています。今のところ，この地域との大きな
貿易摩擦は起きていませんが，日本としては今後
はアジア諸国との間に貿易摩擦が起きないよう配
慮していく必要があると思います。

teria. This will probably continue to be a problem in the years to come.

Q : How will Japan deal with its huge trade surplus?

A : The United States is not the only country which is disgruntled about Japan's huge trade surplus. Other countries also feel that some kind of measures must be taken. At the end of March 1994 the Japanese government announced **the External Economic Reform Measures** including market-opening policies. This package aimed to reduce the current account surplus of 3.4% in fiscal 1992 to 2.8% of the gross domestic product in fiscal 1994. It also aimed to remove restrictions which hindered foreign corporations from doing business in Japan.

We've concentrated so far on the trade friction between Japan and the United States. But Japan's trade surplus is also growing with the so-called **newly industrializing economies** (NIES) of East Asia, and the member states of **the Association of Southeast Asian Nations** (ASEAN). Japan's trade surplus with these two groups has been larger than its surplus with the United States since 1992. At present there are no major trade disputes with the nations of this region. But Japan needs to ensure that such disputes will not arise.

42 | 円高と国内産業の空洞化

日本の輸入全体に占める製品輸入の割合は，1983年にはおよそ27%でしたが，1992年にはどのくらいの水準になったでしょうか。

① 20%　② 30%　③ 50%

A：日本の市場は閉鎖的であるとして，しばしば批判されてきました。しかし，最近の円高の進行とともに製品の輸入は急激に増えました。正解は③の50%でした。（通産省の調査）

Q：**円高**になると製品輸入が増えるわけですね。

- 円高で製品輸入増

A：そうです。円が高くなると，日本の製品の生産コストは相対的に高くなります。外国から買った方が安くなりますから，日本の企業は生産から撤退し，製品の輸入が増えます。こういったケースは，衣料品や靴，おもちゃなどに多いですね。

Q：確かに，スーパーなどで買うシャツなど，韓国や台湾，中国などから輸入されたものが目立ちますね。

A：さらに，日本の企業が外国製品に対抗するために，**生産拠点**を生産コストの安い海外に移し，そこで生産したものを日本に輸入するケースもあります。例えば，カラーテレビです。これはかつて日本の花形輸出商品だったわけですが，今では輸出より輸入の方が多くなっています。**生産設備**が海外に出ていってしまう，いわゆる「**産業の空洞化**」という現象です。

- 産業の空洞化

Q：日本経済の成長パターンは長い間，輸出主導型と

The Appreciation of the Yen and the Hollowing out of Domestic Industry

> Manufactured goods accounted for 27% of Japan's imports in 1983. What percentage did they account for in 1992?
>
> ① 20%　② 30%　③ 50%

A : The Japanese market has often been criticised for being closed. Recently, the yen has appreciated greatly, and this has led to a surge of manufactured imports. The answer is number three, 50% (Ministry of International Trade and Industry survey).

Q : The **appreciation of the yen** has certainly led to an increase in imports of manufactured goods.

A : Yes, it has. First of all, the higher the yen is, the more it costs to produce goods in Japan. Foreign goods are cheaper and, therefore, more attractive. So Japanese companies stop producing and instead import these goods. This is certainly the case with respect to clothing, shoes and toys.

Q : Yes, when you go into supermarkets these days, you often see such things as South Korean, Chinese and Taiwanese-made shirts.

A : In addition, many Japanese firms are shifting their **production bases** overseas where production costs are cheaper. Color televisions are a prime example. In the past, Japan was a major exporter of color TV sets. Today, more are imported than exported. **Production facilities** are moving overseas. This process has been termed the **"hollowing out of industry."**

Q : Japan's economic growth has been export-oriented for a long time.

● 増える現地生産

● 円高不況時も
空洞化を懸念

いわれてきました。つまり，外国から原材料を輸入し，それを製品に加工して輸出することで稼ぐという構造ですね。これが円高の影響で崩れてきたという見方もできるわけですか。

A：部分的にそういう事態になっていることは事実です。今度は自動車の例を見てみましょう。自動車は日本の輸出産業の花形で，毎年，日本の輸出額全体のおよそ20％を稼いできました。日本自動車工業会の調べによると，この自動車の輸出台数が，1985年の673万台から，1992年には567万台に落ちています。特に大きな影響を受けたのは，アメリカ向けの輸出です。1985年のアメリカ向けの輸出台数は313万台，日本企業のアメリカでの現地生産台数は36万台でした。これが，1992年には，輸出台数は177万台に減り，日本企業の現地生産は180万台に増えています。一部のメーカーは日本へ逆輸入しています。例えば，アメリカ本田は1992年に45万8000台を生産，そのうち2万台を日本に輸出しました。もっとも自動車の場合は，円高の影響というより，アメリカとの貿易摩擦を回避することが理由だったと考えられていますが。

Q：とはいえ，現地生産が輸出より多くなったのですから，国内生産が影響を受けるのではないですか。

A：自動車の生産台数で見ますと，1993年の生産台数は1122万台で，1985年に比べておよそ100万台減っています。これはちょうど輸出の減少分に見合った数です。ただ，自動車産業の従事者数自体には大きな変化はなく，まだそれほどの影響を受けているとはいえません。しかし，円高がさらに進むと，国内産業が空洞化する心配が出てきます。

Q：これまでも空洞化が懸念されたことがあったと聞きましたが。

A：1986〜87年の円高不況のときがそうでした。あの

In other words, Japan has earned money by importing raw materials, processing them and selling them overseas. Some people find this whole economic system is starting to buckle under the rapid rise in the value of the yen.

A : Yes, this can certainly be seen in some sectors of the economy. Cars for example are a major export. For several consecutive years, they accounted for about 20% of Japanese exports. According to a survey by the Japan Automobile Manufactures Association, Inc., Japan exported 6.73 million cars in 1985. By 1992 the number fell to 5.67 million cars. Car exports to the United States have been most affected. In 1985 Japan exported 3.13 million vehicles to the United States, while 360,000 cars were produced by local Japanese subsidiaries in the U.S. However, in 1992 exports to the U.S. fell to 1.77 million cars, while the number of vehicles produced by local Japanese subsidiaries increased 1.8 million. Some Japanese manufacturers are reimporting the cars produced overseas. For example, Honda Motor Company's U.S. subsidiary in 1992 produced 458,000 vehicles, of which 20,000 were exported to Japan. Actually, in the case of cars, people think Japanse firms set up production bases in the United States to head off trade disputes, rather than because of the strong yen.

Q : In any case, Japan produces more cars in the U.S. now than it exports. Is domestic production affected by this?

A : Japan produced a total of 11.22 million cars in 1993, only one million less than in 1985. The decrease amounts to the decline in exports. The number of workers in the industry, however, hasn't changed so much. So it can be said that car production in Japan hasn't been all that affected yet. However if the yen continues to be strong, there is a fear that Japanese industry will hollow out.

Q : Worries about the hollowing out of domestic industry have been expressed before.

A : That was during the years 1986–1987, when business was depressed

ときは，造船や鉄鋼，石油化学などの分野が，アジア諸国からの脅威にさらされ，**人員削減や工場閉鎖，新規ビジネスへの進出**などが真剣に検討されました。しかし，コストダウンや技術革新がうまくいったことや，その後バブルといわれるような好景気が訪れたこともあって，産業構造転換の議論はどこかへ消えてしまったといえます。

Q：それが今回の不況，円高の中で再燃してきたというわけですか。

A：そうですね。円は1ドル100円を割っているわけですから，一段と深刻な状況になっています。例えば家電業界などは，日本で作った部品を海外で組み立てることで，生産コストを下げる努力をしてきました。しかし，現在の円高の中では，部品生産も海外に移さざるをえない状況になっています。

● 迫られる構造調整

Q：日本経済は構造調整を迫られているわけですね。打開策はないのでしょうか。

A：1993年の日本の**経常収支の黒字**は1400億ドルに達しました。この額は，G7の他の国の**経常収支赤字**の合計額とほぼ同じ水準です。まさに日本の一人勝ちといえるわけですが，日本の黒字は今や十分に国際的な問題になるほどに大きくなっていることを日本はもっと自覚すべきだ，という声も出ています。日米間の交渉でも，日本の輸出を減らすことに重きがあったのではなく，輸入を増やして黒字幅をどれだけ減らすことができるかが求められていたわけです。産業構造の転換，つまり競争力のなくなった産業は後発の国々に明け渡す覚悟を持つとともに，次世代技術の開発を積極的に押し進めていくことが必要になっています。手をこまねいていれば，産業の空洞化がさらに深刻化する可能性も出てきます。

by the strong yen. During that time, Japan faced stiff competition from other Asian countries in areas such as shipbuilding, iron and steel and petro-chemicals. Manufacturers in Japan seriously considered **staff reductions, factory closures** and **new business ventures**. But all talk of industrial restructuring disappeared once they were able to cut costs successfully and come up with new technical innovations. Japan then entered a short-term economic boom known as the "bubble economy."

Q : But the current recession and appreciation of the yen have caused manufacturers to turn back to restructuring, haven't they?

A : That's certainly true. The yen has risen to the level of ¥100 to the dollar, so the situation is rather serious. Home appliance manufacturers, for example, have been trying to reduce production costs by exporting parts to their assembly plants overseas. But the recent appreciation of the yen has forced them to produce even those parts overseas.

Q : It seems the pressure is certainly on Japan to restructure. But isn't there any way to come to an compromise on trade?

A : In 1993 Japan's **current account surplus** reached $140 billion. This figure nearly matches the combined **current account deficits** of all the other G7 industrialized nations. Japan is unrivaled in the size of its current accounts. There is criticism that Japan needs to be more aware of the problems that its large surpluses are creating internationally. Even in U.S.-Japanese trade negotiations, the focus has been on increasing imports in Japan rather than restraining its exports as a means of reducing its trade surplus. Japan is being required to restructure, that is to surrender sectors in which it is no longer competitive to developing countries, and actively develop a new generation of technologies. Sitting around doing nothing will only increase the possibility that the hollowing out of the industrial structure will worsen.

43 | 日本で働く外国人

法務省の調べによると1984年12月末現在，就労が目的で日本に在留する外国人の数は約2万人でした。それでは1992年の同じ時期ではどれくらいだったでしょうか。

① 約2万5000人　② 約5万5000人　③ 約8万5000

● 外国人雇用の
　現状

A：経済活動が国際化するのに伴い，海外で活躍する日本人が大勢いる一方で，日本で働く外国人も増えています。クイズの答えは③の約8万5000人です。

Q：4倍以上にも増えたのですね。この人たちは，どんな仕事をしているのでしょうか。

A：8万5000人の内訳を在留資格で見ますと，演奏や演劇，スポーツといった「**興行**」が26.6％で2万3000人，通訳やデザイナーなど外国人ならではの知識や感性を生かした業務に就く「**人文知識・国際業務**」が25.6％の2万1900人，システムエンジニアなどの「**技術**」が10.8％の9200人となっています。また労働省の調査によれば，従業員1000人以上の企業の26％，6000人以上の企業の66％が外国人を雇用しています。業種としては金融，保険業，サービス業などが多くなっています。

Q：企業は，どんな理由で外国人を雇用しているのでしょうか。

A：「優れた人材だから」という答えのほかに，「海外取引先や外国人顧客との渉外要員」「外国人ならではの技術，技能」「海外戦略強化」などが挙げられています。ところで今お話ししてきたのは，

Foreign Workers in Japan

> According to the Ministry of Justice, the number of foreigners in Japan with working visas was about 20,000 as of December 1984. Approximately how many foreigners were working in Japan in December 1992?
>
> ① 25,000 ② 55,000 ③ 85,000

A : With the internationalization of business activities, there are a lot of Japanese working overseas and a lot of foreign workers in Japan. The correct answer is number three, about 85,000 foreigners.

Q : So the number of foreign workers has expanded nearly four times since 1984. What sorts of jobs do they do?

A : First of all 26.6%, or 23,000 people, were classified as involved in **entertainment**, such as music, drama or sports. Another 25.6%, or 21,900 people, were classified as specialists in the humanities and **international services** which non-Japanese possess special qualification for, such as interpreters and designers. And 10.8% or 9,200 people, were technical specialists such as system engineers. The Ministry of Labor reports that 26% of companies with over 1,000 employees, and 66% of companies with over 6,000 employees employ foreigners. Most of the businesses are in the finance, insurance or service industries.

Q : Why do companies employ foreigners?

A : The same survey found companies employ certain foreigners because they are especially talented, they are needed as liaisons with foreign customers or for overseas transactions, or they have a particularly rare skill. And some companies want to strengthen their

ポイント

あくまで正規に就労資格を持って働く外国人についてです。

Q : といいますと。

A : '93年11月に発表された労働省の報告書によると，現在すでに60万人の外国人が日本で就労していると推計されています。これは日本の雇用労働者の1％を超える数字です。この中には今お話ししたような合法的に就労している外国人や，就労に関して制限を受けない南米などからの日系人のほかに，非合法な形で働いている人もたくさん含まれています。

● 日本政府の受け
入れ方針

Q : 合法，非合法という話が出ましたが，日本は**外国人労働者**に対してどのような受け入れ体制をとっているのですか。

A : 現在日本政府は，技術者・専門職従事者といった**熟練労働者**や外国人ならではといった能力を持つ人には門戸を開放していますが，**単純労働者**は基本的には受け入れていません。1992年7月の「**雇用対策基本計画**」を見ると，「外国人労働者問題については，日本の経済社会の活性化や国際化をはかる観点から，専門的技術的分野の労働者は可能な限り受け入れる」としています。その一方で，「単純労働者の受け入れについては，雇用機会の不足する高齢者への圧迫，**労働市場**における新たな二重構造の発生，受け入れに伴う新たな社会的費用の負担など経済社会に広範な影響が懸念されることから，慎重に対応する」と述べています。

Q : しかし，**建設現場**などでは，明らかに単純労働をしていると思われる外国人をあちこちで見かけますが。

A : おもにアジア諸国から**観光ビザ**などで入国したにもかかわらず，在留資格以外の仕事につく労働者が急増しているのです。1992年に**入国管理法違反**

overseas strategy. Of course, everything we've just talked about applies only to foreigners working legally in Japan.

Q : What does that mean?

A : The Ministry of Labor report in November 1993 estimated that 600,000 foreigners were working in Japan. So foreign workers comprise just over 1% of the labor force in Japan. This includes the foreigners just discussed who are legally working in Japan, those from South America who are of Japanese ancestry and are hence not restricted, and those who are working illegally.

Q : You talked about legal and illegal workers, but what kind of system does Japan have for **foreign workers**?

A : Right now, Japan only admits **skilled** foreign **workers**, such as technicians or specialists or those who possess some unique ability. It does not in principle allow **unskilled laborers. The Basic Plan of Employment Measures** of July 1992 said Japan should allow foreign workers as much as possible into specialized and technological areas to promote internationalization and activation of its economy. On the other hand, it takes a cautious stance regarding unskilled workers, saying allowing unskilled labor into Japan would create a double structure in the **labor market** and decrease employment opportunities for older workers. Also, it could have a broad impact on economic society, such as creating a new social-cost burden.

Q : But you often see foreign workers doing unskilled labor, such as at **construction sites**.

A : Most of these workers are from Asian countries and they enter Japan on **tourist visas**. So an increasingly large number of illegal laborers are working in jobs that they are not permitted to do

● 増える不法就労

で摘発された外国人のうち，不法就労で摘発された人はおよそ6万2000人にのぼり，前年の約2倍，5年前の約6倍となっています。しかしこの数字は氷山の一角であり，実際はもっと多くの数にのぼると考えられます。また，就学生，留学生といった資格で日本に入国した人々は，学業のかたわら1日4時間までアルバイトをすることができるのですが，それを口実にほとんどフルタイムの労働をする人も多くいて，問題視されています。

Q：こうした人たちがなぜ増えているのですか。

A：日本側の要因としては，'80年代後半の好景気による日本の労働力不足があります。特に彼らは，日本人の働きたがらない，いわゆる**3K（危険，汚い，きつい）労働**を，日本人よりも低い賃金で働くということで，日本企業から重宝がられています。労働者側の要因としては，出身国で働く場が不足している，円高が定着し日本との間に大きな所得格差があるといったことがあります。

Q：けれども，世界第2位の経済大国である日本が，熟練労働者以外受け入れないというのは閉鎖的だという声もありますが。

A：そういった声もあって，政府は'93年度から未熟練の外国人を研修生として受け入れ，工業技術や技能を身につけた後，実習という形で一定期間の就労を認める「**技能実習制度**」を導入しました。人材育成に協力することで，開発途上国の経済発展を促そうというものです。しかしながらこの制度も，本来の目的にそった形で機能しているかどうかは疑わしい，という声もあります。

Q：ところで，昨今の景気低迷の影響で日本国内の失業問題も深刻になりつつありますね。外国人労働者はどうなんですか。

A：1980年代後半は日本経済が好調で労働市場全体

according to their visa status. Approximately 62,000 illegal workers were found to be in violation of **immigration control laws** in 1992. This is twice the number in 1991, and six times that of five years ago. But it seems this figure is just the tip of the iceberg, and there are in reality many illegal foreign workers including workers on student visas. Students from overseas are allowed to work four hours a day. They enter the country with student visas, but actually they work full time. Their status is regarded as questionable.

Q : Why is the number of illegal workers rising?

A : During the prosperous economy of the late 1980s, Japan suffered a labor shortage. Japanese tend to shy away from **"3D" jobs**, that is jobs which are **"dirty, demanding and dangerous."** These workers were valued as providing cheaper labor than Japanese workers. This was the background in Japan. These foreigners faced job shortages in their own countries and they could get sufficiently high salaries here because of the yen's appreciation.

Q : But as the second strongest economic power, Japan is criticized as being exclusivistic for only permitting skilled foreign workers.

A : This has been pointed out by many people. The government began admitting foreigners as basic technical trainees in fiscal 1993. They are allowed to work for a certain period as practice after training under what is called **the Technical Intern Training Program**. Training personnel helps promote economic progress in developing nations. But we cannot ignore the fact that this system is also a loophole for foreign workers, with a few exceptions.

Q : By the way, unemployment is becoming more serious because of the sluggish economy. How is this affecting foreign workers?

A : In the late 1980s the Japanese economy was booming, and the labor

327

● 不況による影響

● 単純労働者の
　扱いが焦点

で人手不足ぎみでした。そのため企業は，日本の大学などを卒業した外国人留学生を積極的に採用しましたし，単純作業の職場でも外国人を雇いました。しかし，'91年以降景気は下降し続けており，外国人労働者や留学生はそのあおりをまともに受けて，解雇されたり，就職先がなかなか見つからないというのが現状です。

Q：日本は外国人労働者の問題について，今後どう対処していくべきなのでしょうか。

A：政府のたてまえとは裏腹に，日本で働く外国人の多くが不法就労者で，正規に就労する人の方が少数派だという現実があります。こうした人の中には，不法就労という立場の弱みにつけ込まれて劣悪な環境のもとで働かされたり，雇い主に賃金を払ってもらえなかったり，**労働災害**にあっても補償が受けられないといった，人道的立場から見ても放置できない問題も生じています。外国人労働者，特に単純労働者を受け入れるかどうかについては，賛否両論があってまだ議論がかたまっていませんが，現在の状況を放置しておくことが良い結果にはつながらないことだけは確かなようです。

market was suffering from a shortage. So companies actively recruited foreign exchange students who graduated from Japanese universities, and employed foreigners as unskilled workers. But the economy has been heading downhill since 1991, and foreign workers and exchange students have been dismissed and are now are unable to find jobs.

Q : How will Japan deal with foreign workers in the future?

A : Contrary to the government's principle, the reality is that the number of illegal foreign workers is greater than that of legal foreign workers. Among them are some who work under poor conditions because they are taken advantage of because of their illegal status. Some are unable to get salaries from their employers or get compensation for **work-related accidents**. From the humane perspective these workers ought not be ignored. As for accepting unskilled laborers, opinions are divided and there is no consensus, however, merely ignoring this situation will not bring about a suitable result.

44 | 国際社会への貢献

> 1992年の世界全体のODA，政府開発援助の中に占める日本のシェアはおよそ何％でしょうか。
>
> ① 8%　② 18%　③ 28%

A：日本はいまや先進国の中でも有数の政府開発援助大国となりました。クイズの答えは②，正確には，18.2％で世界第1位です。金額でいいますと，111億5100万ドルとなっています。第2位はアメリカで，107億6200万ドルです。

● 経済援助が中心

Q：国際貢献といってもさまざまな形があると思いますが，日本の国際社会への貢献というと，やはり**経済援助**というイメージが強いですね。

A：日本は第2次世界大戦後，驚異的な経済復興を遂げて，経済大国日本の地位を築き上げましたが，国際社会における政治的な役割は相対的に小さなものにとどまっています。国連においても安全保障理事会の常任理事国ではありませんし，政治的な指導力もほかの先進諸国に比べると見劣りがするとよく指摘されます。

Q：日本が，第2次世界大戦の敗戦国であるということと関係があるのでしょうね。

A：そうですね。日本は二度と軍事大国にはならないとして，専守防衛の**自衛隊**のみを組織し，防衛費も，名目GNPの1％程度に抑えてきました。また東西冷戦におけるアメリカの**安全保障体制**に完全に組み込まれたことがそれを可能にしてきました。その結果，日本の国際社会への貢献は，主に

Contribution to International Community

> **What percentage of global official development assis-tance (ODA) did Japan contribute in 1992?**
> ① 8% ② 18% ③ 28%

A : Japan is one of the largest contributors of ODA among the indus-trialized nations. The correct answer is number two, 18%. The exact figure was 18.2%, the largest share of any nation, and that amounted to a total sum of $11.151 billion. The second largest donor was the United States, with $10.762 billion.

Q : There are many ways of contributing to the international commu-nity, but it seems Japan usually contributes in the form of **economic aid**.

A : After the Second World War, Japan achieved incredible growth, and built itself into an economic superpower. But its international polit-ical role has remained relatively small. It is not one of the perma-nent members of the United Nations Security Council, and its political leadership is much more limited than that of other indus-trialized nations. Other nations have often pointed out these facts.

Q : Does this have something to do with the fact that Japan was a defeated nation in the Second World War?

A : Yes, it does. Japan can never again become a military superpower. It only has **Self-Defense Forces** for its own protection. And the budget allocated to the forces is about 1% of the nominal gross national product (GNP). This was possible because the U.S. **secu-rity system** totally absorbed Japan during the Cold War. As a result, the government has been able to contribute to the world

● 日本の経済協力
　の特徴

● 援助対象国は

　ODA（**政府開発援助**）などの経済援助を中心に
なされてきたのです。

Q：日本の**経済協力**にはどのような特徴がありますか。

A：それを説明するためには話を戦後の日本にさかの
ぼらなければなりません。日本は今でこそ援助大
国ですが，50年近く前は焼け野原でした。そこか
ら立ち直り，驚異的な経済発展を成し遂げたわけ
ですが，その復興に大きな役割を果たしたのが，
海外からの援助でした。アメリカの「**ガリオア・
エロア基金**」（占領地救済資金・占領地経済復興
援助費）による援助は，食料，肥料，衣料品など
の緊急物資とともに，鉱業原料や，繊維，機械な
どを供与するものであり，総額は，1945年から51
年までの累計で17億1630万ドル，1946年には，日
本の名目GDPの12.6％に達しました。**世界銀行**
の融資も，**インフラ整備**，電力，鉄鋼業などを対
象に総額8億6000万ドルにも達し，日本の産業基
盤の整備に大きく貢献しました。この経験を生か
すために，日本の経済協力は開発途上国の発展の
基盤整備を意図するものが中心となっています。
これまでの二国間のODAを分野別に見ると，運
輸，通信，エネルギーという経済インフラの比率
が30〜40％と高い比率を占めており，OECD諸
国平均の18％を大きく上まわっています。

Q：地域的にはどんな国に対する援助が多いのですか。

A：'92年度のODAを地域別に見ると，インドネシ
ア，中国，フィリピン，インド，タイという順と
なっていて，アジア諸国が全体の6割以上を占め
ています。そしてアフリカ，中南米がそれぞれ1割
程度となっています。

Q：日本のODAに対しては，ほかのOECD諸国のも
のに比べて贈与の比率が低いといわれていますね。

A：確かに日本の贈与比率は39％と，OECD諸国平

mainly by supporting economic development such as through **official development assistance** (ODA) and other means.

Q : What are the features of Japanese **economic cooperation?**

A : To answer that question, we have to go back to post-war Japan. Though Japan is now a large donor nation, it was just a scorched plain nearly 50 years ago. Japan was able to rebuild and achieve amazing economic development, but aid from overseas played a major role in its reconstruction. Through Government and Relief in Occupied Areas–Economic Rehabilitation in Occupied Areas (**GARIOA–EROA**) the United States sent emergency supplies such as food, fertilizer and clothing. They also donated things such as mining resources, textiles and machinery. The total cost of the project from 1945 to 1951 amounted to $1.7163 billion. In 1946, the amount was 12.6% of Japan's nominal gross domestic product (GDP). Financing from **the World Bank** added $860 million, and this was directed toward areas such as **infrastructure**, electrical power and the steel industry. This contributed greatly to establishing Japan's industrial base. Putting this experience to use, Japan's economic cooperation aims mainly at building a base for development in developing countries. If we look at bilateral ODA, 30–40% of Japan's aid is directed toward developing economic infrastructure, such as transportation, communications and energy. This is much higher than the average of 18% among OECD nations.

Q : Which countries have received aid from Japan?

A : In 1992, over 60% of Japanese ODA went to Asian nations, such as Indonesia, China, the Philippines, India and Thailand, in that order. Africa and Latin America each received 10%.

Q : I've heard that the percentage of pure grants or donations in Japanese ODA is quite low compared to that of other OECD nations.

A : The percentage of grants in Japanese ODA is 39%, which is much

● 少ない無償資金
　協力

均の79％を大幅に下回っています（'90年）。これ
は有償資金協力の適用が多い，アジア諸国の比率
が高いことにも原因がありますが，政府としては
今後無償資金協力を拡充していくことを「ＯＤＡ
第5次中期目標」（'93年〜'97年）の中で明らかに
しています。しかしこの計画では，同時に，有償
資金協力の着実な推進もうたっています。**有償資
金協力**は，**無償資金協力**よりも多額の供与が可能
なので，経済インフラ整備のために必要な，大規
模かつ長期的なプロジェクトに向いています。ま
た，途上国にとって返済義務のある援助資金です
から，その使い道も慎重に検討されることになり，
結果的に途上国の自助努力を促し，経済開発を後
押しすることにもなるという側面もあるからです。

Ｑ：日本のＯＤＡは，いわゆる「ヒモ付き」援助だと
　　いう批判の声もよく聞かれますが。

Ａ：「ヒモ付き」といわれる割には，意外とタイイン
　　グ・ステイタス，つまり開発計画のための資材な
　　どの調達に際して，援助供与国の企業のみが契約
　　の入札に参加できるというタイプの援助の比率は
　　低く，ＯＥＣＤ諸国が平均33％なのに対し，日本
　　は15％となっています。

Ｑ：日本のＯＤＡが本当に途上国の人々の生活に役立
　　っているのでしょうか。

Ａ：これまで産業基盤整備を中心とする援助の比率が
　　高かったことから，生活に密着した分野では，経
　　済援助による恩恵が直接には実感しにくかったと
　　いう側面もあるかもしれません。1993年にＯＥＣ
　　Ｄ諸国が行った経済協力審査では，日本のＯＤＡ
　　活動に対し，「要員の不足や大規模化するプロジ
　　ェクトの支援体制が充分でない」ことに懸念が表
　　明されています。また，援助物資や機械が実際に
　　使われないまま，棚ざらしになってしまったケー

lower than the OECD average of 79% (1990). One of the reasons for this is that many Asian countries use the economic loan system or receive aid which must be repaid. The government, however, has released "the fifth mid-term plan for ODA" for the period from 1993 to 1997, according to which the percentage of pure grants will be expanded. It also calls for the promotion of the loan system. Japan can assist with larger sums of money through **repayable aid or loans**, rather than **pure grant money**. So this type of aid is suitable for large-scale, long-term projects required for building an economic infrastructure. Since developing nations are required to repay this capital, they have to carefully consider how to use it. This may actually result in encouraging self-sufficiency and economic development.

Q : Japanese aid is often criticized for being "tied aid."

A : Japan has been criticized for only allowing Japanese companies to bid on the contracts and for procuring resources for development projects. But although Japan has been so criticized, Japan's percentage of such tied aid is comparatively low, only 15% compared to the 33% average among OECD countries.

Q : Does Japanese ODA actually contribute to improving the standard of living in developing countries?

A : Until now, a high percentage of aid was focused on building an industrial base, so the average person may not have actually felt the benefits in their daily lives. But an OECD economic aid survey in 1993 reflected a concern related to Japanese ODA that there was a shortage of qualified personnel and an insufficient support framework for large-scale projects. In some cases, the aid materials and machines were left to rust on the shelves. So Japan should try to improve this area in the future.

● 今後の日本の
　経済協力

スがあることもしばしば報じられており，今後の改善が必要と思われます。

Q：今後の日本の経済協力はどのような方針で進められていくのでしょうか。

A：これまでの日本のODAに対する批判や，東西冷戦構造の崩壊，地域紛争の多発などの動向を考慮して，日本政府は'92年6月に「**政府開発援助大綱**」を発表しました。そこでは，環境と開発の両立，途上国の**軍事支出**や**武器輸出入**の動向を注視して，国際紛争を助長するような援助を避ける，途上国の民主化への取り組みに注意を払う，といった原則が明らかにされています。また，地球環境の保護にも重点を置くという意味から，'92年に開かれた地球サミットで，今後5年間に環境分野で9000億円から1兆円供与することを表明しています。

Q：日本の国際貢献は経済協力中心のスタイルでこれからも進められていくのでしょうか。

A：1991年の湾岸戦争の際に，自衛隊の掃海艇が派遣されたり，'92年以降カンボジア，モザンビーク，ルワンダなどの**PKO活動**に自衛隊が参加するなど，これまで資金面の援助が中心であった日本の**国際貢献**のあり方が変わりつつあります。また東西冷戦構造の崩壊や，民族紛争，難民問題，および環境問題は，今後の日本の経済協力，ひいては国際貢献のあり方にさまざまな議論を投げかけています。日本は国連安全保障理事会の常任理事国入りを目指していますが，それに伴い，どのような形でどこまで，国際貢献を行っていくのか，世論のコンセンサスづくりが急務だといえます。

Q : What are the future plans for Japanese economic cooperation?

A : The Japanese government has taken this criticism, the collapse of the Cold War structure, and the frequent outbreak of regional conflict into consideration, and it announced **Japan's Official Development Assistance Charter** in June 1992. The outline set principles of ensuring that development was compatible with the environment, avoided provoking international conflict through **military expenditure** and the **export and import of weapons** in developing countries, and supported democratization in developing nations. The government has also pledged to emphasize protecting the environment. At the Earth Summit in 1992, it announced a donation of between ¥900 billion and ¥1 trillion over five years to environmental protection.

Q : Do you think Japan will continue contributing to the international community in the future mainly through economic cooperation?

A : Japan dispatched mine-sweepers belonging to its Self-Defence Forces to assist in mine removal in the Persian Gulf after the Gulf War in 1991. It has also sent troops for **peace-keeping operations** to Cambodia, Mozambique and Rwanda since 1992. So I think Japan's **international contribution** is shifting away from a focus on purely monetary aid. There are now varying opinions on how Japanese aid can best contribute to the world, in the wake of the end of the Cold War, ethnic conflicts and refugee and environmental issues. Japan is also bidding for permanent membership in the United Nations Security Council. With that aim in mind, Japan will have to quickly build a public consensus on how it should direct its future contributions.

戦後の経済成長率の統計は，終戦から6年たった
1951年の分から公表されています。さてそのときか
ら現在に至るまで，実質経済成長率がマイナスにな
った年は何回あるでしょうか。

　　① 0回　　② 1回　　③ 3回

● 戦後日本の経済
　成長率

A：戦後の日本経済は大変順調に推移してきました。
　　クイズの答えですが，戦後，**経済成長率がマイナ
　　ス**になったのは，②の1回だけです。

Q：わずか1回だけですか。マイナス成長になった年
　　はいつですか。

A：第1次石油ショックの影響が深刻になった1974年
　　で，**GDP**（国内総生産）の実質の伸びは，マイ
　　ナス0.6％でした。ここ40年余りの間にマイナス成
　　長がわずか1回だけというのは，戦後の日本の経
　　済成長が大変順調だったことを象徴していると思
　　います。

Q：このところ景気が悪い悪いといわれていますが，
　　成長率はマイナスではないんですか。

A：1993年はプラス0.1％，1994年の予想値はプラス
　　1.0〜1.5％で，かろうじてプラス成長を確保しそ
　　うです。

Q：実際の景気の落ち込みよりも，心理的な落ち込み
　　の方が大きいということですかね。

A：そうですね。今まで日本経済は，がむしゃらに経
　　済の発展，企業の成長を目指して，脇目も振らず
　　に走ってきたわけです。石油危機や円高不況もな

The Japanese Economy at a Turning Point

> Statistical data on Japanese post-war economic growth
> has been compiled annually since 1951, six years after
> the end of World War II. How many times has real eco-
> nomic growth been negative since 1951?
>
> ① Zero   ② Once   ③ Three times

A : The Japanese economy has been transformed very favorably since
the war. Only once has the **economic growth rate** proved negative, so the answer to the quiz is number two, "once."

Q : Only one time? In what year did that happen?

A : It happened in 1974, when the economy was crippled by the first oil
crisis. The real growth of the gross domestic product, or GDP, was
minus 0.6%. But the fact that the Japanese economy has registered
negative growth only one time in more than forty years shows how
satisfactory economic progress has been.

Q : Business has been dull lately, but economic growth has not slipped
below zero, has it?

A : It was 0.1% in 1993 and the prediction for 1994 is from 1.0 to 1.5%,
so it looks like Japan will be able to attain a slight positive growth.

Q : So the economic slump is more psychological than physical?

A : I agree. Japan set a furious pace in economic development and companies with their sights set on growth rushed straight ahead. They
were somehow able to overcome the blows delivered by the oil cri-

んとか切り抜けてきたわけですが，今回はバブルがはじけたという形で，初めて外部要因でないものでつまずいたわけです。またこれまでは，「欧米に追いつき追い越せ」でやってきたのに，その目標がどうやら消えてしまったという目標喪失感もあるかもしれません。いずれにしても今，日本経済は大きな曲がり角にきています。

● 日本経済の課題
  といえば

Q：これまでお話ししてきたいろいろなテーマの中でも，日本がいま，抱えている課題について紹介してきましたが，ここで簡単にまとめるとどうなりますか。

A：第1部でお話しした日本式経営に関していえば，その根幹といわれた**終身雇用制**が大きく揺らぎ始め，高齢化社会になりつつあるにもかかわらず，企業は中高年齢層を削減しようとしています。またサラリーマンの間では，生活の豊かさとは何かを，あらためて考えなおそうという動きが出ています。更に国際経済の中での日本を見れば，貿易摩擦の激化や円高に伴う国際競争力の低下などで，これまでのような**輸出拡大路線**を続けていくことは難しくなってきました。そのうえ**地球環境**問題も出てきて，エコロジーやリサイクルという考え方も必要になってきました。そこで日本経済の構造転換をしなければならないということになるわけです。

Q：'70年代初めの石油危機の後にも，**構造転換**が必要だと叫ばれていましたが。

A：当時いわれたのは，エネルギー多消費型社会をいかに変革するかというものでした。したがって省資源が叫ばれたわけですが，それも結局は，高い石油を使って，いかに安くモノを作るかということでしかなかったのです。今は，そのモノ作りをどうするか，という根本的な見直しが必要とされているのです。

sis and the appreciation of the yen. But now the bubble has collapsed and for the first time they have been tripped up by an internal factor. For many years Japan was just trying to catch up with western nations, but now it seems to have overtaken them, and has lost a sense of purpose. In any case, the Japanese economy is now standing at a turning point.

Q : We have introduced many of the issues the Japanese economy is currently facing, so could you summarize them briefly?

A : In the first section, we talked about Japanese-style management and how the basis for it, the **lifetime employment system,** is now being shaken up. Even though the average age of the population is rising, companies are trying to reduce their number of middle-aged workers. Workers are starting to rethink their concept of real wealth. Furthermore, it is now becoming more difficult to maintain an **export-driven strategy,** in the face of intensified trade friction and the loss of international competitiveness accompanying the yen's appreciation. In addition, we now have to think about **global environment** issues, such as ecology and recycling. Therefore, Japan must make a structural readjustment in its economy.

Q : But **structural readjustments** were called for during the beginning of the 1970s after the oil crisis.

A : At that time, people talked about how to reform society with its large consumption of energy. There was an appeal for energy conservation, but this just aimed at making cheaper goods with high-priced oil. Now the issue is a basic rethinking of how to make these products.

ポイント

Q：具体的にはどういうことなんですか。

A：例えば，これまでは「いかにいいモノを安く作る か」という点に重点が置かれていましたが，これ からは「いかに使いやすく，また再利用が可能で 環境に優しいモノを作るか」に重点を変えるべき でしょう。この使いやすさという点では，ソフト 作りにもっと力を入れる必要があります。という のも日本企業は従来，ハード作りにはその能力を 発揮してきましたが，ソフトの面では米国企業に 依存しているケースが多々あるからです。例えば パーソナルコンピューターが典型的な例です。コ ンピューターの部品の半導体や液晶パネルなどは， 日本企業がその大部分を供給していますが，その ソフトは，ほとんどが米国企業のものです。

Q：さて，今後の日本経済はどうあるべきかという問 題になりますが。

● 平岩リポート とは

A：細川政権当時の首相の私的諮問機関である「**経済 改革研究会**」が，1993年12月にまとめた報告書が ありますのでご紹介します。この研究会の会長が， 経団連の当時の平岩会長であることから，「**平岩 リポート**」と呼ばれています。

Q：この報告書では，どんな方針が打ち出されたので すか。

A：まず経済構造改革の目標として，「内外に開かれ た透明な社会」「生活者を優先する経済社会」「世 界と調和し，世界から共感を得られる経済社会」 などの項目を挙げています。また中長期的な政策 としては，「規制の緩和」「内需型経済の形成」 「世界に自由で大きな市場を提供し，かつ多角的 な海外支援を実施すること」などの政策を掲げて います。

Q：もう少し具体的にいいますと。

Q : What does that mean specifically?

A : Well, Japanese companies have tended to emphasize making good quality products at low prices. But the focus should be shifted toward how to make products which are simple to use, recyclable and environmentally friendly. In terms of simplicity of use, effort should be put into software products. Although Japanese companies have demonstrated their ability in hardware products, many of them have relied on U.S. companies for software products in the past. A typical example would be the personal computer. Japanese companies have been large suppliers of computer parts such as semiconductors and liquid crystal displays. But software was mostly supplied by U.S. companies.

Q : Now, let's talk about the future of the Japanese economy.

A : **The Advisory Group for Economic Structural Reform**, a private advisory panel formed under the Hosokawa administration submitted a report in December 1993. The council was headed by Gaishi Hiraiwa, the chairman of the Federation of Economic Organizations so it was also called the **"Hiraiwa Report."**

Q : What were their suggestions for economic policy?

A : There were several basic targets for economic reform, including "a transparent society, open inside and out," "an economy giving priority to consumers," and "harmonization with the world and an economy understood by the international community." There were several goals for mid and long-term policy, including "deregulation," "the building of a domestic demand-driven economy," and "the creation of a large, free market that is open to the world, and implementation of multifaceted foreign aid."

Q : Does the report give any specific suggestions on what should be done?

A：平岩リポートは，報告書をとりまとめる期間が短かったこともあって，具体的な施策については，あまり触れられていません。しかし大まかな方向性は示されました。例えば規制緩和についていえば，「経済的な規制に関しては，原則的には自由にし，規制は例外的に設ける」という方針を打ち出しています。また内需型経済の形成および市場開放については，「企業がこれまでの輸出依存型体質を改めるほか，規制の緩和や，住宅などの社会資本を充実することによって，日本経済を内需型経済構造に変革する。また外国企業が日本の市場にアクセスしやすくなるようにするため，輸入に関する制度を改善する」ことなどを打ち出しています。

• 国際社会と日本

Q：最後に，国際社会で日本はどうあるべきかについて，ひとこと。

A：平岩リポートにもありましたように，今後の日本は「世界と調和し，世界から共感を得られる経済社会」にならなければならないと思います。例えば発展途上国への協力も，経済協力や生産技術の移転にとどまらず，教育，医療といった分野での協力も必要となってくるでしょう。いずれにしても日本経済の発展だけではなく，世界経済全体が発展していける環境づくりに一役買うことが，「顔の見えない国」という批判もある日本の国際化にもつながっていくのではないでしょうか。

A : The Hiraiwa Report does not give many specific proposals, because it was conducted over a short period. But it did suggest a general direction. In deregulation, for example, the council called for the abolishment of economic regulations, in principle, keeping them at a minimum. It also mentioned building a domestic demand-driven economy and liberalizing the market. It recommended that companies restructure to alter their export-dependent nature and that the government transform the economy to a domestic demand-oriented structure, through deregulation and by reinforcing social capital such as housing. The council also promoted reforms of the import system to broaden access by foreign companies.

Q : Finally, how should Japan behave within the international community?

A : As mentioned in the Hiraiwa Report, Japan needs to foster an economy that is in harmony with other nations and can be understood by them. In aiding developing nations, for example, Japan should not just work on economic assistance and technology transfer but provide assistance in areas such as education and medicine. In any case, it cannot focus solely on its own economic development; it has to help create an environment in which the entire world economy can develop. Japan has a bad reputation for being a "faceless nation" and taking concrete steps will help it take its place in the international community.

日本語索引

- ( ) は語句中の省略可能な箇所，および略語の正式名称，あるいは正式名称の略語を示した。
  - 例：ＩＬＯ(国際労働機関)
    気候変動に関する政府間会議(ＩＰＣＣ)
- [ ] は語の言い換えを示す。
  - 例：家電[家庭電化]製品
- 欧字の略語の配列は，そのカナ読みに従った。
  - 例：ＩＬＯ→アイエルオウ→アの項目　ＮＩＥＳ→ニーズ→ニの項目

English Index

- [ ]は語の言い換えを示す。　例：home [household] appliance
- ( )は語句中の省略可能な箇所，および略語の正式名称，あるいは正式名称の略語を示した。　例：in-house (labor) union
- 定冠詞のつく語は，定冠詞をその語の後ろに置いた。　例：United States, the
- 文中に名詞が複数形で表れている場合は，原則として単数形で示した。

たいやく えいご はな に ほんけいざい
対訳：英語で話す日本経済Q＆A
A Bilingual Guide to the Japanese Economy

1995年5月26日　第1刷発行
1999年6月1日　第14刷発行

著　者　　NHK 国際局 経済プロジェクト
　　　　　株式会社　大和総研　経済調査部
訳　者　　株式会社　NHK情報ネットワーク バイリンガルセンター
　　　　　株式会社　翻訳情報センター
発行者　　野間　佐和子
発行所　　講談社インターナショナル株式会社

　　　　　〒112-8652　東京都文京区音羽1−17−14

　　　　　電話：東京（03）3944−6493（編集部）
　　　　　　　　　　（03）3944−6492（営業部）

印刷所　　株式会社　平河工業社
製本所　　株式会社　堅省堂

落丁本、乱丁本は　講談社インターナショナル営業部宛にお送りください。送料小社負担にてお取り替えいたします。なお、この本についてのお問い合せは、編集部宛にお願いいたします。本書の無断複写(コピー)、転載は著作権法の例外を除き、禁じられています。

定価はカバーに表示してあります。
Copyright © 1995 by NHK Overseas Broadcasting Department Economic Project and Daiwa Institute of Research Co., Ltd., Economic Research Department

ISBN 4-7700-1942-4

講談社バイリンガル・ブックス

英語で読んでも面白い！

- 楽しく読めて自然に英語が身に付くバイリンガル表記
- 実用から娯楽まで読者の興味に応える多彩なテーマ
- 重要単語、表現法が一目で分かる段落対応レイアウト

46判変型 (113 x 188 mm) 仮製

英語で話す「日本」Q&A
Talking About Japan Q & A

KBB 1

講談社インターナショナル 編　　　　　320ページ　ISBN 4-7700-2026-0

外国の人と話すとき、必ず出てくる話題は「日本」のこと。でも英語力よりも前に困るのは、日本について知らないことがいっぱいという事実です。モヤモヤの知識をスッキリさせてくれる「日本再発見」の書。

英語で話す「アメリカ」Q&A
Talking About the USA Q & A

KBB 21

賀川 洋 著　　　　　304ページ　ISBN 4-7700-2005-8

仕事でも留学でも遊びでも、アメリカ人と交際するとき、知っておくと役に立つ「アメリカ小事典」。アメリカ人の精神と社会システムにポイントをおいた解説により、自然、歴史、政治、文化、そして人をバイリンガルで紹介します。

英語で話す「世界」Q&A
Talking About the World Q & A

KBB 19

講談社インターナショナル 編　　　　　320ページ　ISBN 4-7700-2006-6

今、世界にはいくつの国家があるか、ご存じですか？　対立をはらみながらも、急速に1つの運命共同体になっていく「世界」——外国の人と話すとき知らなければならない「世界」に関する国際人必携の「常識集」です。

英語で読む日本史
Japanese History : 11 Experts Reflect on the Past

KBB 4

英文日本大事典 編　　　　　　　　　　224ページ　ISBN 4-7700-2024-4

11人の超一流ジャパノロジストたちが英語で書き下ろした日本全史。外国人の目から見た日本史はどういうものか、また日本の歴史事項を英語で何と表現するのか。新しい視点が想像力をかき立てます。

日本を創った100人
100 Japanese You Should Know

KBB 25

板坂 元 監修　英文日本大事典 編　　　　240ページ　ISBN4-7700-2159-3

混沌と激動を乗り越え築き上げられた現在の日本。その長い歴史の節目節目で大きな役割を果たした歴史上のキーパーソン100人を、超一流のジャパノロジストたちが解説。グローバルな大競争時代を迎えた今、彼らの生き方が大きな指針となります。

英語で話す「日本の謎」Q＆A　　外国人が聞きたがる100のWHY
100 Tough Questions for Japan

KBB 11

板坂 元 監修　　　　　　　　　　　240ページ　ISBN 4-7700-2091-0

なぜ、結婚式は教会で、葬式はお寺でなんてことができるの？　なぜ、大人までがマンガを読むの？　なぜ、時間とお金をかけてお茶を飲む練習をするの？──こんな外国人の問いをつきつめてゆくと、日本文化の核心が見えてきます。

英語で話す「日本の心」　　和英辞典では引けないキーワード197
Keys to the Japanese Heart and Soul

KBB 12

英文日本大事典 編　　　　　　　　　328ページ　ISBN 4-7700-2082-1

一流のジャパノロジスト53人が解説した「日本の心」を知るためのキーワード集。「わび」「さび」「義理人情」「甘え」「根回し」「談合」「みそぎ」など、日本人特有の「心の動き」を外国人に説明するための強力なツールです。

英語で話す「日本の文化」
Japan as I See It

KBB 22

NHK国際放送局文化プロジェクト 編　ダン・ケニー 訳　　196ページ　ISBN 4-7700-2197-6

金田一春彦、遠藤周作、梅原猛、平川祐弘、西堀栄三郎、鯖田豊之、野村万作、井上靖、小松左京、中根千枝の10人が、日本文化の「謎」を解く。NHKの国際放送で21の言語で放送され、分かりやすいと世界中で大好評。

茶の本
The Book of Tea

KBB 28

岡倉天心 著　千 宗室 序と跋　浅野 晃 訳　　264ページ　ISBN 4-7700-2379-0

一碗の茶をすする、そのささやかで簡潔な行為の中に、偉大な精神が宿っている──茶道によせて、日本と東洋の精神文化の素晴らしさを明かし、アジアの理想が回復されることを英文で呼びかけた本書は、日本の心を英語で明かす不朽の名著。

武士道
BUSHIDO
KBB 30

新渡戸稲造 著　須知徳平 訳　　　　　　　　312ページ　ISBN 4-7700-2402-9

「日本が生んだ最大の国際人」新渡戸博士が英語で著した世界的名著。「日本の精神文化を知る最良の書」として世界17ヵ国語に翻訳され、1世紀にわたって読みつがれてきた不滅の日本人論。国際人必読の1冊。

ニッポン不思議発見！　日本文化を英語で語る50の名エッセイ集
Discover Japan: Words, Customs and Concepts
KBB 14

日本文化研究所 編　松本道弘 訳　　　　　　260ページ　ISBN 4-7700-2142-9

絶望的な場合ですら、日本人は「そこをなんとか」という言葉を使って、相手に甘えようとする……こんな指摘をうけると、いかに日本人は独特なものの考え方をしているか分かります。あなたも「不思議」を発見してみませんか。

ニッポン見聞録　大好きな日本人に贈る新・開国論
Heisei Highs and Lows
KBB 8

トム・リード 著　　　　　　　　　　　　　216ページ　ISBN 4-7700-2092-9

国際化の進む日本ですが、アメリカのジャーナリストが鋭い目と耳で浮き彫りにしたニッポンの姿は、驚くほど平穏でいとおしく、恥ずかしいくらい強欲で無知なものでした。トムが大好きな日本人へ贈る新・開国論。

「Japan」クリッピング　ワシントンポストが書いた「日本」
Views of Japan from The Washington Post Newsroom
KBB 6

東郷茂彦 著　　　　　　　　　　　　　　256ページ　ISBN 4-7700-2023-6

アメリカの世論をリードするワシントン・ポストに書かれた「Japan」……政治、外交、経済、社会のジャンルで取り上げられた日本の姿を、国際ジャーナリストが解説し、その背後にある問題点を浮き彫りにする一冊。

NHK「ニュースのキーワード」
NHK: Key Words in the News
KBB 26

NHK国際放送局　「ニュースのキーワード」プロジェクト 編　232ページ　ISBN4-7700-2342-1

日本で話題になっている時事問題を解説する、NHK国際放送の番組「ニュースのキーワード」から「総会屋」「日本版ビッグバン」「ダイオキシン」など、33のキーワードを収録しました。国際的観点からの解説が、現代の日本の姿を浮き彫りにします。

ベスト・オブ・天声人語
VOX POPULI, VOX DEI
KBB 23

朝日新聞論説委員室 著　朝日イブニングニュース 訳　　280ページ　ISBN4-7700-2166-6

「天声人語」は「朝日新聞」の名コラムというよりも、日本を代表するコラムです。香港返還、アムラー現象、たまごっち、マザー・テレサの死など、現代を読み解く傑作56編を、社会・世相、政治、スポーツなどのジャンル別に収録しました。

誤解される日本人　外国人がとまどう41の疑問
The Inscrutable Japanese

KBB 20

メリディアン・リソーシス・アソシエイツ 編　賀川 洋 著　　　224ページ　ISBN 4-7700-2129-1

あなたのちょっとした仕草や表情が大きな誤解を招いているかもしれません。「日本人はどんなときに誤解を受けるのか？」そのメカニズムを解説し、「どのように外国人に説明すればよいか」最善の解決策を披露します。

ビジュアル 英語で読む日本国憲法
The Constitution of Japan

KBB 18

英文日本大百科事典 編　　　　　　　　　208ページ　ISBN 4-7700-2191-7

難しいと思っていた「日本国憲法」も、英語で読むと不思議とよく分かります。日本国憲法を、59点の写真を使って、バイリンガルで分かりやすく解説しました。条文中に出てくる難解な日本語には、ルビや説明がついています。

イラスト 日本まるごと事典
Japan at a Glance

KBB 17

インターナショナル・インターンシップ・プログラムス 著　248ページ（2色刷）　ISBN 4-7700-2080-5

1000点以上のイラストを使って日本のすべてを紹介──自然、文化、社会はもちろんのこと、折り紙の折り方、着物の着方から、ナベで米を炊く方法や「あっちむいてホイ」の遊び方まで国際交流に必要な知識とノウハウを満載。

英語で折り紙
Origami in English

KBB 3

山口 真 著　　　　　　　　　　　　　　160ページ　ISBN 4-7700-2027-9

たった一枚の紙から無数の造形が生まれ出る‥‥外国の人たちは、その面白さに目を見張ります。折るとき、英語で説明できるようにバイリンガルにしました。ホームステイ、留学、海外駐在に必携の一冊です。

英語で日本料理
100 Recipes from Japanese Cooking

KBB 15

辻調理師専門学校　畑耕一郎、近藤一樹 著　268ページ（カラー口絵16ページ）　ISBN 4-7700-2079-1

外国の人と親しくなる最高の手段は、日本料理を作ってあげること、そしてその作り方を教えてあげることです。代表的な日本料理100品の作り方を、外国の計量法も入れながら、バイリンガルで分かりやすく解説しました。

ドタンバのマナー
The Ultimate Guide to Etiquette in Japan

KBB 27

サトウサンペイ 著　　　　　　240ページ（オールカラー）　ISBN 4-7700-2193-3

サンペイ流家元が自らしでかした「日常のヘマ」「海外でのヘマ」を一目で分かるようにマンガにした、フレッシュマンに贈る究極のマナー集。新社会人必読！知っていればすむことなのに、知らないために嫌われたり、憎まれてはかないません。

アメリカ日常生活のマナーＱ＆Ａ
Do As Americans Do

KBB 13

ジェームス・Ｍ・バーダマン，倫子・バーダマン 著　　　256ページ　ISBN 4-7700-2128-3

"How do you do?" に "How do you do?" と答えてはいけないということ、ご存知でしたか？　日本では当たり前と思われていたことがマナー違反だったのです。旅行で、駐在で、留学でアメリカに行く人必携のマナー集。

日米比較 冠婚葬祭のマナー
Do It Right : Japanese & American Social Etiquette

KBB 2

ジェームス・Ｍ・バーダマン，倫子・バーダマン 著　　　184ページ　ISBN 4-7700-2025-2

アメリカでは結婚式や葬式はどのように行われるのか？　お祝いや香典は？……そしてアメリカの人たちも、日本の事情を知りたがります。これだけあればもう困らない。日米冠婚葬祭マニュアル、バイリンガル版。

英語で話す「仏教」Ｑ＆Ａ
Talking About Buddhism Q & A

KBB 24

高田佳人 著　ジェームス・Ｍ・バーダマン 訳　　　240ページ　ISBN4-7700-2161-5

四十九日までに7回も法事をするのは、「亡くなった人が7回受ける裁判をこの世から応援するため」だということ、ご存じでしたか？　これだけは知っておきたい「仏教」に関することがらを、やさしい英語で説明できるようにした入門書です。

まんが 日本昔ばなし
Once Upon a Time in Japan

KBB 16

川内彩友美 編　ラルフ・マッカーシー 訳　　　160ページ　ISBN 4-7700-2173-9

人気テレビシリーズ「まんが日本昔ばなし」から、「桃太郎」「金太郎」「一寸法師」など、より抜きの名作8話をラルフ・マッカーシーの名訳でお届けします。ホームステイなどでも役に立つ一冊です。

まんが 日本昔ばなし 妖しのお話
Once Upon a Time in *Ghostly* Japan

KBB 29

川内彩友美 編　ラルフ・マッカーシー 訳　　　152ページ　ISBN 4-7700-2347-2

妖しく、怖く、心に響く昔ばなしの名作を英語で読む。人気テレビシリーズ「まんが日本昔ばなし」から、「鶴の恩返し」「雪女」「舌切り雀」「耳なし芳一」「分福茶釜」など8話を収録しました。

ベスト・オブ 宮沢賢治短編集
The Tales of Miyazawa Kenji

KBB 5

宮沢賢治 著　ジョン・ベスター 訳　　　208ページ　ISBN 4-7700-2081-3

「注文の多い料理店」「どんぐりと山猫」「祭の晩」「鹿踊りのはじまり」「土神ときつね」「オツベルと象」「毒もみの好きな署長さん」「セロ弾きのゴーシュ」の代表作8編を精選。ジョン・ベスターの名訳でどうぞ。

銀河鉄道の夜
Night Train to the Stars

KBB 10

宮沢賢治 著　ジョン・ベスター 訳　　　　　　　176ページ　ISBN 4-7700-2131-3

賢治童話の中でも最も人気の高い「銀河鉄道の夜」は、賢治の宗教心と科学精神が反映された独特の世界――天空、自然、大地がみごとに描かれ、光と音と動きに満ち溢れています。ジョバンニと一緒に銀河を旅してみませんか。

ベスト・オブ 窓ぎわのトットちゃん
Best of Totto-chan : The Little Girl at the Window

KBB 9

黒柳徹子 著　ドロシー・ブリトン 訳　　　　　　232ページ　ISBN 4-7700-2127-5

小学校一年生にして「退学」になったトットちゃんは、転校先の校長先生に「君は本当はいい子なんだよ」と温かい言葉のシャワーで励まされます……バイリンガル版で、あの空前の大ベストセラーの感動をもう一度！

マザー・グース　愛される唄70選
Mother Goose : 70 Nursery Rhymes

KBB 7

谷川俊太郎 訳　渡辺茂 解説　　　　　　　　　176ページ　ISBN 4-7700-2078-3

「マイ・フェア・レディー」や「お熱いのがお好き」という題名も、マザー・グースからの引用だったってこと、ご存じでしたか？ 英米人にとって必須教養であるこの童謡集を、詩人・谷川俊太郎の名訳と共にお楽しみください。

ビジネスマン必携！

対訳 英語で話す日本経済Q&A
A Bilingual Guide to the Japanese Economy

NHK国際放送局経済プロジェクト・
大和総研経済調査部 編

46判（128 x 188 mm）仮製　368ページ
ISBN 4-7700-1942-4

NHK国際放送で好評を得た番組が本になりました。クイズと会話形式で楽しく読んでいくうちに、日本経済の仕組が分かり、同時に英語にも強くなっていきます。日本語と英語の対応がひと目で分かる編集上の工夫もいっぱい。

対訳 おくのほそ道
The Narrow Road to Oku

松尾芭蕉 著　ドナルド・キーン 訳
宮田雅之 切り絵
A5判変型（140 x 226 mm）
仮製　188ページ（カラー口絵41点）
ISBN 4-7700-2028-7

古典文学の最高峰のひとつ「おくのほそ道」をドナルド・キーンが新訳しました。画家、宮田雅之が精魂を込めた切り絵の魅力とあいまって、この名作に新しい生命が吹き込まれた、必読の1冊です。

対訳 竹取物語
The Tale of the Bamboo Cutter

川端康成 現代語訳
ドナルド・キーン 英訳　宮田雅之 切り絵
A5判変型・横長（226 x 148 mm）
仮製　箱入り 180ページ（カラー口絵16点）
ISBN 4-7700-2329-4

ノーベル賞作家の現代語訳と傑出した芸術家の作品、そして日本文学の研究に一生を捧げたジャパノロジストの翻訳が合体した、大人のための「竹取物語」。

英文版 ジャパン：四季と文化
Japan : The Cycle of Life

[序文] 高円宮憲仁親王殿下
[イントロダクション] C.W. ニコル
A4判変型（228 x 297 mm）
上製　296ページ（オールカラー）
ISBN 4-7700-2088-0

日本の文化は「四季」によって育まれてきました。日本人の生活、文化、精神から切り離せないこの「四季」を、美しく新鮮な数々のカラー写真でビジュアルに紹介します。

第1部　自然と風土
第2部　人々の暮らしと伝統行事
第3部　文化と伝統

英語と日本語で楽しむ

対訳 サザエさん（全12巻）
The Wonderful World of Sazae-san

長谷川町子 著　ジュールス・ヤング 訳

- 吹き出しの中にオリジナルの暖かい雰囲気を大切にした英語、
  コマの横に日本語がつく対訳形式。
- お正月、こいのぼり、忘年会など日本独特の文化や習慣には、
  欄外に英語の解説つき。

46判変型（113 x 188 mm）仮製

第1巻	170ページ	ISBN 4-7700-2075-9
第2巻	168ページ	ISBN 4-7700-2093-7
第3巻	198ページ	ISBN 4-7700-2094-5
第4巻	164ページ	ISBN 4-7700-2149-6
第5巻	176ページ	ISBN 4-7700-2150-X
第6巻	160ページ	ISBN 4-7700-2151-8
第7巻	168ページ	ISBN 4-7700-2152-6
第8巻	168ページ	ISBN 4-7700-2153-4
第9巻	172ページ	ISBN 4-7700-2154-2
第10巻	172ページ	ISBN 4-7700-2155-0
第11巻	176ページ	ISBN 4-7700-2156-9
第12巻	168ページ	ISBN 4-7700-2157-7

対訳 日本事典 (全1巻)
The Kodansha Bilingual Encyclopedia of Japan

講談社インターナショナル 編

B5判 (182 x 257 mm)
上製 箱入り
944ページ (カラー口絵16ページ)
ISBN 4-7700-2130-5

ビジネス、海外駐在、
留学、ホームステイなど、
さまざまな国際交流の場で、
幅広くご活用いただけます。

特色

「日本」を国際的な視点で理解できる幅広い知識と、
実用的な英語が身につきます。

1. 現代の政治制度、最新の経済情報を豊富に記載し、日本を総合的に理解できる。

2. 分野別の構成により、テーマに沿って自然に読み進むことができる。

3. 豊富なイラストと図版を収録し、完全対訳のレイアウトと欄外のキーワードで、重要単語や表現の日英相互参照に便利。

4. 日本国憲法、重要な国際条約、年表をいずれも日英併記で巻末に収録。

5. 英語からも日本語 (ローマ字) からも引けるインデックスつき。

内容構成

地理 / 歴史 / 政治 / 経済 / 社会 / 文化 / 生活